Samuel Dana Horton

Silver in Europe

Samuel Dana Horton

Silver in Europe

ISBN/EAN: 9783743320789

Manufactured in Europe, USA, Canada, Australia, Japa

Cover: Foto ©ninafisch / pixelio.de

Manufactured and distributed by brebook publishing software (www.brebook.com)

Samuel Dana Horton

Silver in Europe

SILVER IN EUROPE

BY
S. DANA HORTON

SECOND EDITION, ENLARGED.

New York
MACMILLAN AND CO.
1892

PREFACE TO SECOND EDITION.

The new matter here added refers primarily to notable events that have occurred since the date of the first edition (April, 1890), but at the same time it has its bearing upon the general direction of the Silver Movement since the last International Conference in Paris, 1881-1882. Mr. Goschen's Proposals of December 2, 1891, are the first actual step forward in Europe made in this behalf since 1881, but, as will be fully explained in an introductory paper on Progress in England (page 291), this step of a Tory Government in 1891 is a pendant to the action taken by the Liberal Government in 1881.

The general argument leading up to it appears to be in fair measure set forth in a tract distributed early last year by the Parliamentary leaders of the Silver Party to their colleagues, the larger part of which is here reprinted. As a statement of the whole case for Great Britain, this paper is deficient in taking for granted, or passing by in silence, the great special interests involved in silver; namely, the agricultural interest, and the interest of trade with silver countries, together with manufacturing for that trade. Of these two "silver interests," which may be classed under the titles *Wheat* and *Cotton*, the former is no longer a stranger in this country—though both were so when I raised the point about them at the Atlanta Commercial Convention in May, 1885. The interests of Lancashire industries, and of the cotton trade generally, are indicated in the extracts which follow on page 319, under the title SILVER IN THE ENGLISH ELECTIONS.

Had time permitted, I should have been glad to remodel the book, changing its form and giving it at least the consecutiveness lacking to a collection of distinct essays.

But the reader will pardon when he observes that most of my papers herein reprinted were like briefs with which (to use the terms of my profession) I had been 'fighting a case' in Europe, and he will pardon all the more readily when he realizes that the 'fighting of that case' is really the thing that Americans are chiefly interested in, whether they are as yet aware of it or no. He will then perhaps discover that that is precisely what his neighbors need to learn—those whom he finds indifferent or visionary or wrong-headed about silver!

If submitting these arguments to the American reader in form as delivered in Europe shall arouse a sense of the realities of the struggle there in progress, then at least it can be said of these disjunct pages that, though the road be a rough one, still we arrive, as the French idiom has it—we "get there," and by a shorter cut.

Among these realities let me mark here points which it may prove peculiarly useful to dwell upon at this juncture, when the air is full of talk of an International Conference, at Chicago or elsewhere. Europeans will never remonetize silver merely because Americans wish them to do so; they will do it only when they recognize it to be their interest. An International "Conference" having as such no original power to establish a coinage system, there is sometimes danger of forgetting that what is really wanted is action rather than talk. Nor is the decision of a ministry, or authorization of a legislature, to take part in a Conference, necessarily anything more than an expression of polite interest.

The real thing desired is an Act of Parliament, an Act of the French Legislative Body, an Act of the German Imperial Diet—beside an Act of Congress.

As most readers are aware that it is no light matter to pass a bill in Congress, they will perhaps shrink back at sight of the task—that has been set for this generation—of getting concordant legislation in Europe. But this generation or its leaders must learn that it is for the interest of England, of France, of Germany that these respective acts be passed. Once it is recognized that the European outlawry of silver is a *blunder*, a *blunder for Europe*, and there is daylight ahead! A campaign against the forces responsible for that blunder may be arduous and long, but if there be good management it must succeed in the end; and what American does not wish to see his country contribute to that management? What we are concerned about, then, is the American contingent in the forces of a reform which must show front in Calcutta, in Paris, and in London, as well as here.

Moreover, the main strategic combinations are simple, in spite of the expansion of the theatre of war. The controlling headquarters are very near together. It was in Paris that the governments of Berlin and London, in 1881, made surrender, for the rest of mankind, of the main principles of demonetization.

A decade has passed since that preliminary victory; heedlessness and neglect have prevailed. The greater the need of effort, of ability, and of caution, now!

The Silver Movement in Europe, unlike the free-coinage movement here, has for its object not the local, but the general, reversal of the outlawry maintained against silver, primarily by European statutes and decrees; America's joining Europe in free coinage when Europe is ready, being taken everywhere for granted. This Movement has its history, its fortunes, its story of good or bad management, of local failures or successes. It is through experience of these that forecast of its future is to be gained, and the knowledge how Americans can assist in promoting good management in Europe, and likewise a sense be acquired of what we must avoid here lest our interposition weaken the efforts of our allies in Europe. Naturally, the action of one partner to a proposed agreement must influence that of the others, and it is plain this country is constantly taking a hand in Silver Diplomacy, so to speak, for good or for evil, and whether we are generally conscious of it or no. Evidently if we are to help and not to hinder, it is doubly important that our information should be correct as to the situation in Europe, and that what we do, and likewise what we omit to do, should be calculated with a view to things as they are!

A word on the task undertaken by the silver reformers abroad.

As they are the sole allies of the American policy, it is hardly less than the duty of educated Americans to recognize what they are doing.

What is their work? It is essentially a work of education; though agitation and management, both political and diplomatic, can direct the work and utilize its conquests. But ignorance is the enemy; and it is a patriotic work that the reformer is doing in his own country. His struggle is not against interests, his attack is not upon the fortunes of any class of his fellows, it is upon their minds. Ignorance, I repeat, is the enemy—though of course by its side are inertia, heedlessness, prejudice, dulness, and the pride of dogma. In short, the reformers are "right." The English silver reformer is a patriotic Englishman, the French reformer a patriotic Frenchman, the German a patriotic German.

The emphasis of this statement is called for by reason of the opposing notions that are widely current among us, both in the gold camp and in the silver camp, as if silver were an American interest alone! Had that been the case, its doom would have been sealed long ago.

The opposition to the Silver Movement is also sometimes painted in deceptive colors. The language of eloquence and of passion before many a constituency has presented an indictment against the originators of the outlawry of silver in Europe, and against its apologists to-day, as well as against the partisans of gold in this country—an indictment for conspiracy against the rest of mankind!

This untenable indictment is a great compliment to the foresight and power of organization of a class which can boast of quite as much dulness as its neighbors.

Of course special interests, and short views about them, affect opinion, and naturally they have played their part here. But in a broad sense, anti-silver legislation was adopted to satisfy opinion based upon avowed and legitimate interests represented in public. Everywhere, in every country, those learned in monetary matters were avowed inspirers of the movement against silver, believing that they were right.

They were wrong! Experience adds annually a new volume of evidence to that effect. But the lapse of time also makes the remedy more difficult. The greater the need of a vigorous campaign of education to the end that the one possible remedy be speedily applied.

April, 1892.

PREFACE.

A rising wave of interest in Silver has within the last year been spreading over the country, deriving momentum from the apparent need that Congress make provision to fill the void in the money-stock of the country left by the retirement of the notes of National Banks. A new stage of discussion and of experimental legislation is thus to be entered, in which the status of the white money-metal in other lands will remain entitled to peculiarly watchful and earnest consideration.

The following pages are designed as a contribution to that end.

It is not to be expected that they will render justice in detail to a subject so multifarious and so pervaded with subtleties and insoluble problems that a library could be filled with its literature. Their theme is the movement for the general restoration of Silver to legal equality with gold. While the reader is invited to consider topics that may appear to bear no close relation to each other, the effect as a whole will be, I trust, to present to him in perspective the changing status of the money-metals, and the changing forces of opinion relating to that great mistake, the general outlawry of silver, which only the chief nations by uniting can repair.

In a review of events the Monetary Congress, held at Paris in September last (1889), naturally comes into the foreground, and as importance can be attached to that assembly chiefly as the scene of an English pro-silver demonstration, it is here referred to in connection with the developments in England, in a chapter which I have entitled THE PARIS MONETARY CONGRESS AND THE ENGLISH SILVER MOVEMENT.

In sequence to this a translation is given of a speech of mine at the Congress, made in reply to notable champions of gold there present, to whose views and authority it will be seen that I make reference, by which further light may be thrown on the opinions current in Europe.

The nature and range of the subjects involved in silver, as they present themselves to the European monetary legislator, are outlined in the QUESTIONS addressed, in 1887, to certain foreign scholars by the BRITISH ROYAL COMMISSION ON GOLD AND SILVER. In the belief that my work will throw light into these recesses, I have printed my ANSWERS to these Questions, which were handed to the Commission in February, 1888.

These are followed by an examination of doctrines relating to monetary legislation that hitherto have prevailed among the learned, a paper entitled the PARITY OF MONEYS, AS REGARDED BY ADAM SMITH, RICARDO, AND MILL—which was printed in London as an open letter answering a question of a member of the Royal Commission, and was sent to members of the Commission, then in session, and to others interested in monetary discussion.*

The pages above referred to, devoted to the growth of opinion in England, formed the historical portion of an address on FEDERATION FOR PARITY OF MONEYS AND THE ADVANCEMENT OF SCIENCE, sent (in response to invitation) to the late meeting of the American Association at Toronto. In that address I endeavored to state the new principles of monetary jurisprudence in a form at once practical and convenient for the general reader, and I therefore present it here.

The important issue raised before Congress and the country by the Report of Mr. Windom, as Secretary of the Treasury, is considered in its general relations in a paper entitled BULLION OR COIN, which is supplemented by an account of the currency proposals of David Ricardo (1816), under the title RICARDO ON BULLION NOTES AND SILVER.

Another subject is also discussed, which explains itself by the title, A PAN-AMERICAN DOLLAR AND THE POLICY OF UNION.

In view of current misapprehensions with reference to the possible action of foreign Powers, I present some considerations ON MEASURES IN AID OF DEMONETIZATION.

A selection of papers embodying proof and justification of views and evidence of facts, set forth throughout the volume, are offered at the close in the form of a documentary chronicle of THE ANTI-SILVER MOVEMENT AND ITS REVERSAL, which serves as appendix.

---

*London: Macmillan & Co., June, 1888.

ERRATA.

Page 74, line 4, for "*observed*" read "*observe*."
Page 80, line 13, for "*and from*" read "*not from*."

TABLE OF CONTENTS.

I.—THE PARIS MONETARY 'CONGRESS' (SEPTEMBER, 1889) AND THE ENGLISH SILVER MOVEMENT. Pages 1–31.

THE ORIGIN AND EFFECT OF THE CONGRESS.
THE SUBJECT OF DEBATE AND PROCEEDINGS.
The organization.
The subject of debate.
The diplomatic situation of silver.
An English and German demonstration in Paris.
Academic debate.
THE ADVANCE OF OPINION IN ENGLAND.
The Commons Committee of 1876.
A fatal mistake.
Bonanzas and Council Bills.
The Monetary Conference of 1878.

1. The attitude of the English representatives at the Conference of 1878.
2. Their attitude at the Monetary Conference of 1881.
3. The work of agitation and education in England.
4. The Royal Commission on the Depression of Trade and Industry (1884–'86).
5. The Royal Commission on Gold and Silver (1886–'88). Its conclusions.
The present situation.
The future.

II.—A REVIEW OF ANTI-SILVER ARGUMENTS. Pages 33–53. Speech in Reply to Mr. Levasseur and Mr. Du Puynode (Paris, September 13, 1889).

Explanatory.
The policy of union.
Why should France object?
The doctrine of the market.
The 'single gold standard.'
Sources of this theory.
England its stronghold.

Based on certain errors.
Mr. Levasseur's position.
His scheme.
How it must look to Englishmen and Germans.
The policy of demonetization.

III.—Questions of the Royal Commission on Gold and Silver, and Answers. Pages 55-106.

Prefatory.
The 'fall of silver.'
The Royal Commission. Its purpose and jurisdiction.
To investigate the effect of well-meant legislation.
To recommend remedies.
Motion to reverse judgment.
Universal bias.
Ten years' delay.
Answer explained.
Preference for gold.
Bonanzas and Council Bills.
Probable future of silver.
Wholesale prices.
Appreciation of gold.
Errors current.

Stability and Parity.
'Contraction.'
Normal stock.
England's condition.
Supply of metal.
'Scarcity' and Parity.
The concept 'standard.'
Various aspects of 'quantity.'
Quantity theory.
Credit and cash.
Methods of economizing specie.
Federation for Parity.
Law of Parity and Gresham's Law.
Effect of restoring silver.
Questions of the ratio.
Provisional measures.
Sensitiveness and stability.

IV.—The Parity of Moneys as Regarded by Adam Smith, Ricardo, and Mill. Pages 107-147.

An Open Letter Answering a Question of a Member of the Royal Commission on Gold and Silver.

The question.
Origin of the doubt.
Cause of Parity.
A fashion of thought.
From Adam Smith to Mill.
A reign of Parity.
Analysis superficial.
Their practical notions.
Money as an object of science.
Mill's classifications.
Herbert Spencer.
Cause of inattention.
'Mercantile system.'

Freedom and *vis medicatrix naturae*.
Nature and art.
Incomplete grasp.
Ricardo's 'few words.'
Mill on Freedom and Money.
Novelty or exaggeration.
The fable of Midas.
Money and Barter.
Pliny and the Utopias.
Mill and 'Ideal Money.'
A visionary hypothesis.
Conclusion.
Appendix. Money and the State.

V.—Federation for Parity of Moneys and the Advancement of Science. Pages 149–168.

An Address before the American Association.

Abstract.
Introductory.
Affirmative statement of the Federalist position.
1. That silver and gold are the money-metals, and that gold is money and silver is money to-day.
2. That parity of money is desirable.
3. That it is the law of each nation which determines what is money in that nation.
4. That the preponderant employment—that is to say, economic 'demand'—for silver and gold is an effect of the laws of nations.
5. That monetary laws establish parity.
6. That permanent parity between silver and gold is producible by a proper regulation of their employment.
7. That concurrent laws for legal equality of the metals in an effective majority of nations will establish parity outside as well as within their direct jurisdiction.
8. That such parity benefits each nation by assuring comparative stability to the valuation in which it is interested.
9. That federation is a condition and a guarantee of such concurrent laws replacing those which now maintain disparity.
10. That the paramount monetary issue of the age is whether a settlement on this basis should be made.

The Dis-Unionist or Anti-Federalist position.
First grouping.
Second grouping.

VI.—Bullion or Coin? Pages 169–198.

(1) *It is futile to treat the silver dollar independently of silver itself.*
(2) *The people of the United States do not take to the silver dollar very kindly.*
The advantages of paper.
Paper based on bullion.
Bullion in banks.
The policy of Seigniorage.
Gratuitous mintage.
Free sale of bullion.
Monetary policy in the future.
Bullion and the general remonetization of silver.
Free mintage, gratuitous mintage, and free sale of bullion.
The policy of the Conferences.
The novelty of Mr. Windom's plan.
Legal equality of the metals.
The parity of bullion.
Resolution of American Bankers' Convention.
Dutch Bank Charter Act.

VII.—Ricardo on Bullion Notes and Silver.
Pages 199–208.

His idea of a standard.
Plans for resumption.
One-pound notes.

Modernness of anti-silver doctrine.
Lord Overstone and Mr. Haggard.

VIII.—A Pan-American Dollar and the Policy of Union.
Pages 209–222.

John Quincy Adams on metrical reform.
Course of events.
The gold mark.
The countries of the franc.
The change of ratio.
Mexican dollar and Brazilian milreis.

Currency of foreign coins.
Proper object of Federation.
The American Conference.
Position of Mr. T. J. Coolidge.
Report of Committee.
A Monetary Union sanctioned.

IX.—On Measures in Aid of Demonetization.
Pages 223–234.

Place where silver is money.
'Monetizing' in one place and demonetizing in another.
Political effect.
Supposed case of Austria-Hungary.
Four methods of demonetization distinguished.
The public and private.
What loss?
Exaggerations on this head.

Sources of misunderstanding.
Supposed case of the Bank of France.
Present use of silver stock.
Intervention of the Government.
Depressing gold price of silver.
Gold party and silver party.
Degree in which demonetization is facilitated.
Forces to prevent.

APPENDIX.

THE ANTI-SILVER MOVEMENT AND ITS REVERSAL. A DOCUMENTARY CHRONICLE. Pages 235-290.

I.—INTRODUCTORY.

Character of the movement.
Successive steps.
Its universality.
The Conference of 1867.

Its sequel in the Scandinavian Union, Germany, Latin Union, United States.
Relative value since 1870.

II.—THE WORK OF THE CONFERENCE OF 1867. Pages 241-251.

REPORT OF MR. DE PARIEU.

The Monetary Treaty of 1865 as a basis of union.
Propositions of France to other nations warmly received, by Europe and the United States.
The Conference.
Its object.
Variety of issues raised.
The program of discussion.
Twelve questions submitted.
Expectation that treaties will be made to give effect to decisions.
Preference for the Latin Union System.

Is the silver franc available?
The primacy of gold in the Roman Empire.
Its present position.
Gold the standard, with silver as transitory companion.
Five francs of gold nine-tenths fine unanimously chosen as the unit.
25-franc piece recommended by Austria and the United States.
Internationality of silver coins unimportant.

III.—THE GERMAN COMMERCIAL CONVENTION OF 1868. Pages 252-254.

The work of the Permanent Committee.
Resolution adopted.
Unity desired.
Silver mark scheme withdrawn.
Principles of the Paris Conference of 1867 adopted.

Decimal system.
Collection of essays to accompany report and petition to the Governments.

IV.—THE PROPOSALS OF THE UNITED STATES BEFORE THE CONFERENCE OF 1878. Pages 255-259.

Propositions stated.
Propositions held in reserve.

Answer of European Delegates.
Reply of American Delegates.

xii   SILVER IN EUROPE.

V.—The Conference of 1881. Pages 259-261.

Declarations of France and the United States.
Evil and remedy.
Concurrent action.

Question of ratio.
Its permanence.
Resolutions for adjourned meeting in 1882.

VI.—The Proposed Conference of 1882. Pages 261-262.

Copy of Identical Note sent to the Various Powers by the Governments of France and of the United States.

VII.—Foreign Coins as Legal Tender and the Policy of Union.
Pages 263-265.

Coinage systems in cases of conquest or union.
Instances in history.
Coinage treaties in the past.
Refer chiefly to weight and device.
Two metals recognized as material of money.

Novel situation produced by the attack upon silver.
The material becomes chiefly important.
Legal equality of metals.
Disadvantages avoided.

VIII.—The Royal Commission on Gold and Silver, 1886-1888.
Pages 266-273.

Extracts from the Final Report.

Part I.
Peculiarity of supply.
Agencies controlling demand.
India Council Bills.
Influence of the Latin Union ratio.

Part II.
Interest of India.
Conditions of a stable ratio.

Apprehensions discussed.

Part III.
Gravity of situation.
Experiment of unregulated use of money-metals.
Breach in 1873-'74.
Proposed remedy.

IX.—The Strength of the English Silver Party. Pages 274-281.

Platform of Bimetallic League, and list of officers.

The Silver Deputation of May 30, 1889. (List.)

X.—The Monetary Congress of the French Exposition (1889).
Pages 282-284.

List of official delegates.

List of Congresses.

Appendix to Chapter VII. Pages 285-290.

Currency Proposals of D. Ricardo.

I.

THE PARIS MONETARY 'CONGRESS'

(SEPTEMBER, 1889)

AND THE

ENGLISH SILVER MOVEMENT.

THE PARIS MONETARY 'CONGRESS' (Sept., 1889), AND THE ENGLISH SILVER MOVEMENT.

The Origin and Effect of the Congress.

The idea of having international meetings, reunions, or conventions at the time of an international exhibition of products is very readily conceived, and sure to recommend itself; and having been put in practice by the French in 1867 and in 1878, it was very natural that the rule should be followed in 1889. But while monetary reform is sufficiently important, one would say, to dictate its own times and places, it is a curious fact that it has been brought to the fore-front in Paris at the date of each of the French Exhibitions, and yet from motives or reasons in each case distinct.

The Exhibition of 1867, the first of its kind, offered the advisers of the Emperor Napoleon an occasion for advancing the primacy of France upon the very path of light—that is to say, in every direction. Far-sighted policy had already brought the unification of monetary systems within their range. It was in August, 1866, that a treaty of monetary union with Belgium, Switzerland, and the new kingdom of Italy had come in force, to which in ·1867 Greece, Roumania, and the Papal States gave their adhesion. Correspondence with other nations had followed upon this notable achievement, with a view to their joining this 'Latin' union, and when in due time the disposition of nations was sufficiently ascertained, a Conference was called in Paris for June 1867, at which were present the delegates of twenty-two nations, including the United States. It is to be noted that at about the same date there was also at Paris a 'Congress of the Exposition,' which dealt with Weights, Measures, and Coins. This has sometimes been confounded with the 'Conference of 1867.'

The origin of the Monetary Conference held in Paris in 1878, the year of the second great French Exposition, is to be sought in Washington, in the second section of the Act of Congress of February 28, 1878, directing the calling of a Conference in Paris within six months. This American Conference is well entitled to be known as the Conference of 1878, albeit there was also a Conference of the States of the Latin Union in Paris in the same year.

The meeting in 1889 of which we are speaking was merely a 'Congress of the Exposition,' and came into being without any distinctive fatherhood of government or signification of political or public interest.

In December, 1888, the Floquet Ministry having the arrangements for the Exhibition on their hands, a list was made of conventions, as we should call them, to be held during its pendency, and among them was suggested a monetary convention. The monetary question, with sixty-eight other subjects,* was put on the list, and an organizing committee was appointed.

Such was the origin of the *Congrès*, as it is called in French.

No purpose was fixed, no jurisdiction assigned, excepting in so far as the word "monetary" has a meaning. The character and effect of the Congress was left to the future, and must depend upon those who thereafter should take it in hand.

In setting forth the outcome of the meeting I shall adopt the language of an 'interview' (in the Paris *New York Herald* of September 15, 1889), the informality of which will be excused in consideration of its directness and brevity.

To one familiar with the political aspects of Silver it was plain that this accidental Congress contained an element of danger to the future of the project of Monetary Federation. It was perhaps unfortunate that this apparently aimless assembly was called, but it had been called, and called under the auspices of the French Government, which, in 1881–'2, had joined the United States in supporting that project. The only thing to do for the

---

* The Exhibition was under the direction of the Ministry of Commerce and Industry. The Monetary Congress was held in a hall in the Trocadero Palace. If I remember rightly there was a Congress on Co-operative Stores, a Fire Brigade Congress, and a Railway Congress about the same time. The latter was, I believe, independent of the Exposition. The list may interest the curious in connection with the coming Quadricentennial, and I have, therefore, reprinted it in the Appendix.

cause was to prevent the meeting from being a failure, and, on the contrary, so far as was practicable, to make it a success.

The subject had long been in abeyance on the Continent. In the years since 1882 the scheme of joint action of nations to restore silver had come to seem very remote, and since 1885 had been, as it were, concealed from view by the nearer, though comparatively trivial monetary issues connected with the fate of the Latin Union. It was in 1885 that the second term of the Monetary Treaty of 1865 expired, and the various Monetary Systems of Europe have an interest in the future of this Treaty Union, either directly or through relations with the parties to it. It is now in full force (as modified) only from year to year, and is liable to be terminated by notice at the will of any of the Signatory Powers. Under the circumstances, it appeared that if the scheme of a new Monetary Union was to be dealt with in Paris with benefit to the cause, it was from England, where silver has long been a subject of agitation—and, if possible, from Germany also—that impulse and reinforcement must come.

In the end the great Deputation of English 'silver men' (see Appendix) which waited on Lord Salisbury and Mr. Goschen on May 30, elicited a response from them which simplified the problem, what was to be done with this Congress in Paris. That response challenged the friends of silver to make a showing in the Congress.

It was a change of venue, but it has not operated to our disadvantage. As I had the opportunity of pointing out to them this challenge opened to English allies of the cause the occasion to break the 'boycott' which the London press has steadily maintained against them hitherto. Independently of all else, this effort was worthy of their energy.

This advantage has been fully gained. It will be evident to English readers that when the London *Times* publishes a column and a half on silver, telegraphed from Paris by Mr. de Blowitz, as it has to-day, a new stage in the progress of the cause of Monetary Union has been reached.

The Congress has, in fact, been a field-day, in which the reformers of England and Germany have displayed their forces. They have made a report upon the good work of conversion that is going on in their countries. That work of conversion is the very life of the cause. There have been only these two chief Powers left to be converted since France and the United States, by the Conference of 1881 and 1882, put the future of silver at their door. Germany waits for England, and England is moving in the path of conversion.

But beside this effect, we have obtained the tactical advantage of bringing the representatives of primitive economic orthodoxy face to face with the leaders of a living reform—requiring the former to face a responsibility which they had never fully realized before. Some of these well-meaning academicians begin to recognize that their anti-silver and anti-parity theories are somewhat incomplete.

The total effect, then, of this interchange of opinion has been excellent. It, in some measure, disarms opposition on the Continent and certainly strengthens the hands of the friends of silver in England.

Beyond this, of course, the Congress can have no effect. It was understood beforehand that it was free to all who were interested in monetary discussions, and that no vote was to be taken. It was only a demonstration of opinion, an occasion for interchange of views. The object proposed has been attained in fair measure. To revive the interest in the subject, which on the Continent had very generally died out, and to answer the challenge of Lord Salisbury and Mr. Goschen, and bring new light into English anti-silver circles, cannot fail to strengthen the cause of Monetary Union.

For certainty of clearness I should make reference to the erroneous information that obtained currency in the United States, at and about the date of its occurrence, as to the scope and character of the "Congress." It seems to have been generally supposed to be an official body* with diplomatic functions, like the Conferences held in 1878 and 1881, and remark was widely made in the press upon its failure to come to a vote; an impression

---

* Official color was, in fact, given to this error (no doubt inadvertently) through the publication, under the auspices of the Departments in Washington, both before and after the Congress, of a Consular report, dated July 8, in which the Congress was referred to in the same terms as the Conference of 1881, and into which some other analogous errors had crept.

quite natural though erroneous; but misleading in a high degree, raising as it did the whole question of the 'foreign relations' of money, and especially of the future of silver.

The list of official representatives at the Congress is given in the appendix.*

The Subject of Debate
and Proceedings of the Congress.

The Organization.

The Congress was opened Sept. 11, with a letter from M. Rouvier, the Minister of Finance, read by M. Magnin, Vice-President of the Senate, Governor of the Bank of France, who was President of the Committee of Organization, and became the President of the Congress. M. Pelligrini, Vice-President of the Argentine Republic, was made Honorary President, and to the names of Léon Say and Cernuschi, Vice-Presidents of the Committee and of the Congress, were added those of Dana Horton, Emile de Laveleye, Grenfell, Levasseur, Luzzatti, and Max Wirth.† The presence of official delegates from the British Indian Empire (Mr. Fremantle, Master of the Mint, and Mr. Murray, of the Treasury), from Japan, and from the South

---

* Of my countrymen I know only of Mr. D. O. Mills and Mr. Edward Tuck as being there. The latter was, I believe, owing to a clerical error, mentioned in some quarters as being a delegate of the United States, but this error was at once corrected by Mr. Tuck. There was no official representation on the part of the United States Government.

† This list is also given in the alphabetic order of countries.

American States, to mention no others,* shows the range of attention excited by the Congress.

The Subject of Debate.

For the debates an ample series of subjects had been set forth, but in the end one paramount subject engrossed attention, and occupied the entire space of the six sessions of the Congress (Sept. 11-14).

The restoration of silver to its former legal equality with gold, in a strong Union of nations, remains, as it has long been, the order of the day.

The Diplomatic Situation of Silver.

A brief retrospect is necessary to indicate the stage now reached in the movement for the adoption of this measure. Silver having become in 1876 the object of agitation in both continents, the proposal of a federation for concurrent free mintage of the two metals was formally made by the United States in a Diplomatic Conference called to meet in Paris in 1878. In 1881 the proposal was renewed by France and by the United States (acting upon the suggestion of France) in a Conference called in Paris for that year. The respective attitudes of nations then disclosed, offered substantial concurrence of all in joint measures to bring about the end proposed, a stable parity of the metals. But the quota of co-operation offered by two of the chief Powers—England and Germany—fell short of that proposed by, and expected from, the others. The partial pro-

---

* The full list will be found in the Appendix.

silver measures offered by England and Germany were conditioned upon complete restoration of free mintage in other States, upon whom, accordingly, the burden of maintaining the parity of the world's money would substantially fall.

France and the United States were not satisfied with this quota from the two other Powers; they required more effective co-operation before they would open their mints freely without limit to new silver. Thus the halting attitude of England—for Germany would have followed England in a further advance—broke up the proposed alliance. Since the Conference of 1881 and 1882 the issue—What England, and in second rank what Germany, is ready to do, has remained the paramount practical issue in this field, down to the present day.

The task evidently pre-ordained for the meetings in the Trocadéro was to collect and focus light upon this situation.

An English and German Demonstration in Paris.

In his opening discourse, M. Magnin pointed the moral of late occurrences in England which decisively establish a new point of departure, and especially of the Silver Deputation* which waited upon the Marquis of Salisbury and the Chancellor of the Exchequer, on May 30, last, and of the response then elicited from the heads of the English Government. The Deputation was pronounced,

---

* See list in Appendix.

it is understood, by so competent a judge as Lord Rowton, to be the strongest Deputation which ever waited upon a Minister of the Crown. The answer of Lord Salisbury and Mr. Goschen seemed to single out the coming Monetary Congress of the French Exposition as an arena where the cause of silver was to be fought for.

The account already given of the Congress shows that the challenge was accepted. The English bimetallists deployed their forces in great strength. Mr. Henry McNiel, the Chief Secretary of the Bimetallic League, was present. Addresses from Mr. Henry R. Grenfell, Ex-Governor and Director of the Bank of England, Vice-President of the League; Sir Henry Meysey-Thomson; Professor H. S. Foxwell, Fellow of St. John's College, Cambridge, Professor of Political Economy in University College, London; Mr. Fielden, the representative of the Workingmen's Organizations of Lancashire; proved that the work put upon Englishmen in 1881 had been manfully performed with a success which seems to promise final triumph. A similar report from Germany, in the address of Dr. Otto Arendt, the leader of the silver agitation in Germany, with a letter from Freiherr von Kardorff, its parliamentary leader, made like answer for Germany, and certified that the government in Germany would second the policy of England, as has been generally maintained.

Academic Debate.

As a supplement to this entirely practical proceeding—in which representatives of English and German opinion made, in Paris, a report of the progress of their countries toward the Monetary Alliance * before proposed, in Paris, by the United States and by France—ample space was offered for academic debate. Fortunately for the liveliness of interest felt in each succeeding session of the Congress, the phases of opinion which make up the opposition to the policy of Parity Union, found ample representation among the Parisian members of the Congress. MM. Levasseur, Frédéric Passy, Fournier de Flaix, Du Puynode, Clément Juglar, Mannequin, Cochut, and MM. Coste and Raffallovich (who were the secretaries of the Congress) presented anti-silver arguments made familiar to monetary students by the Conference of 1867 and by the opposition speakers in the Conferences of 1878 and 1881,—bringing down to date, as it were, the arguments of the gold party in Europe—while the affirmative was represented by a list of speakers, among whom M. Cernuschi was prominent, and which numbered, beside those already mentioned (and myself) M. Emile de Laveleye; M. Alphonse Allard, of Belgium; M. Boissevain, of Holland; M. Lalande, of Bordeaux; and M. Moret, Ex-Minister of Foreign Affairs of Spain.

---

* This Quadruple Alliance is assumed to secure the adhesion of lesser Powers.

The Advance of Opinion in England.

I now set forth in brief outline the course of events which led to this demonstration in Paris of British interest in the Restoration of Silver.

Silver became the object of public attention in England in 1876, which was the date of the phenomenal fall in its 'price' and of the opening of those discussions in Congress and in the Silver Commission then appointed, that were closed with the final passage of the Coinage Act of February 28, 1878. A Select Committee of the House of Commons, of which Mr. Goschen was Chairman, made its report on the Depreciation of Silver in the summer of 1876.

The Select Committee of 1876.

The conclusions of the Report were as follows:

"Your Committee are of opinion that the evidence taken conclusively shows that the fall in the price of silver is due to the following causes:

"1. To the discovery of new silver mines of great richness in the State of Nevada.

"2. To the introduction of a gold currency into Germany in place of the previous silver currency. This operation commenced at the end of 1871.

"3. To the decreased demand for silver for export to India.

"It should be added—

"4. That the Scandinavian Governments have also substituted gold for silver in their currency.

"5. That the Latin Union, comprising France, Belgium, Switzerland, Italy, and Greece, have, since 1874, limited the amount of silver to be coined yearly in the mints of each member of the Union, suspending the privilege, formerly accorded to all holders of silver bullion, of claiming to have that bullion turned into coin without restriction.

" 6. That Holland has also passed a temporary act, prohibiting, except on account of the Government, the coining of silver, and authorizing the coining of gold.

"It will be observed that two sets of causes have been simultaneously in operation. The increased production of the newly-discovered mines, and the surplus silver thrown on the market by Germany have affected the supply. At the same time the decreased amounts required for India, and the decreased purchases of silver by the members of the Latin Union, have affected the demand. A serious fall in the price of silver was, therefore, inevitable."

A Fatal Mistake.

The Committee made the radical mistake of putting among the causes of the change of ratio between silver and gold, not only without qualification but even first on the list, the Nevada Bonanzas—a factor whose efficiency in lowering silver existed purely by favor of other factors mentioned, and which therefore should be placed in a distinct and subordinate position, with clear indication of its nullity from the point of view of state policy. The same error applies to the factor which in the list above is numbered 3, and which is better known under the name of the India 'Council Bills,' a factor which is also *nil* except by reason of the others. These two factors belong to the second line of fructifying causes. Granted the action of governments—that is to say, the laws and decrees which closed the mints of Europe to silver, the gold-rate of silver might naturally suffer some *increase* of its fall by reason of enlarged new supply from the Bonanzas, and likewise by reason of diminished demand for India. But in the absence of these anti-silver laws and decrees it would have suffered no fall whatever. The "demand" for mintage to which the Committee refers, was in the case of the Latin Union a demand of character absolutely distinct, a fixed-ratio demand, a preordained employment equalizing silver with gold at that ratio.

The truth thus ignored by the Committee is the very pith and marrow of the whole business, so that their report is a brilliant, and most unfortunate, exemplification of the obscurity of monetary questions. It was twelve years later that the truth which the Committee of 1876 might have seen but failed to see, was officially recognized, namely, by the Royal Commission on Gold and Silver.

Yet the course of reasoning which leads to this truth seems not too difficult. It was merely necessary to study with unprejudiced eye both sides of the policy of demonetization which had been adopted on the Continent; or in other words to inquire what would have happened to the ratio between the money metals if free mintage had been maintained in Europe for silver as well as for gold.

This inquiry was really imposed by the mandate under which the Committee did its work. One would suppose it a natural course for a legislator brought face to face with a business catastrophe following directly upon a revolutionary series of laws of outlawry directed specifically against the object chiefly involved in the catastrophe, to inquire whether the catastrophe could have occurred, or what would have happened, if these peculiar laws had not been passed ; that is to say, if the object in question, silver, had been left alone where it was. Yet, it was this which Mr. Goschen's Committee omitted.

The causes marked 2, 4, 5, 6, taken together, are the Acts of Demonetization. Without these Acts the " fall in the gold price of silver " could not have occurred. These acts were within the control of governments ; they could be reversed or repealed, and thus an end could be put to the ' fall.' A proposition to that effect from Mr. Goschen's Committee or from the House of Commons would have met with cordial support in other nations. On the other hand the factors which the Committee marked 1 and 3 were not within control. No one would seriously propose to close the mines of the Rocky Mountains ; nor to cancel that debt of India to Europe which led to the use of Council Bills for clearance between the continents, by which debit and credit were balanced as far as they would go, and the unnecessary shipment of specie avoided. Hence in putting into the front rank these ancillary and subordinate factors, the Committee established a bar to action. With such impossibilities in the foreground it was plausible to treat the intervention of Governments in reference to Silver as quite out of the question.

The error went to the very life of reform. It was a dogma of paralysis. No estimate was made of the evils to arise from the situation thus analyzed, and no remedial measures were suggested. The unfortunate result is seen in that sluggishness of the forward movement to recognize the neglected truth, of which the following pages are a brief record.

To assist the reader unfamiliar with the subject to make these several conclusions his own, I pursue in some detail the query, what effect bonanzas of silver could have had on the ratio between silver and gold if silver had remained freely coinable money in Europe just as it was before the Acts referred to were passed. What could happen?

Let us follow in imagination the advent in Europe of this tiny stream of Nevada Silver, turning itself into coin at Paris and Brussels, Utrecht, Berlin, and so on, and gradually adding itself to the thousand millions dollars' worth of silver coin already there, with other thousands of gold (beside paper) in use side by side with them. What would be the result?

A little more silver money in Europe! That is all! What difference would that make? How could that affect the ratio of gold to silver?

Any change that occurred must naturally take the form of a premium on gold. How could an increase of the silver stock produce that effect—a gradual increase, say of

5 per mille, or one per cent., or 2 per cent., as compared with the moneys of Europe? Nay, let us ask whether if all the bonanzas, unrelieved by Indian demand, had been unloaded in France alone, they could have driven gold to a premium? Impossible! Even the suspension of specie payments by the Bank of France did not do that. Indeed, France would have held less silver metal in any case than she holds to-day, when, in spite of the fall of silver bullion her silver coin is not at a' discount. Of course our supposition really implies that the new silver, so far as it went to the European continent, would be distributed among all the money-using populations of the continent.

The reader will find this supposition pregnant with suggestions; especially when he realizes that but for the closing of the mints to silver through ill-advised statute and decree, new life-blood would have poured into the circulation of Europe, most welcome to the veins depleted by the collapse of credit in the years of disorganizing liquidation after 1872. And not even the wildest doctrinaire would have prophesied a premium on gold.

So much was lost by the Committee's failure to penetrate below the surface of their subject! Yet the points I have referred to were apparent to some who were studying the subject at the time—among whom I may myself be numbered. The report of the Congressional Commission appointed in 1876 is in striking contrast to that of the Committee of the House of Commons.

The Conference of 1878.

The second section of the Act of Congress of February 28, 1878, proposed the restoration of silver by concurrent action of nations.

In pursuance of that Act an invitation was issued by Mr. Evarts, then Secretary of State, to the Governments of the principal European nations, which was accepted by all, with the exception of Germany. The Conference met in Paris in August, 1878, as the guest of the French Republic, in the Palace of the Ministry of Foreign Affairs.

The resolutions adopted in this Conference, together with those adopted in the Third International Monetary Conference, which was called by France and by the United States in 1881, are set forth in the Appendix.

The advance of opinion in England on the subject presents itself in the following successive stages :

1. *The attitude of the English representatives at the Monetary Conference of* 1878.

The speeches of Mr. Goschen at Paris put the veto of English science and sagacity upon the further rejection of silver money upon the Continent. This, logically, was not only an abandonment of the case for England's anti-silver laws, but it operated as an admission that the opposite of such rejection, the restoration of silver (proposed by the United States), was a measure which would benefit the United Kingdom. It was thus an affirmation of the internationality of money.

THE CONFERENCES OF 1878 AND 1881.

But the requirements of logic were not applied. No prospect was held out of any active measures to be adopted by England in pursuance of the proposal of the United States.

2. *The attitude of the English representatives at the Monetary Conference of* 1881.

The attitude of Mr. Fremantle, Sir Louis Mallet, and Lord Reay was an advance beyond this position. Although promising no further change in the local sytem of Great Britain than the acceptance of silver as a deposit for Bank of England notes up to the limit of existing statute, to which was added for India the maintenance of free coinage of rupees, the recognition of the interest of the Empire in the policy now proposed by two Great Powers was made more clearly and more strongly. An analogous admission was contained in an offer of co-operation from Germany, which had closed its sales of melted thalers in 1879, and had accepted the invitation to the Conference. But the co-operation offered by England and by Germany was not held sufficient to warrant the United States and France in opening their mints. As a sequel the silver question was left at England's door. It was plain that under no circumstances could the accession of Germany offer so important a consideration to France and the United States to induce them to establish concurrent free coinage of silver, as the accession of England; and at the same time it was probable that Germany's adhesion would follow that of England.

3. *The work of agitation and education in England.*

France and the United States not finding that the situation warranted them in restoring silver mintage, it became incumbent upon those interested to set on foot in England a work of education and agitation which should at length secure the desired change in her policy. The International Monetary Standard Association (Bimetallic League) in England, and likewise the Internationale Doppel-Waehrungs Verein in Germany, were founded in the interval between the adjournment of the Conference of 1881 and the date of its intended re-convocation in 1882.

Of their labors—through the press, by tracts and lectures, public meetings, and the rest—I will not attempt to give here a detailed account. Suffice it to say, that since 1882 a work of education and agitation has been carried on; that public-spirited men have been rallying to the cause from time to time; while the doctrine of monetary union and parity of the money-metals, has been preached in the high-ways and bye-ways. In the meantime the evils which we had prophesied have been descending, chiefly upon England, and have given cumulative force to the teachings of reformers.

I may conveniently mention here a measure* of external strategy which has been amply urged as efficacious for the ripening of conviction in England, namely, that the Ameri-

---

* Stoppage at a future date, in case Europe should refuse to come to terms, was embodied in the Senate amendment to the House Trade-Dollar Bill, reported by Mr. Morrill for the Senate Finance Committee in January or February, 1885. In the House it formed the alternative measure with

can Congress should fix a limit of time to the continued mintage of new dollars. In the never-ending strife in America between those who saw only the silver side of the shield and those who saw only the gold side, the merits of this great stroke for the cause of silver federation have failed of practical recognition. But the event has justified what was said in favor of fixing a limit.

The results obtained in England to-day—the present strength of the pro-silver movement in England—attest the sagacity of the propositions urged upon Congress. The conviction that is ripening slowly under unfavorable conditions, would have ripened quickly under favorable

---

which free coinage was defeated in the spring of 1886; a defeat which seems to have operated as a stimulus to the silver movement in England. (See pages — and —.)

The history of the silver debate in the House in 1886 is briefly this: On February 16 Mr. Bland's free coinage bill, which was supported by two other members of his Committee, was reported by Mr. James for the Committee on Coinage, adversely, "with an expression of their unqualified condemnation." The bill was put upon the calendar, and Mr. Dibble, of South Carolina, in concert with the majority of the Committee on Coinage, offered the following amendment as a substitute:

"That unless meantime, through concurrent action of the nations of Europe with the United States, silver be remonetized prior to July 1, 1889, then and thereafter so much of the act of February 28, 1878, entitled 'An Act to authorize the coinage of the standard silver dollar and restore its legal tender character,' as authorizes and directs the Secretary of the Treasury to purchase silver bullion and cause the same to be coined, shall be suspended until further action by Congress."

The vote was taken April 8, 1886. It stood, on the Free Coinage Bill, nays, 163; yeas, 126; not voting, 34; on the Conditional Limitation Bill, nays, 200; yeas, 84; not voting, 39.

conditions, and such favorable conditions would have been provided by the bill for Conditional Suspension of the Dollar Coinage, which was supported by the international bimetallists in Congress in 1885 and 1886.

It would have operated as the strongest pro-silver measure within the reach of Congress. Failing this reinforcement the slow processes of education and agitation in England were continued.

4. *The Royal Commission on the Depression of Trade and Industry.*

An overt public act appeared when the Royal Commission on the Depression of Trade and Industry was appointed in 1884. Among its members was Mr. Gibbs, Director and former Governor of the Bank of England, Mr. Goschen's colleague at the Conference of 1878, now the President of the Bimetallic League. Its final report was made two years later, in 1886. In its diagnosis of economic malady the disturbance of the money basis of trade and industry caused by the outlawry of silver in divers nations was marked as a region which deserved to be explored by a Special Commission. The report is given in the Appendix.

5. *The Royal Commission on Gold and Silver.*

Such a Special Commission was proposed to Parliament, and was appointed on September 6, 1886. Its Report (presented November 8, 1888), based upon volumes of evidence and exhaustive study by men of distinguished competence, is a memorable landmark in the advancement of science. It is an achievement of moral as well as intellectual dignity. With it the doctrines which many of its members had been wont to hear denounced as heresy, if not as lunacy, have become admitted truths of monetary science.

The full extracts from the Report which are given in the Appendix, leave only for this page the gist of the conclusions arising from this elaborate investigation.

The outcome is a victory. The American proposals of 1878 are justified by the English propositions of 1888.

Six of the Commissioners urge that Her Majesty's Government call the representatives of nations together to offer concurrent free mintage of silver at a ratio to be agreed upon. The other six are not prepared for so pronounced and far-reaching a declaration; but the principle of international concert is admitted, and a goodly part of the opinions subscribed to by Lord Herschell, Mr. Fremantle, Sir John Lubbock, Sir Thomas Farrer, Mr. J. W. Birch, and Leonard H. Courtney, M. P., are very much at home as part of the platform of the Bimetallic League.

The following suggestions (presented in abbreviated form) proceed from these gentlemen who are known to the now anxious partisans of anti-silver laws as the "gold men" of the Royal Commission.

Negotiations with other countries—§§ 135–136.

It might be worth while to meet the great commercial nations on any proposal which would lead to more extended use of silver, and so tend to prevent the apprehended further fall in its value, and to keep its relation to gold more stable ; * * * probably in the direction of an agreement that each nation should annually coin a certain amount of silver, not necessarily the same in all countries. It is worthy of consideration whether foreign governments might not be approached with a view to a larger coinage of silver than at present, in conjunction with an arrangement on the part of India for keeping open her mint, and on the part of the Bank of England, as to a reserve of silver.

Issue of small notes based on Silver—§ 137.

We think that the best suggestion in relief of the tension of the existing situation is to be found in the issue of small notes based on silver as substitutes for the half sovereign. Twenty-shilling silver notes might also be issued. These would probably pass largely into use without any alteration of the law of legal tender, and the Bank might safely be required to issue such notes to some fixed amount, in exchange for silver bullion taken at the average market price; or upon conditions of retaining silver of equal nominal amount. The objections on the part of expense, and the danger of forgery, are met by the example of the United States, where enormous note circulations for small amounts is current.

The Present Situation.

It is plain that the harvest of conversion in England is coming into sight. It is a harvest that took a long and weary seed-time after a long and weary breaking of the ground. England has unfortunately been busy with other things, and she remains busy. She could not leave Ireland in order to study silver and gold: one might say she could not stop worrying, or worrying about, Ireland, according as one's sympathies are Liberal or Tory. In less troubled times she would have been free more quickly to learn new truths, or rather to recognize old truths in the garb which new experience lends them, and thus would not have blocked the advance of a reform of which she is to be the chief beneficiary.

What has been accomplished is indicated by the Deputation of May 30th, and by the demonstration in Paris, of which an account has been given.

In an appendix will be found a list of names, which needs no comment as setting forth the strength of the English friends of Silver Federation.

Their course is complicated by the parallel advance into public notice of two other monetary questions, namely, the questions of withdrawing and recoining light gold coin, and of issuing one-pound notes (perhaps ten-shilling and two-pound notes).

The condition of the gold coin has excited the attention of monetary writers now for many years. A considerable proportion of the gold coin in England is under-weight.

According to a rough approximation current in England, sovereigns lose two pence worth of gold in ten years, which is not far from one per cent, and there has been no important recoinage since 1817. The half-sovereigns suffer more in proportion from wear than the sovereigns.

The proposal made by Mr. Lowe (Lord Sherbrook) then Chancellor of the Exchequer, in 1869, to cut down the sovereign about four pence, and charge the deduction as seigniorage, was intended to bring about assimilation between the English and French units, making the sovereign equal to a twenty-five-franc piece, but the peculiar merit was no doubt observed, that this measure would have provided the means of putting the coinage on a uniform basis. The proposition was rejected. A few years ago Mr. Childers, as Chancellor of the Exchequer, brought forward a plan of cutting down the half-sovereign by a tenth, making it a gold token, and so covering the expense of a general reminting by the gold thus saved.

This also was rejected.

The expectation has been general that Mr. Goschen's fame as a financier is to receive an added lustre by his coping successfully with this problem, which has foiled his predecessors. The special point of query is, where the money is to come from? Among the competing sources is the issuing of silver tokens, which in 1889 gave the difference between 14.28 (the weight of English change relatively to gold) and 21 to 22, say fifty per cent., as profit to the Treasury, less expenses. Another source which has been mentioned is a tax on circulating notes, which seems to imply that an alteration in the law is to be made, which is expected to go further than merely withdrawing the existing prohibition upon the issue of notes by the Bank of England under five pounds. The way has, in part at least, been paved for such change of English policy by the favorable experience of Scotland, which was allowed to maintain its one and two-pound notes. Having greatly recommended themselves there, they have, from time to time, been brought to general attention as a possible example well worthy to be followed in England.

A beginning was made with the light gold coin by a law passed in June, 1889, ordering the withdrawal of gold coined before the present reign, and it has been understood that large purchases of silver were made, followed by a considerable increase in the issue of silver change.

Public attention has also been directed to the question whether half-sovereigns are to be reissued or not; that is to say, whether the melted gold is to come forth in the shape of twenty or of ten-shilling pieces, a matter which lies within the control of the Crown. Such a withdrawal of small gold would be regarded as intended to make room for silver.

It is plain there is material for a currency debate, if Parliament can find time and taste for it.

In the meantime no positive steps are known to have been taken by the Government to give practical sequence to the proposals for concerted action of nations made by either wing of the Royal Commission.

The Future.

The future is in the making. It depends on the will and upon the ability—that is to say, on the knowledge and energy, the grasp—of a few men, and upon the permission or acquiescence of many others.

Circumstances favorable to success exist. The question is, whether advantage will be taken of them. That is the question! It is not new. The circumstances have been favorable since 1881. And many opportunities for action have occurred since then, of which no use has been made. And the statute of limitations has been running against all settlement.

I am very willing to believe this page may find readers to whom the principal statements above made will seem so obvious as to be trivial and unnecessary. To such a reader I have a word to say in explanation of them.

Of the many who now wish well to the project of restoring silver to legal equality with gold, a very large number act, or suffer, under the belief either that the project is so sound and sensible that it will "get itself" adopted, or that the unstable condition of the money basis of the property and investments of mankind will, if left to itself, provoke a crisis so disastrous as to make concurrence of nations in remedial action an inevitable measure of self-protection.

To those who hold these views—which are exceedingly natural and utterly erroneous—the remarks which my critic finds so obvious as to be trivial and unnecessary, are by no means obvious. On the contrary, their truth is excluded by the views of these excellent friends of parity and peace.

And yet these are the very people whose support is needed to make the project of restoring silver to its ancient parity a success. So, while the truths I have stated are not obvious to them, still less are they trivial or unnecessary. On the contrary, they are the truths most necessary to be understood, to be grasped, to be held with the utmost vigor of conviction.

If those who are now friends of the project in the United States were only so convinced of the truths first above stated as to be willing to use their influence in favor of it, the project would very speedily become a reality.

II.

A REVIEW OF ANTI-SILVER ARGUMENTS.

REPLY TO

Mr. LEVASSEUR and Mr. DU PUYNODE.

A REVIEW OF ANTI-SILVER ARGUMENTS.

REPLY TO MR. LEVASSEUR AND MR. DU PUYNODE,

In the Monetary Congress of the Exposition in Paris, September 13, 1889.*

EXPLANATORY.

The following pages are a translation from a stenographic report, in French, as printed (with some trifling corrections) for the official journal of the Congress. These remarks were made in response to a request, coming from various sections, that I should speak, and were made not only without notes but with nothing which could properly be called preparation.

If a friend on the silver side should reproach me for neglecting the cause by not making a set speech, I should

---

* PIERRE-EMILE LEVASSEUR (b. 1828), member of the Institute, Professor in the College of France. The list of his financial and economic works begins in 1854, and numbers among other important titles: *The Gold Question* (Paris, 1858). *The History of the Working Classes in France from Cæsar's Conquest to the Revolution* (Paris, 1859).

MICHEL GUSTAVE PARTOUNAU DU PUYNODE (b. 1817), Doctor of Laws, a founder and chief editor of the *Journal des Economistes*, President of the Council-General of the Department of the Indre. The list of his financial and economic works begins in 1843, and contains among other important titles: *Money Credit and Taxation* (Paris, 1853), and *The Great Financial Crises of France* (Paris, 1826.)

be able to make good a defence on the following lines, which are worth mentioning, not for any personal reason, but because they may throw light on some of the obstacles to the success of the federation project. In the effort to promote that project, in which I have been active since it was conceived, the exposed and defenceless condition of the cause in respect to prolixity has often impressed me; for even slight verbal excesses repel and repress, rather than encourage, the wished-for growing interest and persuasion, when one is dealing with such a subject—which can well be pictured as a morass of problems, intersected by a few safe paths, easy to walk on, but also easy to stray from. The work of agitation and education which has been going on in Europe for so many years offers ample and varied illustration of what I mean.

So far as an appearance on the platform at the Trocadéro was concerned, I felt that my country's attitude as to silver was sufficiently known, and that, personally, my past services as a founder and promoter of the federation project relieved me from the need of saying much. My contributions upon the subject are numerous and not unknown to monetary students, while speeches in support of the policy which I had, I believed, justified in 1876, in a Treatise on Silver and Gold, were made in Paris in 1878 and 1881, before official delegates of nations, the majority of whom were at last in favor of it. Our friends from England and Germany, it appeared to me, were entitled to the floor. This view, I may add, I had occasion to press in the proper quarters long in advance of the meeting of the Congress.

Beyond the reception of reports from these still delaying but expected allies in the coming Parity Federation, it seemed to me that the opponents of this policy should have their say. They should then be fully met on our side, face to face, hand to hand, argument to argument—*in reply*, to use a term more familiar to a lawyer than to a professor, and with their flanks exposed under the burden of proof. This course I thought, under the circumstances, more suitable than the academic procedure, which may be described as a series of essays spoken or read, and perhaps formally directed against each other, but in a vague and inconclusive manner—a sort of parade charge through a monetary bog, after which each party returns to its own camp.

In preparing this translation to be offered to the public I have in several instances observed that there was too great condensation of statement, and hence I have inserted *in brackets* a few phrases or sentences in order to explain by amplifying.

A Review of Anti-Silver Arguments.

Mr. President and Gentlemen:

I shall address you very briefly, limiting myself to criticism, partly from the scientific and partly from a practical point of view, of the position taken by speakers who are opposed, or who believe themselves opposed, to the movement for the restoration of silver to its former condition of money equal to gold; equal, that is, before the law.

I regret that Mr. Levasseur is not here to-day, for I desire particularly to indicate the great importance of certain practical conclusions which he has set forth and defended here. Mr. Levasseur has also told us that to be a partisan of what is called "the Single Gold Standard," is not a certificate of old age; there are still young men as well as old men who are in favor of it. He also observed that there is a great difference of opinion on this topic, and he sought to investigate the source of this difference. It appears to me, however, that he has not noticed the true cause. The true cause is this, that there was an orthodoxy, and that this form of religion is disappearing, or, rather, transforming itself into a new orthodoxy.

We respect the economists of the past. Eleven years ago, gentlemen, I crossed the sea to bring you the proposals of the United States—proposals for a Monetary Federation—based upon the principle of Union which had been consecrated by the consent of all the economists of France and of other countries. These propositions have been discussed here before you during some days, by Englishmen, by Germans, by Hollanders, who have expressed their adhesion to them. The fundamental difference between the new principle and the old is this: we think that the accord of monetary laws should relate to the material and not to the form. The Monetary Unions known to the past have dealt chiefly with the coins, the mintage, the stamp; and the material of which money is made has been a little neglected. We came, therefore, not as innovators, but merely, as it were, to propose an amendment, and ask for it the support of economists who had already given their adhesion to the principle of Monetary Union.

You see, gentlemen, it is perfectly natural, this difference of opinion of which the Honorable Mr. Levasseur has spoken; there are economists who propose an amendment of science, and to obtain its acceptance—of course, that takes time.

But we, who have desired for so long a time that you, who are opposed to us, should accept an amendment of monetary science, we have the right to recall to your minds that it is not probable that monetary science should remain without improvement, without growth. We have asked you to understand us. Gentlemen, I do not wish to speak ill of any one; I have no idea of making an attack upon friends who are here, and met together in an international reunion. But I pray you to accept from me a complaint. You have not yet done us the honor fully to understand our propositions, and it is for that reason that you are here to oppose the pro-silver movement in England and in Germany, of which these gentlemen have spoken.

I beg you to observe, gentlemen, that the thing we are speaking of is practical in its nature. I ask those gentlemen who have spoken, and those who are about to speak; I ask Mr. Passy* and others who are to address you: Give us the reasons why England should not accept the proposition to form a Monetary Alliance with France. [Applause.]

If you can show that monetary union is not a good policy, I beg you to do so. But I will say this to you, if it is not a good thing that Paris or France should have a stable parity of money with London, with Calcutta, with San Francisco, with Buenos Ayres, then demonstrate, I pray you, why it is a good thing that Paris should have a stable parity of money with Marseilles, with Bordeaux, and with Calais. [Applause.]

There is the point! This is a practical matter, gentlemen. We are not here for the purpose of making academic eulogies on certain doctrines of science; it is with a view to action, to results, with a practical object, that we desire to compare our ideas.

I have complained, gentlemen, that our adversaries have not yet done us the honor of understanding us. I

---

* FREDERIC PASSY (b. 1822), member of the Institute of France, Deputy. The list of his economic and political works begins in 1856.

assure you that the divergency that exists between our opinions can be harmonized, if our adversaries will do us this honor. For us, gentlemen, it is necessary to understand your position, your opinions. If we cannot do that we can have no hope of persuading you. We began with the study of the opinions you share, and it was because we understood them that we have been able to add the corrections of which I have spoken.

I now allow myself, gentlemen, to call attention to certain remarks which fell from speakers who have preceded me to-day. There is an order of fact and opinion, the significance of which was indicated by the honorable gentleman who has just spoken, Mr. Du Puynode, in referring to the two metals *as subject to the laws of the market*. I adopt for a moment the language used by the distinguished speaker; I also say they are in the market. But I ask, what market? I aver that it is a market in which a decision of the English Parliament can determine the position of a metal. Mr. Du Puynode cannot deny that. It is impossible. Everyone knows that if the English Parliament passes a law, a law for gold money in England, or a law for silver money in England, it will be gold in one case, or silver in the other; that will be money in England. The market we are in, then, is a market in which great nations are, so to speak, buyers.

Very well, we are here to say, or rather these English and German representatives are here to say, after the invitation of France and the United States (1881): Yes, we are ready that our countries respectively shall enter this market as buyers, and we know that if we do so, if these nations combine, they can fix the relative importance of gold and silver. There are no other nations that have the power to neutralize what these nations shall determine.

I shall now ask you, gentlemen, to consider for a moment the origin of these ideas on the "single gold standard," which have been set forth by speakers who are among the partisans of this metal. What is the source, what is, so to speak, the history of the evolution of this theory?

My researches into the history of monetary policy * have enabled me to ascertain that in the past, in most nations, the system of money was this: There was a principal money and a secondary money. Everywhere throughout the world there was the "single standard," if you desire to call it so, of silver, and another "standard," but a secondary one, of gold. [There was, therefore, a combined single and dual standard.]

From the legislative point of view silver was superior, gold the inferior. This is the system of money which has continued down to our century.

Mr. Du Puynode has cited to you, and, I believe, Mr.

---

* The statements of historical facts given in this and following pages, which are at variance with the hitherto accepted versions of history, are set forth, and I believe, justified in "Historical Material," and "Contributions to the Study of Monetary Policy," in the Document of the Monetary Conference of 1878 (Washington, 1879), and in "The Silver Pound and England's Monetary Policy since the Restoration" (London: Macmillan & Co., 1887), copies of which works were distributed to members of the Congress through the hands of MM. Guillaumin & Co., publishers, 14 Rue Richelieu, Paris.

Mannequin and another of our speakers, have cited to you, a great work of Lord Liverpool.* Now, Lord Liverpool thought he could transfer, from silver to gold, this position of legal superiority. But he was not an enemy of silver. His propositions embraced free coinage of silver in England.

Mr. Mannequin has cited to you the names of Locke and Newton. But they were as much in favor of two money metals as we are. This has been proved. I shall have the honor of bringing to your attention manuscripts of Newton, which I discovered in the Archives in London, and also a report of Locke which had not been generally known, all of which I published two years ago.† It is now proven that for Locke and for Newton and for all the elder English authorities the true system was a system of money made of the two metals, the one superior, the other in a legal position, so far as the thought, the intention of the legislature was concerned, a little inferior— that is all.

And now I pray you, gentlemen, to glance (in passing) at the practical importance, for our question of the origin of the theory of the single gold standard, of the fact that we have here to-day the representatives of public opinion in England [to tell us that conversion in favor of silver is proceeding in the home and native soil of that erroneous doctrine].

---

* A Treatise on the Coins of the Realm in a letter to the King. London. 1805.
† See preceding note, page 42.

Eleven years ago, during the Monetary Conference of 1878, I had the great pleasure of making the acquaintance of Michel Chevalier,* to whom I was presented by M. de Parieu. Chevalier spoke to me of the object of the Conference, and said words which remain and always

---

* MICHEL CHEVALIER (b. 1806, d. 1879), member of the Institute of France. He was sent, in 1833, by Mr. Thiers, to study the methods of transportation in the United States. He published *Letters on North America* (2 vols., Paris, 1836); *Material Interests of France, Public Works, Roads, Canals, Railways* (Paris, 1838); *History and Description of Modes of Transportation in the United States* (Paris, 1840). In 1840 he succeeded Rossi as Professor of Political Economy in the College of France. Among his numerous succeeding works I mention here his Treatise on *Money*, the first thorough and comprehensive work on the subject, and his *Probable Fall of Gold* (Paris, 1859), which was translated and reprinted in England by Cobden. He was made member of the Academy of Moral and Political Sciences in 1851; was Counsellor of State under the Empire; a Deputy, and Senator.

I have always regarded him as the controlling spirit in the monetary thought of his time, and as the chief spiritual progenitor of the decisions of the International Monetary Conference of 1867, and hence of the Anti-Silver Movement.

The saying of Chevalier, above quoted, seemed to me the symptom of an admission extending to the innermost core of the subject; the admission, namely, that if we succeeded in one way we should succeed in the other; that if England should join with the other nations, the parity of the metals would be maintained—the contrary of which opinion still plays its part as a tenet; it is not yet dislodged entirely from the convictions of the learned. Reference will be found to this point on a later page.

The present representatives of the Chevalier tradition in France, the gentlemen who addressed the Congress on the anti-silver side in such force, including the accomplished young journalists who acted as its Secretaries, illustrate the persistence of the mathematician's idea of the

THE SINGLE STANDARD.

will remain in my memory: "*You will never succeed in converting England.*"

There, gentlemen, is the basis of the opinion of all those who oppose this movement for the restoration of silver, which is now going on in England and Germany. France and the United States, as you are aware, were gained long ago. The main support of the opinions of those who oppose us, is still and always England, and it is because it was believed to be descended from ancestors so worthy of respect as Locke and Newton that this idea, opinion, or theory of the Single Gold "Standard"—an idea which belongs properly to mathematical sciences—has been accepted in political and economic science.

Gentlemen, look about a little, if you will, and consider what is your idea. Everyone makes his ideas for himself. What is your idea of a "standard"? It is a weight,

---

"standard," to which I have referred on pages 45 to 47. The same remark would be justified by the existing opinion in academic circles in other European capitals, though such opinion makes itself heard chiefly when attack is made upon the existing primacy of gold, which is *de facto* the established "standard" of Christendom, that is to say, privileged by law and by administrative regulation in Europe and America as the ruling money, freely coinable and receivable everywhere. In each country the gold party is still in some measure inspired with faith in its metrical and mathematical concept "standard" (*étalon*), which it adopted from the exact sciences in the course of the long-continued agitation for perfecting and unifying weights, measures, and units.

I may here appropriately observe that if Michel Chevalier had not begun life as an engineer—with an engineer's confidence in physical weights, measures, and units—the monetary history of his time might have been a very different one.

says one. Very well, put it in a glass case where we keep standards of weight. No, no; that is not all. This weight is circulating through the country. Then in the case of money the weight is not everything. But where is the "standard," gentlemen, where is the "standard," if it is in the pockets of the people, and if it is a weight? I beg you, gentlemen, to make an effort to give substance, to represent in its reality, your idea of a "standard," and you will see there is something wrong in it.

[You cannot with impunity predicate of values that quality of physical fixity and invariableness which the word "standard" represents, by reason of its general application to the constants with which science measures space, time, matter, and force.]

There is money, gentlemen—what is money by law. Talk of that and I understand you, and I care very little what you say of a "standard."

Very well; this theory of the single standard made of gold took its rise in this way. There was a misunderstanding — that is all — a misunderstanding about the former "constitution of money," which was, as I have explained, silver as principal money, gold as secondary money, but both of them money, and both fully money; the difference in their rank being a difference in the intent of the legislator, not in their employment by the people. Rights of coinage and legal tender power were the same. But, in the plan of the legislator, the basis of the system was silver. If it should become necessary to change the ratio, then it was the gold coin whose weight must be increased or diminished. That was the legal difference between the two kinds of money. Here, then, was the misunderstanding [a confusion of concepts, an exaggeration, you see, of the legal theory of unity at the expense of the facts, the actual and lawful duality], and it was believed that the authority of Newton and Locke and of other guiding spirits made for this [exaggeration which ignored the fact, for a] theory, or rather for a definition—a tendency of opinion about money—which belongs rather to the physical sciences than to political economy.

Based upon this error came the prestige of the United Kingdom to fortify it; the fact that the laws of this great people, the people most advanced and best known in the world of international trade—the chief maritime nation—gave a marked preference and privilege to *gold money*. The law for free coinage of silver still existed on the statute book, but it had not been put in force. Well, the prestige of the English system impressed itself upon general opinion; nothing occurred to disturb the impression; and when the great agitation for the improvement of weights and measures and units [that is, of real " standards "] came, there was this error about the nature of money at the foundation [of the general opinion of the learned in these matters], and the experience and the authority of the United Kingdom sustaining it. Thus it came to pass that the mathematician's enthusiasm, enthusiasm for the metric system, misled economists [and statesmen] into the disastrous path which the International

Conference of 1867 recommended—the effort to abolish silver money.

Here, gentlemen, you see the origin of opinions which still—even to-day—have maintained a certain influence.

But, gentlemen, before leaving the tribune I allow myself the pleasure of noting that, after all, the opposition in France on the part of the masters, the professors of science, does not amount to very much—

MEMBERS. [Oh! Oh!]

Mr. HORTON.—According to the opinion of Mr. Levasseur!

This is not merely my opinion, gentlemen; it is the opinion of Mr. Levasseur; for he has proposed to you the free coinage of silver.

A MEMBER. But under what conditions!

Mr. HORTON. I will tell you the conditions. I regret that Mr. Levasseur is not here.

The PRESIDENT. He was obliged to leave Paris this morning. He asked me yesterday to present his regrets to the Congress. It was my forgetfulness that prevented my doing so.

Mr. HORTON. You were all here; you all heard Mr. Levasseur. According to what I heard, he was for the free coinage of silver, at the market rate, was it not?

MEMBERS. [Yes! Yes!]

The SECRETARY, Mr. COSTE. That is to say, that before coining a five-franc piece he would want not merely silver enough to coin it, but a third more.

A MEMBER. They would have to begin again when the rate changed.*

---

* NOTE.—The member who said this was in error as to Mr. Levasseur's proposition, at least unless both myself and Mr. Coste are wrong. "Beginning again when the rate changes" implies what Americans have known as the "cart-wheel dollar"—the effort to coin a dollar "with silver enough in it to make it equal to a gold dollar." To do this it would be necessary to change the weight (and perhaps to recoin the existing stock) whenever a change should come in the gold price of silver.

The effect of Mr. Levasseur's proposition would be—so at least I understood it and explained it at the time to some of his friends,—that the Government would buy all the silver that should be offered to it, and pay in five-franc pieces. In self-defence it would be obliged to coin up the bullion. To maintain its silver coin at par with gold would be necessary for self-preservation, and hence it could tolerate no discrimination against silver coin.

The Government must therefore use silver coin on the same terms with gold in its own transactions. In that case there would be, *de facto*, unlimited legal tender for silver, so far as such transactions are concerned. In presence of such an arrangement, with this avenue for use wide open, the little fence set up on the side of compulsory legal tender (limiting it to 1000 or 500 francs) would be of no avail. The limitation would be nullified in practice, even if it were not repealed out of hand.

So, as I said in the above lines, What difference would it make?

I may usefully recall here that the vocabulary of money is very deficient in the means of clear thinking and precision of statement on these heads; and French, which expresses "legal tender" by "liberatory force," or "power," is no better off.

I have endeavored to reinforce the plain English of monetary talk (which is not yet plain enough), by introducing the word "partial"—*partial legal tender*—in the special sense of money which, *in certain quarters*, is legally receivable without limit. With us, for example, the national bank notes and silver certificates are partial legal tender, being receivable for public dues.

Mr. HORTON. Mr. Levasseur gave a great many arguments; he was very eloquent; I remember with pleasure that he said many brilliant things, and that they were aimed at us, and all was very well said; but at the end, he proposed the free coinage of silver.

The SECRETARY, Mr. COSTE. Permit me to say that Mr. Levasseur added that the silver coin should have its legal tender limited to 500 francs.

Mr. HORTON. Five hundred francs, or 1,000 francs, or something like that.

The SECRETARY. It was I who, in first addressing the Congress, took occasion to point out that it ought not to go beyond 1,000 francs, and in fact that the legal tender power should not be so high, but Mr. Levasseur indicated 500 francs as the limit.

Mr. HORTON. According to my remembrance he spoke of 500 francs, but he also spoke of 1,000 francs, and added at the end, " something like that."

But what difference does it make? If all the opposition which exists against the movement in England and Germany, the object of which is to persuade these nations or governments to ally themselves with France and the United States—if all this opposition, I say, melts down and disappears in a proposition like that of Mr. Levasseur, I have great pleasure in assuring my friends from England and Germany that we need have little solicitude for the future. If these gentlemen who are opposed to us are of that way of thinking, they are on the right track;

they have made good progress; they are at last coming over to be our friends and to stand by our side.

These gentlemen from England have come here on the invitation of the Direction of the Exposition; they have given a report on the progress which has been made since the silver question was left, so to speak, at England's door, at the close of the Conference of 1881 and 1882; and these other gentlemen have come from Germany for a similar object. They are curious to see if the men of science who are here assembled can say anything to convince them that they are wrong; that they must turn back, retrace their steps, and abjure their opinions.

Well, gentlemen, when the practical outcome of a discourse so eloquent as that of Mr. Levasseur is the free coinage of silver, I assure you we are very near a general agreement.

Mr. FREDERIC PASSY. It is not free coinage at the rate of $15\frac{1}{2}$.

Mr. HORTON. A word more! The honorable Mr. Du Puynode, who has spoken of England as the native land of the single gold standard, also added some words of encouragement as to the condition of England in these late years. One would suppose—that is, if I heard him rightly—that there had been no "hard times"[*] there.

Mr. DU PUYNODE. I said there had been hard times, but that the crisis has passed for England.

Mr. HORTON. If the crisis has passed we are all rejoiced, are we not?

---

[*] *Crise.*

But what I wish to point out to you is this: the practical question for this assembly is to know whether the outlawry of silver has been an efficient cause of hard times in the past. If that is the fact, the thing to do is to prevent the outlawry of silver in the future. [Applause.]

Well, on this question, I have heard nothing, and yet it is the chief practical question. We are not here to inquire if we are feeling well. [Laughter.] We want to know if there is something to be done to ward off any disease that is in the air. [Applause.]

Now, gentlemen, I have one word to add touching the attitude of those who defend the outlawry of silver. I point out to you that the very existence of their opinions to-day is due to the fact that their propositions were not adopted. The demonetization of silver!—we can use the words if we wish—but the great fact, the important fact, is that the demonetization of silver did not take place; the movement was checked, and it went no further.

If that movement had gone on we should have witnessed a different state of affairs—[we should have witnessed disasters far beyond all that has oppressed mankind since 1873.] This is what we wish to explain, and what the speakers who oppose the restoration of silver ought to be denying. But they cannot do this.

The sale of melted silver dollars in Germany was closed ten years ago. Gentlemen, if you wish to get to the root of this question—I give you notice of this because we expect you to do so, to recognize the significance of the issue which our friends from England and Germany have

THE POLICY OF DISUNION.

put before you—ask for yourselves, or let us ask you to tell us, what would have been the result if the French dollars* which we had the pleasure of inspecting this morning in the Bank of France, had been sold?

There is the point; the point about which you should take sides. Your advice is asked; people wish to know whether you are in favor of demonetizing silver. If you are not in favor of it, we beg you to say so—Mr. Levasseur has already done this—and we ask all speakers who are opposed to the silver movement in England and Germany to tell us what ground they would have taken if such a sale had occurred, and what would happen if they should succeed in inducing the governments to undertake a general attack against silver.

I thank the assembly for its kindly reception. [Applause.]

---

* 1,250,000,000 francs' worth in 5-franc pieces.

III.

QUESTIONS

OF

THE ROYAL COMMISSION

ON

GOLD AND SILVER,

AND

ANSWERS.

PREFATORY.

The following letter and enclosure gave the occasion and motive for preparing these pages:

GOLD AND SILVER COMMISSION,
8, RICHMOND TERRACE, LONDON,
August, 1887.

SIR: The Commission appointed by Her Majesty's Government in the course of last year to investigate the recent changes in the relative values of the precious metals have made some progress with their inquiry, and have taken a considerable body of evidence from persons in this country; but they feel that they would have imperfectly discharged the duty imposed upon them if they had not had recourse to some of the many competent authorities on the subject who reside in foreign countries.

It is, however, obviously impossible to elicit the views of these gentlemen by the usual method of oral examination, and the Commission have therefore drawn up the enclosed paper of questions, comprising the more important points on which they are anxious to obtain the opinion of those who have studied the subject.

Should you feel disposed to assist the Commission in this way, they would be very much obliged if you would favor them with written answers to any or all of these questions.

If, however, you are unable, for any reason, to comply with the invitation of the Commission, they desire me to convey to you their apologies for having ventured to trouble you with this letter.

I forward under another cover a copy of the First Report of the Commission, which has been recently issued.

I have the honor to be, sir, your obedient servant,

(Signed) GEO. H. MURRAY,
Secretary to the Commission.

To Mr. S. DANA HORTON.

The above circular letter was sent to a limited number of persons in different countries, and replies, to the number of eight I believe, including the replies of the Hon. David A. Wells and the following, were printed in the appendices of the Commission's Report.

The enclosure is as follows:

QUESTIONS.

1. *To what do you attribute the fall in the value of silver, as compared with gold, since 1874?*

2. *What probability is there of a continuance of the fall?*

3. *To what do you attribute the fall in the wholesale prices of many commodities which has been in progress during the last 10 or 12 years?*

4. *Has it extended to (a) retail prices (b), wages and other payments for services rendered (c), land and houses?*

5. Has the fall resulted in any material prejudice to the commercial or general interests of the world?

6. Do you consider that the countries using the gold standard, or any of them, are suffering from an injurious contraction of the currency which might have been obviated or mitigated by an increase in the supply of gold?

7. To what extent and in what way are prices affected by the quantity of the metal or metals used as standards of value?

8. What is the relation, if any, between the supply or quantity of the precious metals and the fluctuations of credit?

9. Has there been during the last 15 years any important development of the system of cheques, bank credits, bills of exchange, or other means of economizing the use of the precious metals?

10. Do you consider that an international agreement could be made for the free coinage of gold and silver as legal tender money at a fixed ratio?

11. Is it in the power of Governments to maintain such a ratio if agreed upon; and would the practice of the commercial world follow the law?

12. *What would be the effect of such an agreement, if carried out, upon* (a) *prices, and* (b) *the production of the precious metals?*

13. *Do you consider an international agreement for bimetallism possible on any other ratio than* 15½ *to* 1 ?

14. *Failing an international bimetallic agreement, what measures could be adopted by the commercial nations of the world for giving increased stability to the relation between gold and silver?*

15. *It is argued that, in the absence of bimetallism, the effect of any disturbance of the currency is limited to half the currencies of the world, and thereby increased in intensity. Do you consider this view correct; and, if so, do you think the evil a serious one?*

16. *If the effect of such disturbances could be spread all over all countries, would greater stability of the standard of value be secured thereby?*

QUESTIONS OF THE ROYAL COMMISSION ON GOLD AND SILVER

AND

ANSWERS.

I.

QUESTION I.

To what do you attribute the fall in the value of silver, as compared with gold, since 1874?

DEFINITION (*relating also to other* QUESTIONS).

The form of the QUESTION "to what do you attribute" a certain phenomenon? opens a wide field. It brings into view the entire range of elements which have combined their influence to produce the phenomenon: and the temptation arises in answering the question either to contemplate with indifference both causes and conditions, or fail to recognize the restraints upon freedom of choice among them. In a certain sense each of these regions is a little world in itself, for there is an endless multiplicity of factors distributed in time and space, without the concurrent existence of which the monetary situation could not have been exactly what it is. For the purpose of gaining any useful generalization as to that situation, the range of view must be limited to the causes and conditions that are close at hand, and they must be distinguished, the controllable forces must be recognized as such, the subject looked at in mass and in perspective.

These observations, however obvious and commonplace, would be germane if it were for a purpose purely scientific that the labors of the ROYAL COMMISSION were undertaken; if it were merely an Economic Academy gradually accumulating the materials for an exhaustive Dictionary or Cyclopædia of Monetary Science. This however is not understood to be its character. However important the contribution which it makes to the knowledge of monetary economy, its function is primarily a practical one, that of a Special Council of State, its function as a scientific body being tributary to its function as a political body. Its members, deliberating upon the remedies of existing evils and the means of preventing future evils, are to act by recommendations, positive or negative, expressing themselves favorably or unfavorably, upon a proposal to modify English monetary laws; and are, at the same time, to exert an influence, favorable or unfavorable, upon the prospect of the adoption of modifications of their laws by the legislatures of other nations, an influence which cannot fail seriously to affect British interests. The point of view of the ROYAL COMMISSION is, then, really that of the learned law-giver at the moment of decision, or of drafting a decree. Although it deals with a subject presenting many problems unsolved or insoluble, its object is to act; as a council of astronomers would reform a calendar, or select a meridian, without determining the chemistry of the sun, or completing a catalogue of the stars.

In so far as the ROYAL COMMISSION shall affect legislation,—whether positively or negatively, passively or actively, by leaving things as they are, or by suggesting change,—it directs the will of nations for good or for ill. Its choice between the two paths which lie before it must mark a turning-point in history. The paths are well distinguished; for a decade of controversy has been exploring these fields of thought, and all mankind have an interest in the decision. Further light is to be thrown upon the questions: Has the general outlawry of silver money pending since 1873, been beneficial to England?—Will the restoration of silver to permanent monetary equality with gold by joint action of nations be beneficial to England?—questions upon which England gave some answer before the nations in the International Monetary Conferences of 1878 and of 1881. Impetus will be given to decision of the questions: Shall England promote Monetary Union or Monetary Disunion?—Shall England aid in giving stability or instability to the foundation of the valuations of mankind?

To deal with these issues is the gist of the mandate of the ROYAL COMMISSION.

The course of definition, then, which I am now seeking to present,—that which, with a view to action, would insure a grasp of the situation as a whole,—is the course which the COMMISSION takes in order to fulfil its trust, to "rise to the height of its great argument." Hence, one who seeks to give answer to the QUESTIONS of the COMMISSION will do well to regard the same perspective in his replies, as far as his vision may reach. But to do this, and to guaranty thorough understanding of these replies on the part of a reader, they must be seen and be shown in their relations; it is necessary not only to declare the standpoint, but to define it with particularity. To this end, a certain energy of precision is required, to overcome an existing tendency toward confusion, an opaqueness of the very atmosphere by which all readers of the day are surrounded. There is an omnipresent never-resting pressure, a momentum of opinion, a gravitation of interest, which resists an adequate recognition of the obvious truths heretofore set forth, and which therefore calls for a corresponding energy in their vindication. I do not here refer merely to the well-known obscurity and difficulty of the subject—by reason of which the questions of the ROYAL COMMISSION, though brief in themselves, would need a volume for exhaustively explicit treatment—but to a peculiar tendency toward error in the minds of many men of learning, the nature and origin of which is given by the following facts:

These anti-silver laws, whose effects the ROYAL COMMISSION is called upon to study, were not adopted without deliberation. The advice of counsel was taken, men of action submitted to men of thought, and the advising counsel were the learned of a generation. It was the general consensus of the learned opinion of the time which these laws were intended to reflect. The republic of monetary learning, an *imperium in imperiis*, an economic church which respects no national boundaries, was unanimous. If believed in the Unification of Money—in security of valuations, in simplification of the means of exchange, in facilitating international trade and investment—an aim nobly in unison with the progressive spirit of an age whose glory it is already to have made giant strides in this direction, by putting nature's forces in harness, as well as by cultivating the faculties of men. This was the aim, the object, the end. What could be more worthy?

But of the means to attain this end what account is to be given? What was this means? The outlawry of silver, the legislative or administrative exclusion of silver from legal privileges hitherto enjoyed equally with gold. Did this tend toward the Unification of Money and the benefits it was to bring in its train? This is one phase of the subject before the ROYAL COMMISSION. In considering it, there are at least two hypotheses that must be entertained, namely, either that this repeal of laws equalizing the metals was wise, or it was unwise. The inquiry can hardly be carried on without entertaining these two suppositions. If the latter supposition, which I aver to be true, be dispassionately examined with some deliberation, it will appear that it entails precisely the conclusions as to the present confused state of monetary learning to which I have referred. It must be assumed then that, in the field of action, lay error. The means was not only inadequate for its special end, sacrificing substance to shadows, but was disastrous in the wider field of its influence.

Failing, however, to perceive all this in advance, the learned world was betrayed into acting as sponsor of a mistaken scheme of Unification, accessory before the fact, aider and abetter in the great overt acts of the anti-silver movement, the anti-silver laws of Germany, which were followed in natural sequence by the anti-silver laws of other states. The event is unique, without precedent. For the first time in history has a theory of the closet been so abruptly transformed into *jus gentium*, the law common to the nations. How far, then, did the interpreters of science feel themselves committed to justify the correctness of their practical suggestions? How far did they recognize the means which they had suggested to attain an end, as merely tentative, as an experiment, as the object of scientific curiosity rather than of partisan attachment? Did they feel themselves committed to the error as well to the truth, to the mistaken means, as well as to the justified end?

The question is of decisive practical importance.

Certainly the average man would naturally regard them as so committed, and, human nature being in full operation, it is quite plain that it required a certain rare elevation of spirit, for one who had borne a part in the anti-silver movement, to grant access to his mind for that course of study of the practical working of the change wrought by anti-silver laws, which showed he had been in the wrong. Beside this the mere momentum of accomplished facts, the complexity and obscurity of the subject, made such study an effort which could not fail to be unwelcome, and would easily seem to be unnecessary. To whatever extent, then, economists failed to support a new and heavy burden of learning and of unlearning, an unique array of forces was summoned to defend error. Conviction must take time, and until it becomes general, fallacious doctrine must here and there be flourishing under the shadow of authority, an abnormal atmosphere of monetary opinion must obscure, refract, or distort the image of truth. It is then, quite in the natural order of events that mighty forces should be at work to prevent recognition of the truth as to the questions before the COMMISSION; a resistance for which the vitality of a race, or of a religion, alone affords adequate parallel.

To prove this steadiness of pressure, the very existence of the ROYAL COMMISSION is itself a witness. It was commissioned in 1886 to perform a task, a goodly part of which a SPECIAL COMMITTEE of the HOUSE of COMMONS, appointed in 1876, might, could and, — it may be argued, — should, have performed. Ten years of the life of a generation, a goodly fraction of the most active years of the XIX century, are thus, in a certain sense, a measure of these forces.

For whatever obstacles to conviction and bent toward fallacy there may be, the special subject now considered supplies outwork and bulwarks and fortress and the very inner and final citadel of strength. One may say, indeed the very configuration of the ground combines the natural advantages for the defence of error.

It is, upon final analysis, the free will of men which affords the staple of discussion, but the free will of men moving as it were, in two distinct masses, the one belonging to the individual acting separately, the other to the organized will of the community, the state, acting through governments. The difficulties of adequate distinction between the two orders of volition, of assigning its true place to each, offer amplest field for a confusion which must surely tend to obscure the duty of statesmanship, whose task consists in overcoming inertia, in stimulus and direction and control of the will of nations. Thus the mere enthusiasm of the votary of science—making " better the enemy of good," as the French phrase has it—may tend, by delaying action, to defeat the true object of inquiry.

It is with a view to these various considerations that the present response to the invitation of the COMMISSION is conceived; and in order, as far as may be, to guard against misapprehensions which may naturally arise, I have presented laconic replies surrounded, as it were, with signals of definition and explanation.

ANSWER.

I attribute the fall in the value of silver as compared with gold, to anti-silver laws and governmental regulations, in the western nations.

EXPLANATION.

Throughout the entire pendency of the breach of parity between silver and gold, the opinion has been currently expressed, that this fall is attributable to certain other alleged causes, which are hereinafter set forth.

(A.) *A Preference for gold or antipathy to silver.*

The error of this view consists (1), in an erroneous in-

ANSWER AND EXPLANATION. 69

terpretation of the word "cause," or (2), in a misapprehension touching the practical operations of business, the use of money.

(1.) The word "cause" is used to designate the *motives* which led the individual rulers of Germany to establish gold, and reject silver, money, and of France to check the rate of silver mintage, etc., and it is assumed that preference for gold and antipathy to silver are an adequate characterization of these motives. Without stopping to inquire whether this characterization is correct it is sufficient to point out that it is irrelevant. What we are concerned with is a deed, an act, not an opinion, or intention, just as in a surgeon's diagnosis of a gunshot wound it is indifferent whether the shot was fired intentionally or by accident.

(2.) A field of importance is, in imagination, opened to this "preference for gold," by flatly ignoring the most obvious facts about the uses of money and the nature of the institution of money. The exertions of the visionary in the defence of anti-silver laws have offered a parallel to the speculations of the mediæval schoolmen. There is no lack of opinions on money which are explicable only on the ground that their authors are ignorant of the existence of laws of Legal Tender, Coinage, Banking, etc., or imagine that, if there are such things, they are of no effect, that the citizen pays no attention to them, acting exactly as he would act if there were no such laws. As is usual in case of delusion, the sense of humor here shines by its absence, for these products of a sophisticated imagination exist for the special purpose of defending nothing less than actual laws of Legal Tender and Coinage,—anti-silver laws, gold-favoring laws,—to which their advocates ascribe great efficacy.

(B.) The slightly increased production of silver from the mines has been regarded as a cause.

(C.) Certain special instances of a reduction of the employment for silver, which are familiar to the COMMISSION, have been treated as a cause.

The error of B. and C. lies in treating as paramount and efficient a factor whose influence is only ancillary and subordinate. While the slightly increased output of silver, and the India Council Bills, etc., exerted a depressing influence on the market ratio of silver to gold, yet they were only enabled to do so by anti-silver laws.

But for these laws they would have had no effect. Their effect is thus a part of the effect produced by the anti-silver laws, hence they are not entitled to be regarded as a cause of the fall, in the proper sense of the words. That these points are so often ignored is due to the confusion analyzed in the DEFINITION. I am not aware that the facts have been categorically disputed. To disprove my point, it would be necessary to maintain that if the Mints of Germany, Holland, France, Belgium, etc., and of the United States, had remained open to free coinage of silver, gold would still have risen above the French par in silver, by reason of Nevada's silver product and India's payments in London; an opinion which is obviously erroneous.

II.

QUESTION II.

What probability is there of a continuance of the fall?

ANSWER.

The chief element in the calculation of this probability is necessarily the action of governments, and the action of governments will presumably be affected to an important extent by the action of the ROYAL COMMISSION.

To discuss the probable action of the United States, of Germany, of France, or of other Powers, without reference to the alternative possibilities of a decision on the part of the British-Indian Empire, a decision which, in its preliminary form of a Report of the ROYAL COMMISSION, is regarded as impending, would be futile. In estimating the importance of this decision, from the international point of view, essential data are embodied in the conclusions of the two International Monetary Conferences called to discuss the proposal of a concurrent regulation of the legal position of the money metals.

In the Conference of 1878, called by the United States, in which Germany was not represented, the delegates of the other principal Powers united in a declaration recognizing "that it is necessary to maintain in the world the monetary functions of silver as well as of gold." In the Conference of 1881, called by France and the United States, the attitude of representatives of the British-Indian Empire and of the German Empire, the chief Powers whose adhesion to the programme of concurrent action was withheld, nevertheless respectively recognized an interest in the carrying-out of that programme, offering certain measures to be adopted within their respective jurisdictions as a contribution to its success.

To whatever extent, then, this action of the two Powers can be held to have any binding effect, the question of principle, touching the main issue within the consideration of the ROYAL COMMISSION, was admitted, and the issue was narrowed to the question of amount, How much these Powers were respectively prepared to do in order to bring about a settlement of the existing conflict of Coinage Systems.

The quota of co-operation actually offered not having been looked upon by other nations as sufficient, a long period of monetary inaction, so far as modifications of monetary laws are concerned, has followed, which seems to imply an expectant attitude, looking especially to a new departure on the part of Great Britain.

III.

QUESTION III.

To what do you attribute the fall in the wholesale prices of many commodities which has been in progress during the last 10 or 12 years.

DEFINITION. *See* QUESTION *I.*

ANSWER.

I attribute the general fall of prices to the anti-silver

laws and regulations adopted and carried out in various states since 1871; but this assertion cannot properly be held to imply necessarily that if there had been no anti-silver laws there would have been no fall of prices, nor that there would have been a rise of prices. No probabilities of this kind can be laid down with precision of detail. But from the point of view of the legislator, responsible for the action of the state, and treating the action of individuals, in all the *minutiæ* of processes of production and distribution, as merely giving the conditions amid which he is to act,—it is sufficient to say with certainty that if there had been no anti-silver laws the fall of prices might not have occurred, and that the greater part of that fall could not have occurred. Whatever doubt may be justified in the matter, the opposition to the outlawry of silver is entitled to the benefit of the doubt; the presumptions are against the outlawry of silver. They are likewise in favor of its being set aside now.

Explanation.

Among the current explanations of the general fall of prices (or appreciation of gold, which is only another mode of describing the same event) prominence is often given to certain notable features of modern economic life; namely, new inventions, improved means of transit, transport, and communication, new methods of business, etc., all tending to lessen the labor of production. It is therefore important to ascertain what place is to be given to these elements of the situation.

Referring to the considerations presented in the definition of QUESTION I, I first observed that these elements, from the standpoint of monetary policy, occupy at best an inferior and subordinate place, as affording merely the conditions with reference to which the legislator has to act. If the tendency of their influence upon prices is downward, and thus to produce an injurious rise in the purchasing power of money, the business of the legislator is, if possible, to counteract this tendency, and if, as has been stated, the maintenance of silver in parity with gold would have this result in any important degree, then the practical question is decided in favor of silver. The same response applies to the reasoning, that sometimes attains currency, about overproduction, which should rather be named under-consumption.

But the anti-silver argument based upon new inventions and improved methods is not content with elevating conditions into causes. It goes further. It is in substance maintained—sometimes in specious, vague, or confusing language—that because new inventions and improved methods are economic benefits, therefore the fall of prices is an economic benefit. Here lies the real strength, because here lies the seductiveness of the argument. In essence, this reasoning is merely a resolute begging of the question, and puts the cart before the horse. This will be apparent from the following analysis.

If a general fall of prices, or rise in the value of money,

is an evil at all, it is an evil because it is a derangement of the terms of existing investments and obligations, and a derangement peculiarly unfortunate ; being more injurious in proportion than its complement, a fall in the value of money, because it disturbs the adjustment of the machinery of business and so checks the normal growth of enterprise. Evidently no peculiarity of origin of the rise in the value of money can divest it of this latter character ; it must be a derangement, no matter how it comes to pass. To deny, then, that such a dislocation of values is an evil at all is an obvious error. It implies, in fact, the impossible opinions that it is not desirable that money should remain stable in value, and that "hard times" are not an evil. From this it is but a short step to affirm that it is the business of statesmanship to prevent prosperity! .

We proceed to consider the argument which defends this evil, as a price, so to speak, paid in order to secure the admitted economic benefits of new inventions and improved methods, and therefore more than made good by the profits of the operation.

The illusions embodied in this view will, I think, be disclosed by the following analysis. What is the difference of effect between an invention that does not lower prices at all—to imagine an extreme case—and an invention which lowers them? Does it not consist in this, that in the latter case it is (what economic science knows as) "the consumer" who has the gain, which in the former case would go to "the producer?" Can there be any doubt that the admitted benefits of new inventions and of improved methods can be obtained without paying such a price, so ruinous a price, as a general rise in the value of money? There should be no doubt. It is not necessary,— it never was (strictly) necessary,—to pay this price. (See C, page 82.)

That this truth is left out of sight is probably due to an exaggeration of the importance of the new inventions and improved methods which have come into play since 1873. Offering, as they do, the strongest, because most seductive, argument to defend the anti-silver laws from the charge of having produced a ruinous dislocation of values, so much has been said about these new inventions and methods since 1873, that men forget what happened before 1873; and forgetting what happened before 1873, they ignore what might have happened since 1873 but for these same anti-silver laws.

Before 1873, a marvellous development of "cheapening" inventions and methods took place, while there was no fall of prices, and also during periods when there was a rise of prices. Why could not the same experience be repeated? Evidently it would have been repeated after 1873, if the conditions of quantity (parity. See Def. of Q. VI) had been maintained by a proper course of monetary legislation. The entire plea of new inventions and new methods is thus put out of court.

It remains to consider some special points which have been relied upon to excite sympathy for this plea. Special reasons are alleged why a fall of prices is a benefit: namely that it tends to improve the relative position of the manual-labor classes. If this entry to its credit were correct (in certain cases), it would be more important, than it is, to note that the debit entries are also to be taken into consideration; that the annual return for manual labor is not to be ascertained by multiplying an average of daily wages by 300, but is a question of fact to be proved by testimony, in which the number of "unemployed," the regularity and certainty of work for the employed, would come under examination.

But the credit entry is not correct. This entry is not to be made correct by the mere observation that the productiveness of work, in obtaining satisfaction of his needs for the worker, has actually increased of late years. To rely upon this observation is to reveal confidence in a false issue. The true issue is: *Would the satisfaction of the worker have been less, if there had been no anti-silver laws?* I am not advised that any apologist of anti-silver laws has even tried to establish the affirmative of this issue.

IV.

QUESTION IV.

Has it extended to (a) *retail prices,* (b) *wages and other payments for services rendered,* (c) *land and houses?*

ANSWER.

On these subjects I have no fruits of original research to present, and can therefore add nothing to the evidence already before the Commission, unless by way of analysis and criticism of that evidence.

In a general way an affirmative reply to QUESTION IV is indicated in the answers to other QUESTIONS, and some brief criticism is also set forth touching certain inferences which have been drawn from the facts toward which QUESTION IV is directed.

V.

QUESTION V.

Has the fall resulted in any material prejudice to the commercial or general interests of the world?

DEFINITION. See QUESTION *I*.

ANSWER.

Yes, so far as a vitiated system of money can affect them. Of course the respective degrees to which various national systems of money have been so affected cannot be stated with precision.

EXPLANATION. *See also* QUESTION *III*.

The general importance of stability of average purchasing power and of parity between monetary systems connected by trade or investment are elementary, rudimentary, principles of monetary policy : very much as the rule of the majority is an elementary principle of representative bodies.

These principles belong in fact to the category of definitions. It is impossible to define good money without including the "parities" which have been violated in these dislocations of values, and it is impossible to define what is desirable so as to exclude what is good. Granted the existence of men, it is desirable that there should be good men, and so, likewise, granted that money exists, it is desirable that it should be good money.

Now to say that the money of Europe has been and is good money—as good money as it would have been if there had been no breach of these parties--is intrinsically absurd, and nothing but the confusion produced by the causes analyzed in the DEFINITION of QUESTION I prevents universal recognition of this absurdity.

If the absence of a certain par between London and Bombay is not a material prejudice, the absence of a certain par between London and Manchester is not a material prejudice; if a past fall of prices of 25 per cent. is not a material prejudice, a future fall of 25 per cent. will not be a material prejudice, or 50 per cent. or 75, 80, 90, a fall which would reduce the business world to universal bankruptcy or repudiation. So long as human nature endures, men who buy and sell will be glad to know what the price is to be, men who invest will desire a return, mortgagees will desire that their security shall be enough to pay the debt, and mortgagors will desire to realize as much as possible from their " equity of redemption."

It is upon the propriety and persistence of such desires as these in men, or in other words, upon the inexpugnable basis of human nature, that the affirmative answer to QUESTION V is based

VI.

QUESTION VI.

Do you consider that the countries using the gold standard, or any of them, are suffering from an injurious contraction of the currency which might have been obviated or mitigated by an increase in the supply of gold?

DEFINITION.

The question is a double question. The first part relates to a matter of fact: "Are certain countries, is any country, suffering from contraction of the currency?"

The countries referred to as "using the gold standard" use this standard and from "choice," but in obedience to statutes which accord the full rank of national money to gold alone.

The second part is a matter of opinion: "Could such contraction, if existing, have been obviated or mitigated by an increase in the supply of gold?"

What is the meaning of "contraction of the currency?" The history of the phrase is a long one. Originally applied to the various species of Paper Money, it is only lately, so far as I am informed, that it has been used to describe the event which I assume the ROYAL COMMISSION has in view, namely, a deficient supply of Metallic Money.

The distinctly artificial or conventional origin and character of Paper Money, which is admittedly a product of law and of governmental action, and the "quantity" of which is subject to governmental control, import distinc-

THE MEANING OF CONTRACTION.

tions which are of vital importance in defining the new meaning of the phrase.

Inasmuch as "contraction" implies that something is contracted, it is essential to have a clear understanding of what that something is; and, the thing contracted being plainly a quantity, it is necessary, in order to appreciate the decrease in quantity, to have an idea what the original quantity was.

What, then, is the starting point, the original quantity, the disappearance or non-appearance of a part of which makes the "contraction?"

In the case of Paper Money, created, as it is, within the view of the public, it is a comparatively simple matter to come to an understanding. The case of Metallic Money is different. Not only is there neither precision, nor concurrence of opinion touching that which is indeterminate, but the principles relative to the subject are still to be agreed upon. Nowhere in the range of monetary discussion is there, in my belief, a greater lack, or greater need, of clearness. In order to an adequate treatment of QUESTION VI, it is therefore necessary to establish some general views with reference to the quantity of Metallic Money.

What, then, is the *normal stock of Metallic Money?*

Three alternatives suggest themselves as giving the desired point of departure:

A. The actual stock, in a given nation at a given time—let us say in Great Britain, in 1874—may be taken as the original quantity, and a subsequent reduction of that stock may be regarded as "contraction."

B. The actual stock in 1874, plus an annual increment (estimated upon some established rule) to be applied as due each subsequent year, may form the first term of comparison. A failure in subsequent years to enlarge the stock to the agreed extent will then be regarded as a deficiency.

C. The supposed requirement (for any given year) may be fixed by the establishment of certain conditions to be fulfilled. Such conditions are, for example, suggested by the once universally-admitted principle that money should be stable in value. The normal stock, then, for the period 1874–1887, would be that stock and increment which should have maintained the general average of prices at the level of 1874.

A deficiency, then, existing by comparison with either of these three requirements might be regarded as a "contraction." Looking, however, to the practical objects which the learned law-giver has in view, the requirement set forth in *C.* would be entitled to precedence. Of course, whether, in any given case, it is in the power of the law-giver to afford any remedy for a contraction, from the point of view either of *A.*, *B.*, or *C.* is a distinct question concerning which nothing is said here. (See below.)

In further explanation of the answer to QUESTION VI, the subordinate query should also be stated whether a contraction is "injurious" or no, upon which point the considerations presented under QUESTIONS III and V are applicable.

ANSWER.

The points elsewhere herein set forth touching the peculiar effect of the breach of established parity between silver money systems and gold money systems, and touching the relation of quantity to prices, and the causation of monetary changes, apply as reservations to limit and explain the following reply:

Yes. England has so suffered, and is so suffering. The experience of other gold standard countries is similar, but naturally not identical. For obvious reasons I shall follow the QUESTION into detail in reference to England alone. A fall of prices (appreciation of gold), depreciation of property, derangement of the calculations of trade and investment, all upon a scale of importance attracting the attention of the law-giver, are ascertained, and are admitted.

A deficiency in the normal stock of Metallic Money in England is also ascertained. The requirements set forth in the third mode of determining the normal stock (C) are evidently lacking. So, likewise, from the standpoint of the second explanation (B), there is a deficiency. Again, as to the actual stock of 1874 (A), the evidence tends to sustain the belief that there is actually less metallic cash in England in 1887 than in 1874. That this contraction is injurious is apparent.

This injurious contraction referred to could have been mitigated and probably obviated by an increase in the supply of gold money; but, while it was not within the power of legislation to command such an increase by increasing the product of the mines, it was, and (for the benefit of the future) is, within its power to obtain a similar result, in profitable degree, by reuniting the broken standard of silver and gold.

DEFINITION OF THE SECOND PART OF THE QUESTION.

The second part of the QUESTION VI: "Could this contraction of the currency have been obviated or mitigated by an increase in the supply of gold," seems to supply its own answer. To whatever condition of things the phrase "contraction of the currency" may be applied, an increase of the supply of gold money must serve as the opposite and negation of it. As surely as subtraction is to be obviated or mitigated by addition, so surely does increase of money obviate or mitigate or, rather, prevent contraction, or deficiency, of money. The stress of the QUESTION seems therefore to lie in the degree of mitigation.

How much effect will be produced by such and such an in increase in the supply of gold?

An increase in the supply of gold may describe two distinct events:

(*a*) an increase of the existing stock in the hands of man, or

(*b*) such an increase as shall, under existing circumstances, render an enlarged stock of money available for a given nation at a given period, or, more definitely stated,

PARITY AND SUPPLY. 85

(a) an increase of the annual output of gold mines, and

(b) the occurence of such a change in the conditions of supply or employment of money-material that an increased amount of gold money comes normally into use in a given country at a given time.

It will be observed that the second case (b) contemplates a greater quota of change supplied to remedy or prevent a deficit than the first case (a).

If we imagine the requirements set forth in (b) applied to England, it becomes apparent that the change referred to must embrace the money-using world as well as England. The general conditions of supply or employment of money-materials, which are to enable gold money to flow into England will therefore demand attention. What is contemplated in QUESTION VI, and thus in the ANSWERS to be made to QUESTION VI, as a "contraction of the currency" is not an event occurring in isolation, but rather an event alone to be understood as a part, by means of an explanation of the whole.

For money-using England as well as the money-using world, there are two money-metals, not one alone. The supply and employment of silver, and the ratio of exchange between silver and gold are decisive factors in the monetary position of gold.

With this observation the question of quantity of gold is brought face to face with an order of events distinct, and, from some points of view, incommensurate. The breaking of the par of silver and gold, and the derangement of valuations arising in exchanges between silver countries and gold countries are in fact comparable to the invasion by one of the forces of nature, of the field ordinarily exposed to the undisturbed working of another force.

The collision of coinage systems merits, therefore, a treatment quite distinct from the issues directly raised by QUESTION VI. Suffice it to say here that the evils consequent upon that breach and collision are obviously to be in some measure remedied, and the future effects of that breach and collision can be entirely prevented by removing the cause—that is to say, by restoring equality between the metals.

Without entering further upon this field, it is legitimate and important to explain that the ANSWERS TO QUESTION VI, although accepting the terms of "quantity" imposed by that QUESTION, make full allowance (if the definitions be clearly understood) for the perturbation due to the break of the parity and the subsequent clashing and conflict of coinages. The definition of the normal stock (see page 82) and of an increased supply of gold (*b*, see above) show that the narrow view touching a "scarcity of gold" is here excluded. It is to be recognized that the peculiar effects of the break of an established parity do not eliminate the element of quantity from the monetary problem in the wider sense. What increased output of gold mines or silver mines would have been needed to cause a rise of silver prices in silver countries, which would have left gold prices where they stood before the divergence of the ratio? Opinions may vary touching the required quantity (as well as the effect of such imagined output upon the course of trade, development of wealth, distribution of capital, etc.), but it will hardly be denied that in the scale of magnitudes some point could be reached where this imagined effect would be produced. Is it not quite probable that a repetition of such an experience as the Great Gold Discoveries in Australia and California would have transferred the change of price-level from a downward movement of gold prices in the Occident to an upward movement of silver prices in the Orient?

Turning from these speculations to the actual condition of the nations in the period 1874-1887, we can profitably seek to define the importance of the break-down of the parity formerly maintained by France and her allies. What would have been the condition of things if the par had not been broken? The question, what increased product would have come from the mines, in that event, is important, but can be laid aside here in order to simplify the issue. We assume, then, the par of $15\frac{1}{2}$ to 1 maintained, but the other great factors of the monetary situation of Europe,—the product of the mines, the expansion of the United States, the Indian railroads, etc.,—such as they have been in fact. Could the local subsidence of the valuations that are expressed in pounds sterling have occurred? It is safe to say that the cause of the greater part of this subsidence would have been removed.

But as QUESTION VI treats the position of gold money as a matter of quantity alone, it is germane to show that, from the standpoint of the legislator, parity is a factor of available quantity.

VII.

QUESTION VII.

To what extent and in what way are prices affected by the quantity of the metal or metals used as standards of value?

DEFINITION. (*See also* QUESTION *I.*)

The phrase " standard of value " in the above question, can only profitably be used as a synonym of money, just as the " metals " contemplated in it are gold and silver, and no other, and " prices " is but a name for the respective equivalents of vendible things in money units.

If to regard a metal as a standard of value carried with it no actual employment of pieces of that metal for the uses known in fact as monetary, that is to say, if the metal were purely a term of mental comparison and nothing more, as might be the case if one were to consider as a matter of curiosity, what a horse was " worth " in platina or in gallium, the question might be treated in a different way.

There would then be no need of laws of Legal Tender, of Coinage, of Banking, there would be no Monetary Systems, there would be no money and no questions of currency, of monetary policy. But this is not the case. It is but a dreamland of the economic visionary to which this latter spiritual meaning of " standard of value " points. Money exists. The actual world of human society has always been, and is to-day, a world of payments as well as of price.

Price has, in fact, always implied action, the potentiality of action, of payment; it exists by contemplation of an actual exchange of one thing for another, and the one thing is the vendible object and the other thing is money, and it can be nothing else, except by favor of a license of speech which has no place in monetary discussion. Many prices are not paid, many exchanges are made without transfer of cash. Cash payments are but a fraction of the totality of transactions, and the rapidity with which cash does its work is a matter of surmise, but, nothwithstanding, the nucleus of these comet-like phenomena is a solid fact in more than the purely material sense. There is a stock of cash, and with it some proportion of prices is paid. But between the actual amount of cash and the sum of possibilities of demand for payment (the totality of transactions) there is a broad space, so broad that it may well be likened to the furthest sweep of the comet in its flight. It is in these interstellar spaces, so to speak, that the visionary finds fields of fancy beyond the reach of the glass of a Montesquieu. The fatal attractiveness of this region of ideal money, of "money of account" or "metal used" mentally "as a standard of value" is well attested by the experience of to-day, there being no lack of minds that have

> Eaten of the insane root
> That takes the reason prisoner.

Hence the necessity of a most rigorous course of definition.

QUESTION VII relates, then, to the effect of the quantity of metallic money upon prices. But there are various distinct aspects in which "the quantity of metal or metals used as money" may be regarded; among which are:

1. The weight of the Units of Coinage.
2. The relation of parity between the two money-metals.
3. The number of existing copies of the Units.
4. The metal not coined which has a monetary use.
5. The metal which may be relied on to recruit the stock of money.

The quantity of substitutes for metallic money is also an element of importance for any practical conclusions.

For purposes of clearness then, treating the question in a practical way, it is necessary to contemplate some normal state of these elements of "quantity," and this can be conveniently attained by turning the eye away from the present amorphous conditions, brought about by the late revolutionary divorce of silver and gold, and regarding the conditions as they were before 1873, when parity existed between the metals, which affected the total stock. In this assumed normal state there was an increment: a yearly increase of the stock. Let us then apply QUESTION VII to the state of affairs as it was in 1873, 1863, 1853, 1843.

There were "prices" in those years, and "prices" in the sense in which the word is used in QUESTION VII, namely, the general mass, or average, of price of things vendible.

We ask whether these prices would have been the same as they actually were if the world's stock of silver and gold in 1843, 1853, 1863, 1873 had been less than it actually was—if it had been half what it was, for example. It is well-nigh self-evident that prices could not have been the same. Indeed, if we carry out the hypothesis with loyal fulness of statement, it will be plain that, in all probability, prices would have been only half what they actually were.

If, on the other hand, we imagine an equal diminution in the world's stock of any other form of wealth, the amount of money-metal remaining what it was, we are led to a very different conclusion.

Of course no one can answer the question in this form with precision. No one can answer QUESTION VII in any form with absolute precision.

But the prevailing force of tendencies can be clearly stated, and if the elements of any given special case are carefully studied, an approximately correct conclusion can be formed. Despite all the fluctuations of business, the constancy of human nature and the inertia of the metals, and of laws, afford ample material for practical decision.

ANSWER.

The general tendency is that prices are in direct ratio to the quantity of money; but this a tendency limited by factors which may be briefly indicated in the proviso "other things being equal." As for the way in which quantity acts upon price it can be regarded as a special instance of " demand and supply."

VIII.

QUESTION VIII.

What is the relation, if any, between the supply or quantity of the precious metals and the fluctuations of credit?

ANSWER.

I do not avail myself of the opportunity to enter fully upon this question on account of the great extent of an inquiry into the multifarious and evanescent phenomena to which it points. I venture, however, to present some elementary observations which may be the more important because they are not infrequently ignored.

To affirm that there is *no* relation between the supply or quantity of the precious metals and the fluctuations of credit is,—if the proper meanings be given to the words,— an error, if indeed it be not actually a contradiction in terms. What are the fluctuations of credit? An increase or decrease in the quantity of obligations expressed in terms of money, which obligations are often transferred or exchanged for a money price. Whether the relation of credits to hard cash be likened to the relation of a comet's tail to its nucleus, of the sun's corona to the sun, of the earth's atmosphere to the earth, it must be a relation and a relation of quantity.

Whatever problems insoluble in the present state of

knowledge, these various relations may present to human curiosity, a considerable body of data has already been acquired which cannot fear to be superseded. So likewise in reference to the relations between credit and cash, enough is known to give security in dealing with the main practical tasks which are to-day incumbent upon the legislator. So far as the practical task is concerned, to which the labors of the ROYAL COMMISSION are directed, what is known of the relations of cash and credit can certainly afford no valid argument against a settlement of the Silver Question by concurrent action of nations.

IX.

QUESTION IX.

Has there been during the last 15 *years any important development of the system of cheques, bank credits, bills of exchange, or other means of economizing the use of the precious metals?*

ANSWER.

As compared with preceding decades, there has been in the last 15 years no important development of the methods of economizing specie.

EXPLANATION.

It may be said, in a certain narrow sense, that an important development of this kind is always going on, for although, regarded as a whole, the movement may be checked or counteracted in times of war or panic, yet local expansion of specie-economizing credit may have been present to minimize the final result.

Among the most notable changes in the direction of economy in the use of the precious metals in late years, I should mention:

The telephone.

The postal order system.

The extension of the telegraph.

The extension of railways.

Question IX, as I understand it, demands a comparison of what has occurred through these and similar agencies, with what occurred before. This comparison seems to me to be clearly unfavorable to the later period. The earlier decades of the development of railways and telegraphs saw more important changes than the latter; the postal order system was preceded by great postal reforms; and the telephone would perhaps operate rather to prevent the necessity of credits than to economize specie. And the great development of systems of Banking and Clearing belongs to the earlier period.

The rate of increase of the ratio of money transactions to metallic stock has therefore probably been reduced of late years. The fact that prices have fallen in spite of the growth of methods of economizing specie, points in the same direction, for it is obvious that, so far as it may go, economizing specie tends to promote a rise of prices.

X.

QUESTION X.

Do you consider that an international agreement could be made for the free coinage of gold and silver as legal tender money at a fixed ratio?

ANSWER.

I do.

XI.

QUESTION XI.

Is it in the power of governments to maintain such a ratio if agreed upon; and would the practice of the commercial world follow the law?

ANSWER.

Undoubtedly.

EXPLANATION.

The exercise of power referred to is in substance identical with that which all governments have been wont to apply with success. Touching the "practice of the commercial world," I assert in favor of an affirmative answer what in the law is known as an estoppel. The established opinions of all economists in a similar case should preclude them from withholding their agreement with this affirmation. This consensus of opinion has been so universal as to have been embodied in the name of a "law."

The theorem known as "Gresham's law" is one of the

commonplaces of economics, and the affirmative answer to question XI rests upon the same basis as Gresham's law. That law is but a generalization touching the working of human self-interest. Under the gravitation of self-interest, men prefer what is crudely called the "cheaper" money to the "dearer" money. That is to say, men gladly part with that which they can most easily spare, and, inasmuch as everything which is paid is also received, it is plain that men are not unwilling to receive payment in anything which they can pay away again. All men are willing to make profit in a monetary transaction; there is a constant pressure in that direction among money-using men, just as every part of a body of water is always pressing down. This is the controlling fact, this is human nature. But this downward pressure of water has two distinct lines of manifestation, the one where resistance is complete, the other where resistance is incomplete; the latter being the current, the fall, movement, tending toward the perpendicular, the former the smooth level of the lake, quiescent, horizontal.

It is the former, which is bodied forth in Gresham's law. The latter in the law I vindicate; the one is the law of disparity, the other is the law of parity. As gravity, operating upon the enclosed waters of a lake, establishes and maintains a level surface, so this gravitation of self-interest maintains parity. The desire, the pressure, exist, but are neutralized by opposing desire, opposing pressure. For the one and the other the resistance, the enclosure, is necessary; that is all that is required for either money or water. Whether it be pond, lake, or ocean, if the enclosure be there, the level surface is inevitable.

Whence comes the strange parity between cheap bronze pennies, light silver shillings, solid gold sovereigns and paper promises to pay five, or a hundred, or a thousand pounds? Evidently the English lake is well embanked around by English law. If analogous enclosure be given to silver and gold money by the monetary laws of nations, a similar level of parity will be produced and maintained. This can be done by giving the two metals equality before the law in a strong body of nations.

XII.

QUESTION XII.

What would be the effect of such an agreement, if carried out, upon (a) prices, and (b) the production of the precious metals?

ANSWER.

In reference to the respective production of the two precious metals, the current estimates of probabilities point to a diminished output of gold and to an increased output of silver. The restoration of silver to monetary equality with gold, presumably at a higher ratio than has obtained of late years, would tend, within limits, to stimulate its production; but the estimate of amounts of increase are frequently exaggerated, sometimes to a preposterous degree. An impulsion to business activity would also tend to enlarge the range of gold mining, and hence to increase the output of gold and to restore the balance.

So far, then, as the annual product of the money-metals is concerned, the total effect of joint action of nations to equalize them, must be to relieve the monetary interests of nations from evils connected with that source ; connected, that is with a prospect of wider divergence between the metals, and of an increasing intensity of employment or demand, for a limited stock of gold. The practical sense of this danger exists in many quarters, where its scientific weight has not yet been formally recognized. This will appear if we imagine the effect of really important Gold Discoveries. Is there any doubt that they would be hailed by economists as a relief? Can it be denied that they would bring a certain relief ? (I refer, of course, to such Discoveries in their character, not of an increase in the world's stock of wealth, of capital, but in the world's stock of money, of circulating treasure. So far as the former character is concerned, the increment in gold would count no more than the same figures in silver or in steel.) But if this be true of what avail are incantations of casuistry to exorcise " the appreciation of gold?" Whatever relief could be wrought by Gold Discoveries which are not to be had, can be attained by Intermonetary Union, which is to be had.

. In reference to both prices and production of metal, the effect would be in some measure dependent upon the ratio adopted.

'Of the probable effect upon prices of the establishment of a ratio, which shall bring the metals more closely together than they stand as bullion to-day, while detailed prediction can at best move within but narrow limits, yet in general it can safely be affirmed that (assuming the currency of existing silver coin to remain undisturbed), this change would directly operate chiefly upon trade between silver-using and gold-using countries, and upon the great stocks of Money only in so far as their purchasing power is affected by the state of this trade. So far as such trade is concerned, it is also to be noted that no injurious effect can be safely predicted, in the estimate of which the following points shall have been ignored, namely:

First. That the change in question is, as far as it goes, a restoration of the *status quo ante*.

Second. That its impact is reduced by being distributed between the two metals.

Third. That in so far as the change is regarded as a settlement, and firm establishment of the foundations of business, there is some credit entry against every debit, a counter-claim for betterment which in goodly measure offsets each item of damage.'

If the ratio of 15½ to 1 were restored, the existing silver in the hands of man must remain *in situ*. (I assume that the United States adapts its silver coin to the new ratio.) The silver coin in gold-money lands is in use at its face value, and the silver coin in silver-money lands is detached from gold, connected with it only by flexible cords of trade. What, then, are the specific dangers to Europe that are to come from the rise of silver other than a fall of "the price of gold in the money of the country" in Mexico or Buenos Ayres or Bombay, etc.? Is it the return of confidence that is feared? In that case measures *can* be taken to prevent undue expansion; and such measures *could* legitimately form a part of the programme of a Monetary Union.

But exaggerated views which represent the foundation of an Intermetallic Union as importing a monetary convulsion are, in many cases, explicable through the analogy of an optical illusion. The inference touching the future is from what is past and known, and what is past and known is naturally regarded, as it were, in one picture; as, for example, all the depressing elements of the last thirteen years may be crowded into one frame. A Restoration of the United Standard is regarded as implying the reverse of all this, and is contrasted with it on even terms, except that the element of *time* is left out of sight, so that everything is imagined as happening suddenly, at one stroke of the magician's wand. Hence exaggeration, which easily rises to any height of error.

It thus becomes important to observe that the nations which are to bring their laws into concord and give legal equality to the two metals will themselves determine the seasonable terms and times for this action, and are not likely to act with undue haste. It also is necessary to recall that the years which have passed since 1873 are past, and with them have gone their "might-have-beens." For instance, the money-metal that " would have been " mined, and was not mined, in these thirteen years to enrich the world's stocks, is to be mined in the coming years, being next in the lode, and it will need years to mine it. These too obvious remarks are called for when the alchemy of learned fancy is in vogue, by which that metal is "taken as mined," just as a resolution in a deliberative body is sometimes "taken as read!"

XIII.

QUESTION XIII.

Do you consider an international agreement for bimetallism possible on any other ratio than 15½ *to* 1?

DEFINITION.

I assume the word "bimetallism" here to mean free coinage and full legal tender of silver and gold at a certain ratio (See, also, *Definition* XV) and that the word "possible" is taken in the sense in which it is usually applied to political events.

ANSWER.

Yes.

EXPLANATION.

No opinion is here implied upon any details of probability, whether at Berlin, Paris, London, or Washington.

The question of the ratio stands in the second rank. The first interest of the nations is concurrence, by which the status of the money-metals may be fixed. The ratio is a matter upon which any nation can afford to make concessions to the needs of others.

At the Monetary Conference of 1881 the Declaration on this subject of the Delegates of France and of the United States, made in the name of their respective governments, was as follows:

'Any ratio, now or of late in use by any commercial nation, if adopted by such important group of States, could be maintained; but the adoption of the ratio of $15\frac{1}{2}$ to 1 would accomplish the principal object with less disturbance in the monetary systems to be affected by it than any other ratio.

'Without considering the effect which might be produced towards the desired object by a lesser combination of States, a convention which should include England, France, Germany, and the United States, with the concurrence of other States, both in Europe and on the American Continent, which this combination would assure, would be adequate to produce and maintain throughout the commercial world the relation between the two metals that such convention should adopt.'

XIV.

QUESTION XIV.

Failing an international bimetallic agreement, what measures could be adopted by the commercial nations of the world for giving increased stability to the relation between gold and silver ?

DEFINITION.

By the words "international bimetallic agreement" as here used I understand a treaty, supported by appropriate legislation, for free mintage of silver and gold as full legal tender at one ratio.

ANSWER.

Measures establishing a steady demand, and especially any measures (short of the treaty above referred to) tending to establish a fixed gold price for silver, would if moving in concurrence, tend to increase stability, but would of course be liable to be counteracted by fluctuation in the output of the mines, and by changes of employment for existing metal used as money, etc.

XV.

QUESTION XV.

It is argued that in the absence of bimetallism, the effect of any disturbance of the currency is limited to half the currencies of the world, and thereby increased in intensity. Do you consider this view correct; and, if so, do you think the evil a serious one?

DEFINITION.

Current uses of the word "bimetallism" attach to it such a variety of meanings that in replying to QUESTION XV it seems desirable carefully to define the sense in which its terms are understood. The actual condition of the monetary systems of the world which I suppose the ROYAL COMMISSION to have had in view is that which exists while the "currencies" are deprived of the benefit of laws of alternative or optional free coinage of the two metals, which establish their practical interchangeability at a fixed ratio. Such a condition has lately been brought about by anti-silver statutes repealing such laws of equalization of the two metals, and must continue until new laws of equalization shall be passed in a body of nations sufficiently strong to attain this end. But the absence of such laws of equalization does not in fact import to-day, and is not here contemplated as implying, in the "currencies of the world," the absence of silver money or of gold money, nor the absence of full legal tender power, nor the absence of freedom of coinage, for either metal; so that whatever "two-metallism" or "bi-metallism" may be regarded as implied by these facts is still present, and to remain. QUESTION XV therefore embodies a comparison between the "currencies of the world" as they have been of late years, and as they formerly were (or would be again) under guarantees of intermetallic parity.

ANSWER.

The establishment of permanent parity between the two money-metals must impart a certain fluidity or elasticity to the moneys of the world, which would act as a wholesome air-brake to deaden the shock of such disturbances as seem to be contemplated in the QUESTION.

This, however, does not assert that anything more than the primary impact can be limited to one metal, or to the nations whose monetary laws attach the principal monetary interests of citizens to that one metal; or that in the present state of instability the area of the other metal can be held safe against the propagation of disorder originally arising in the domain of the first. So far as the evil is concerned, it is at least sufficiently serious to recommend the relatively trivial effort required to prevent it.

XVI.

QUESTION XVI.

If the effect of such disturbances could be spread over all countries, would greater stability of the standard of value be secured thereby?

DEFINITION.

At first glance it would not appear that the spread of disturbances could serve toward securing greater stability. But I assume the QUESTION is only intended to convey the idea of greater stability *than is attainable under certain circumstances.* And, as is explained in the preceding section (XV), this implies exposure to the first impact of some disturbances and to the rebound of others. It is further to be observed that although the QUESTION is stated in the most general terms it presumably refers to the actual condition of things to-day.

The QUESTION has in view the future of the countries which now have gold as their "standard of value" to the extent of excluding silver from free coinage. It can thus be stated as follows: Could Europe and North America attain greater monetary stability or protection against "monetary disturbances" if the metals were fused into one United Standard—a measure which would give gold, the lighter metal, the advantage of being ballasted, as it were, by silver the heavier metal, amid the winds and waves of monetary disturbance?

ANSWER.

Yes. The United Standard would give Europe and America greater monetary stability than the Disunited Standard.

January, 1888.

These answers were sent to the COMMISSION in print, being privately printed in Lausanne, with the title "The United Standard."

IV.

THE PARITY OF MONEYS

AS REGARDED BY

ADAM SMITH, RICARDO, AND MILL.

AN OPEN LETTER

ANSWERING A QUESTION OF A MEMBER

OF THE

ROYAL COMMISSION ON GOLD AND SILVER.

The Question as stated was,

Assuming that demand is the most potent factor in determining the value of the precious metals: and that Governments have power, by adopting or rejecting them for coinage, to increase or diminish their value, is it clear that this power goes to the extent of enabling them thereby to fix the precise relative value of gold and silver?

In order to simplify the issues I have thought it best to pass by whatever may be debatable in the above assumptions, and consider merely the question alone, the terms of which may be slightly modified in the interest of precision. The text of the following pages is therefore—

Is it clear that the power of Governments goes to the extent of enabling them to establish a stable ratio between gold and silver?

To Sir THOMAS H. FARRER, Bart.,
Abinger Hall, Dorking.

DEAR SIR: The question suggests a query which seems to me to lead directly to the completest answer, and that is, *How has it come to pass that the doubt it expresses can exist?*

The elements of an answer which, on general principles, one would expect to cover the ground, are contained in facts which are plainly in sight. The question is an economic question. The merely political side of the action contemplated is not in the field of view. We are not asking whether this or that nation will or will not pass certain laws; we ask what will happen if they do pass them. In other words, when we speak of laws, we mean laws, not Bills which failed to pass.

Now, there is no doubt, in spite of all the mirage which can be conjured up, that the quantity of gold and silver in men's hands is limited; and, regarded as a total, a stable quantity—unchanging to a marked degree. The predominant demand and use for these metals is monetary, and the laws of nations control this demand. How is it possible, then, that the power of these enactments can be gainsaid? If the laws of nations work together to main-

---

PREFATORY NOTE.—The question was handed me by Sir Thomas Farrer in 1887, while I was his guest at Abinger. The answer was made the year after in print, his name being given with his permission. The pamphlet on the title-page gave AMICUS CURIÆ as the author.

tain parity, how can they fail to produce it? What is there which can resist them? Nothing! For the laws of supply and demand (the theory of supply including that of "cost of production") are really law, and not dreams.

The only apparent chance for escape is the mirage I have referred to, the confusion about the limits of the supply. An important phase of this mirage may be described as an idea that the time is coming when there will be not enough "to go around" of one metal, and at the same time too much "to go around" of the other. Has it not the air of a dream? Who, indeed, has the right to predict the coming of such an event? There never was such a time. Money of the two metals has been known since the age of fable. It was, if I remember the story correctly, about 2700 B. C. that the Chinese are said to have stamped the "second metal" as "treasure current in the peaceful city." Certainly there has been abundant opportunity for experiences of the kind described. Yet there never has been a time like that which our soothsayers predict. And there is nothing in sight in the conditions of production of the metals to promise such a time for the future. Here we may hold ourselves cited to consider "cost of production," and the sins of thought that are perpetrated in its name. The errors grow out of the careless use that is sometimes made of a phrase which needs for its adequate handling a most delicate adjustment.* It is necessary to keep constantly in view—and

---

* When X., for example, speaks of it, he gives me the impression of a man who thinks a glass should be equally good at all ranges without adjust-

no doubt this is difficult for the economist, busy with the eventful lives of ordinary commodities—that gold and silver are precious, that they are imperishable and rare, that the utmost find of any year is no more than a feeble fraction of the stock in hand, so that an inherent intrinsic monopoly value attaches to them, against which mere "cost" of producing fresh bullion alone is powerless, for its utmost force is spent in feebly augmenting the supply.

The above answer, then, may fairly, as I have said, be supposed to cover the ground. In my belief it does cover the ground. And yet the doubt expressed in the question exists in some minds. What is the origin of this doubt? Is there some "fashion of thought" which, like a defect of sight, or color-blindness, vitiates the effect of evidence?

The doubt so expressed will appear all the more strange when we regard its habitat in a certain light. It is a doubt touching the power of laws to maintain parity between two kinds of money. This doubt arises, where? In a land

---

ment. Whether it is chairs, of which the use is limited and the available supply, in a sense, unlimited, or silver, of which the use is unlimited and the supply limited, it is the same "cost of production" for him. It never has occurred to him that the "cost" he speaks of, approximately bears the relation to the general *cost of providing money* that the water spouted into the air by a whale bears to the general level of the ocean. In fact, one would suppose from what he says, that now for the first time in the history of the world has silver mining been profitable. Fortunately the Welsh gold mines have made a diversion, for it is plain, if the published accounts are correct, that the "cost of production" of gold is going to fall as low as certain mines are supposed to have brought the cost of producing silver, so that one fall will neutralize the other!

which for generations has been the scene of a series of remarkable parities, kindred to that which is now our theme.

Are not bronze pennies at par with silver shillings?
Are not shillings at par with sovereigns?
Are not sovereigns at par with legal-tender bank-notes?
Are not five-pound notes at par (per pound sterling) with twenty-pound notes?
Is not the price of gold bullion so steady that one can say there is parity between it and money?

To these questions the answer "yes" must arise in antiphonal chorus. On both sides of the shield—the silver side and the gold side—these affirmatives are admitted, these parities are recognized as fact. There is a chain of parities extending from bronze to bullion and bank-notes. It is very germane then to appeal from the parity that is denied to the parity that is admitted, and so to ask, How comes it that these parities exist? How comes it that every one admits the fact?

To the latter question the answer is obvious. No matter how novel may be the idea of inquiring into the why and wherefore of these parities; whether they have been recognized in their true character or no, they are matters of common daily experience, or easy observation. The parities to which every one is witness are, in fact, as common as prose. Perhaps they never have been called by their true name, but, as in the case of men who talked prose without knowing it, the moment the idea is suggested, it takes a firm place in the mind.

As for the cause—the reason why these parities exist—I confidently appeal to you with the remark that the entire structure of monetary laws enacted by Parliament, and carried out by officials or obeyed by citizens, is harmoniously arranged to maintain them. The effect is a regulation of the employment for these various things, for the pennies, the shillings, the sovereigns, the notes, and the bullion; and thus the work of maintaining this equipoise is done. But the "causing cause" of the phenomenon is the statute enacted at Westminster. Can you suggest any other explanation? Or may I venture to believe that this explanation is quite as difficult to dispose of as the idea of gravity, an idea which has been ineradicable since the days of Newton?

I come back now to my query, How has it come to pass that the doubt expressed in the question can exist? The answer to my query will, I think, present itself most clearly in following the story of the notions about money lately current in the learned world. Is there a warp or flaw or aberrant and deflecting element in the medium through which money is regarded? If there be such which affects our theme, it may well prove to be that "fashion of thought" of which I have spoken, which, operating like a defect of sight, or color-blindness, vitiates the power of evidence and argument. And in ascertaining that there is such a fashion of thought not only shall we find the answer to our query, but also with it, possibly, lenses which in some cases may do something to restore the normal sight.

In relation to this idea of a "fashion of thought," I ought perhaps to explain more clearly what I mean. When a habit of looking at certain things in a certain way is intensified, and, as it were, gains precedence through a high degree of certainty that this is the right way of looking at these things, then this habit, which for the time is a second nature, may become militant and agressive. The *fakir* who astonishes through his fortitude under self-inflicted torture, is proving the marvellous power of the will to control the senses. It is not merely that he is enabled to bear pain without flinching, it is also that he is strong enough in spiritual force to ignore or stifle pain. Why may not an analogous power be exercised with reference to the use of mental powers, so that ratiocination is benumbed, and the attack of argument and evidence foiled completely by the mind's unconscious efforts of self-defence against them?

Now, if there be anything in the notions current about money among the learned in these last decades, which operates in the way thus described, it is plain that its roots lie deep, as a part of the historical development of economic theory, or of the mental habits of the time. Of course I cannot expect to deal exhaustively with such a matter in these pages. That could not be done without writing a book, and a book of considerable length. I can only touch here and there in the "stream of evolution," and report the result of analysis. But no one is likely to suppose that these lately current notions could be what they are in England, but for the influence of great economic writers, and so my task can safely lie in a review of what such men said. Beyond that lies the field of what they thought, or can be safely supposed to have thought, *or to have left unthought,* that bears upon this matter of the Parity of Moneys. You will readily agree with me that chief among the forces towards which inquiry should turn, are the writings of Dr. Adam Smith, of David Ricardo, and of John Stuart Mill. They are certainly competent to have "set the fashion" of thought. What had they to say of money?

As I approach their writings, I remark certain general characteristics of the times in which these great men lived, which are the necessary soil, or atmosphere, or framework—to give a choice of similes—in which their thoughts must be regarded.

First. The world in which they lived was a world in which silver and gold were money, equally money. There was no "Silver Question" in those days—in the sense in which there has been a Silver Question since 1873. On the contrary, so far as the great world was concerned, there was no break between the metals. There was a little sparring from time to time, like a family quarrel, but in the main there was no great conflict of coinage systems; in general, there was intermetallic, intermonetary peace.

Second. So far as the relative value of the metals is concerned, there had been what, to our eyes, is a phenomenal steadiness. The ratio of the year when Mill died (1873) was but little different from that of two centuries before. Locke, as monetary adviser of the government, observed the same ratios, close to 15.50, which were noted in Lombard Street while the later editions of Mill's "Political Economy" were coming from the press. Indeed, a very slight percentage covers the *maxima* of fluctuation in that period.

This being the case, one naturally asks whether the cause of this stability was ever made the subject of formal inquiry. If such inquiry had been made, then the whole matter which is now before us might have come under most competent analysis. Can you, Sir, with your comprehensive range of reading, point to such an inquiry? But though I ask the question, I will not fear to go onward and assume its answer. If correction comes—and no one can be more competent than yourself to administer it—I must submit to it. I know of no such inquiry, and have no reason to think it exists.

Furthermore, I observe that while no doubt a path-finding genius directed to this forbidding field of money would have found a rich vein in such inquiry, yet it is not in accordance with ordinary experience that such work should be done. Is not science, like nature, notoriously opposed to doing things by a very sudden leap? That certainly is my impression. It seems to me that the old rule of doing what thy hand findeth to do is generally observed in the growth of knowledge ; that those who enlarge its borders most usefully occupy themselves with problems which really require practical solution—that is to say, which make very emphatic demand for solution. They are perhaps likely to accomplish more in this line than in dealing with questions which are not yet, so to speak, on the order of the day.

Now, to follow the figure, the great problems before you, which the Royal Commission must act upon in one way or another—the Parity of Moneys, the forces that produce it—were not only not on the calendar for Mill, the latest of the authorities I refer to, but there was really no " notice " that the question would come up at all. There was no idea abroad of abolishing one of the Precious Metals as a money-metal, and still less were there overt acts pointing clearly toward such outlawry, during the time when the first edition of Mill's Economy was being published (1848). This point, I mean the novelty and the modernness of the anti-silver doctrine—to study the effects of whose partial triumph the Royal Commission was created—is one which I am perhaps bound to consider as not yet admitted. I therefore refer to the discussion of the points involved, and to the evidence presented, in "The Silver Pound," a work of which copies were presented to the Royal Commission nearly a year ago. I believe it will plainly appear, from the considerations there set forth, that the idea of excluding silver from its equal place side by side with gold is a novelty which had not in 1848 made its entrance in the world of thought. It is true that later, among the sequences of the gold inundations from California and Australia, came isolated suggestions about demonetizing gold, but that was all. It was not till after this idea had spent its force that men began to think of getting rid of silver. Neither the Treatise of Lord Liverpool nor the anti-silver statute of 1816 were intended to promote that general exclusion of silver, for which the turn of fortune and of events has, in our generation, shown them to be in fact the remoter motive forces. They were, so to speak, the material innocently accumulated, to which, more than a generation later, the enthusiasm of metrical reformers communicated the spark that inflamed. There was, I say then, no notice to John Stuart Mill, in the days when his great work on Economics was being written, that the cashiering of silver as money-metal, or its reduction to the ranks, would ever come upon the order of the day. Hence there is no likelihood of finding in Mill's writings that exhaustive, thorough examination of the questions growing out of such an event, which his great competence would otherwise justify us in expecting.

As I write this I recall a conversation I had, in 1876, with one of Mill's earnest students, whose appreciation I can well believe would have been very gratifying to the author. It was General Garfield. With his objection to my ideas of joint action of nations to hold the money-metals to their level, came a reference to John Stuart Mill —If all this was true, *why did not he, the Master, say so?* My answer was then, as now,—Mill did not live to see the sequel of the great legislative attack upon silver by Germany and the other nations.

I repeat, then, it is probable that no specific and intended scrutiny of the problems to which your question points, or of the then existing evidence, is to be found in Mill; and, of course, still less in Ricardo or in Dr. Smith.

NOTIONS ABOUT MONETARY SYSTEM. 119

Coming now to their writings, I observe, first, that there is a very marked note of neutrality (if, indeed, one should not say unconcern, or inertness, or even fickleness) on the crucial point, the matter of the "standard" which they respectively think should be adopted or maintained in England. That intensity of feeling which is to develop itself after 1867 in favor of gold and against silver, a feeling which is to rival in temperature the passions of party, gave no premonition in Smith or Ricardo, and shows itself in Mill only as predisposition, or as diathesis, to borrow a term from medicine.

Dr. Smith speaks of all accounts being kept in silver, yet of gold as being the majority of the circulation, and he mentions and briefly discusses the idea of changing the ratio, and then, apparently as an alternative, suggests in a tentative way, that lighter coins might be made, and be legal tender only for a guinea. Throughout his work, silver is the metal ordinarily named as the synonym of money, and a "regulated proportion between silver and gold" is mentioned as the natural outgrowth of national development.

Ricardo, in distinction from Smith, uses gold as the common name for money, but this is only a conventional convenience of speech, just as he assumes for convenience that money is stable in value. *Per contra* in his "Plan of an Economical and Secure Currency" for England, he proposed, not gold, but silver, as "the standard." Moreover, on what is seen to-day to be the vital point of the whole matter—Wherefore and how came gold to be chief metallic money in London in his day?—he squarely opposed Lord Liverpool* and makes incisive reference to a little flight of fancy of Dr. Smith.†

Mill, though objecting to a "double standard," so far from showing disrespect for silver as a money-metal, follows Lord Ashburton in pointing out that the inconveniences of the "double standard" are avoided, and its advantages obtained by what he (erroneously) supposed to be the system of France. His idea was that silver was the standard (or as I should call it, unit and sole legal tender), while gold held a (supposed) anomalous position which I should describe as that of a trade coin, with a name which served to give it a certain rating, that could be varied by agreement.‡

This brief but comprehensive glance at the practical ideas of Smith, Ricardo, and Mill, about the "standard" as an object of state policy is, I think, conclusive, as re-

---

* Of Lord Liverpool's idea of a preference for gold because England was so rich, he says (p. 222), "it is not because gold is better fitted for carrying on the circulation of a rich country, that gold is ever preferred for the purpose of paying debts." In another place he observes that the use of gold in the eighteenth century in England was due to "the inaccurate determination of the Mint proportions." (p. 271.)

† Referring to Dr. Smith's idea that "during the continuance of any one regulated proportion between the respective values of the different metals, the value of the most precious metal regulates the value of the whole coin," Ricardo makes the significant comment: "Because gold was in his day the medium in which it suited debtors to pay their debts, he thought that it had some inherent quality by which it did then, and always would, regulate the value of silver coin." (p. 224.)

‡ Mill's Principles of Political Economy, edition of 1848, Vol. II, p. 4.

MONEY AS AN OBJECT OF SCIENCE. 121

spects a certain branch of this inquiry. One cannot look in their writings for anything definite and thorough about the nicer issues now before us. As no germ of incitement is to be found in their writings for a revolution of one metal against the other, so there is nothing positive as to the possibility of that absolute intermetallic peace, of which we are now treating, and which is the object of the policy of Monetary Union. In the world of practical life, Smith, Ricardo, and Mill take the metals, so to speak, for "what they are worth," but do not dogmatize either about parity or disparity.

But you will say that, notwithstanding this, I have already pointed to their teaching as responsible for a fashion of thought about parity of Moneys which I regard as fraught with error, and you will ask where that teaching is. It is this which I propose now to show.

And first of their general impressions of the subject, its character, importance, the standing of money in the commonwealth. From that point of view, upon which it seems to me it is inevitable that one who wishes to deal competently with monetary legislation should place himself, it is of importance to know how far he can look to Smith, Ricardo, and Mill for instruction about matters of principle. What, for example, had these authorities to say of the importance of monetary legislation, of the occasions which call upon the legislator for interference, and of the mode and the purpose of such action? Incompleteness, or onesidedness, in the scientific treatment accorded by these writers to the subject of Money must prove to be misleading. As there is no doubt that they would be referred to as authorities, so their message would prove a source not of instruction, but of confusion. Now, in fact, at least as I understand the matter, they omit to deal with it exhaustively, or even methodically. To whatever extent, then, their influence—whether by omission or commission, the influence of what they taught, or what they did not teach—remains a power, it requires revision. As for my views of what the course of this revision should be, I have expressed them from time to time since 1876, but will briefly set down herewith as a postscript a statement on the subject of Money's place among the functions of government, which can conveniently be compared with the views of Mill which I now quote, and also with what once were the views of Herbert Spencer.*

The omission or defect to which I have referred is greatest in Mill, less in Ricardo, least in Smith. But it is not merely because Mill wrote last, with a greater expanse of monetary experience in sight than the others, that the defect is more marked in his case. It is also because of the scope and plan of his work. An analogous remark applies to Ricardo. In Smith's great book the historical element predominates : it was a conspectus of the economic condition of societies. Ricardo's work, *Principles of Political Economy and Taxation*, was a series of generalizations, which might be called in some measure a supplement and criticism of Smith. But Mill's twelve hundred pages contained not only *Principles of Political Economy*, but

---

*See note to page 125.

MILL'S CLASSIFICATION.   123.

Some of their applications to Social Philosophy. It professedly covers the ground of Economics in a wider sense, the economic side and the political side, and in the latter of course the field of economic statecraft, the sphere and duty of government. Book IV is entitled *Influence of the Progress of Society on Production and Distribution*, while the last book, Book V, treats, in eleven chapters, *Of the Influence of Government.*

Where, then, does Money stand, as an object of legislation and of administration? What is the scientific classification of this matter of legal tender for payment, and the regulation of the Mint, which Adam Smith had referred to as from early ages the object of governmental care? Mill, in Book V and Chapter I, deals with the whole matter. He treats of the functions of government—where does he find a place for Money?

I doubt if any member of the Royal Commission is prepared for the answer. Life is said to be measured rather by sensations than by time, and when, under the mandate of the Sovereign of a great Empire, gentlemen have been studying, for nearly two years, a question which has considerably interested the world since 1876, it is inevitable that they should rapidly outgrow a certain circle of ideas, which once may have been quite familiar. If the man could wear the cap that fitted him as a child, there would be no shock in realizing what it is Mill says about Money.

Mill[*] treats money as "coining," and puts it side by

---

[*] Vol. II, page 377.

side with weights and measures—a matter of convenience, to save the trouble of assaying. As for the regulation of Paper Money and of Credit generally, I find no mention of them here, though they are elsewhere exhaustively discussed by Mill. So coinage is put side by side with weights and measures. That is all! Let us pause for a moment to consider where this doctrine will carry us. Imagine a cabinet, a parliament, charged with the conduct of the monetary interests of a great nation, drawing its inspiration on that subject from such teaching. Evidently, if Money be cut down, in the case now before you, to the limits of the theory as stated, the sovereign and the rupee are but weights of metal. You will agree with me, I doubt not, if it is true that the sovereign and the rupee are only weights of metal, this alone and nothing more, then the Royal Commission has been dealing all this time with a matter of the size of the Troyes Pound or the Imperial Gallon. Shall we say, if Mill is right, there may yet be a " Trojan " Question or a " Gallonial " Crisis ?

Is the implication quite clear ? To make this page more luminous, let me apply the same method in another field— for example, to great works of art that have been the grace of civilization, and so are more attractive than dry-as-dust theories of economy. Let those who have visited Rome and Paris, and Dresden know that the theory I am attacking is like that which should treat the Antoninus of the Capitol as a mixture of copper and tin, the Venus of Melos as carbonate of lime, and the Sixtine Madonna as pigment. I am sorry to add there is nothing in the rest of Book V to redeem the defects of this view. Evidently the writer's thoughts were elsewhere, or the mere inconsistency of this with other parts of his work would have occurred to him. Of course it is not at all implied by this that such defects are common; indeed, I have elsewhere said enough to disprove this. Nor, indeed, is it just to my admiration for the great thinker to allow the implication to pass that he may not in any case have taken a broader view than is here revealed by his book. One would not build an indictment upon a slip of the pen. But print is a persistent force, and fame gives posthumous power for harm to the indiscretions of the great. Disciples have a fatal facility for building systems on the oversight of the master.*

---

* An illustration is given in the use lately made in some quarters of Mr. Herbert Spencer's utterances on this subject. See "Journal of the Inst. of Bankers," Pt. VI., Vol. VII., p. 399. The reference is, I believe, to "Social Statics" (c. xxix.). A glance at the book seems to me to show that it is unjust to Mr. Spencer to hold him responsible for the letter of what there is printed. The book was written about 1850, and the preface of the American edition (1864) states that the reprint must not be taken as a literal expression of the author's present views, and this preface is reprinted in the edition of 1868, and referred to in the new preface.

The chapter in question reveals complete unconsciousness of laws of legal tender. The essential character of money, which Adam Smith with his catholic good sense was aware of, is thus ignored. The author deals with money by taking it for granted. He objects to "interference with currency," and thinks that mints are unnecessary—but he never objects to making silver and gold legal tender, or explains how governments could exist without money! His unconsciousness of the facts also comes to the surface in his characterization of Scotland as a land of *free-trade in currency*, in which, of course, money is implicitly included.

How, then, did it come to pass that monetary legislation was lightly dealt with by Smith, Ricardo, and Mill? What was the source of this "fashion of their thought"? Asking, as we do, how they regarded the Parity of Moneys, and such Parity being obviously an equilibrium supported by legislation, it is in the path of these inquiries that we shall surely discover the key to what they may have to say which bears upon the matter. We have seen that they lived securely while there was comparative legal equality between gold and silver, and that this condition of things seemed so entirely normal and natural, that its causes were not examined in a scientific spirit. I now inquire whether there was not an active influence, no longer negative, but positive, working against truth—a fashion of thought which produced what I might call an innocently studied neglect of the scientific basis of monetary legislation, and hence a marked bias in reference to it.

I find such an influence. I find it in the natural exaggeration of the enthusiasm of the great conflict in which these great men spent their mental life. A spirit of reaction was naturally engendered by this conflict, which obscured the truth about money, but failed to reveal itself as a prejudice to these lovers of truth, because no serious consequences or erroneous conclusions growing out of their default could show themselves at the time.

These thinkers arose to attack and destroy false systems. For them the Commercial or Mercantile System, together with its various developments of vexatious state interference, was the Enemy. Their teaching was aimed

THE MERCANTILE SYSTEM. 127

to persuade the world to renounce this devil and all his works.

The Mercantile System, which, to use Dr. Smith's words, "represented national wealth as consisting in the abundance, and national poverty in the scarcity of Gold or Silver," was a doctrine and a policy. Gold and Silver, then, were involved in the struggle. But in that case monetary legislation also was necessarily involved in it together with them. Economic legislation generally was, in its purpose and effect, monetary legislation, the aim being to increase the national store of gold and silver. The great work of these men was thus an effort to abolish a doctrine and a policy relating to the precious metals which implied all manner of artificial regulations on the part of the state. Was not this a conflict likely to excite an enthusiasm that would be capable of exaggeration, which everyone would regard as entirely pardonable, if not indeed laudable? How could the question escape exciting a "political being" like man, whose nature it is to put his heart into politics. I find it perfectly natural on their part to be disposed to draw the line against monetary legislation generally—or, if this could not be done entirely, at least not to admit the subject into the inner circle of their "system" or scheme.

But the real effective strength of this disposition can only be realized when we consider the general orbit of thought upon which these great men were swept along with their time, leading and yet led. What is the distinguishing mark of the whole age of thought? Freedom, the rule of Nature, one phase of which is well suggested by the words *laissez-faire*, and non-interference. Set the individual free; remove all barriers to his development, was the watchword in the camp of science. This, then, was the principle. But like all principles it needed for its rightful application a sound understanding of its natural limits. Exaggerate the force of it, let it carry men to extremes, and you will see the gaols open and the Mint closed!

There is, by the way, what seems to me a curious parallel to the whole situation now before our view, which I will mention, as I do not remember ever to have seen it referred to. This idea of a state of freedom and rule of nature* is but the same principle applied to the social life of men as that *nature* in whose light the Father of Medicine regarded the bodily frame. The appeal of the eighteenth or nineteenth century for the health of the economic body is still to that healing power of nature (*vis medicatrix naturæ*, as the modern Latin phrase has it) which Hippocrates must have revealed to Aristotle. But mark the sequel! The principle of medicine being *to allow nature to act*, it is said to have been discovered by the Mediæval Church that various operations of medicine, and, in general, surgery, were rather *an interference with nature*, and hence they were forbidden to ecclesiastics. Are we not bound to trace and identify a similar superstition among economic writers? Were they not infallibly led to treat

---

* Quesnay's first work seems to have been his *Droit Naturel*.

certain departments of the medicine of the state as an interference with nature?

I trust you will kindly absolve me from any intent of disrespect toward the theories of nature.* Of course thought is no more likely to divest itself of the antithesis between nature and art than between right and left or between the equator and the poles. But there are limits; and there is a disposition to overpass them—a natural disposition! I recall an illustration of this extreme view, which may be suggestive, namely, a comparison between Varro's modest line " that Nature gave the fields and human art made the cities "—and Cowley's

" God the first garden made, and the first city Cain!"

Now, I entirely disclaim accusing Mill of regarding monetary laws as a work of Cain. But it could fairly be said the mood of the passage from Mill just referred to, and of others I shall cite, is represented by Cowper's

" God made the country, and man made the town."

As for the great Father of Economic Science, Dr. Smith, I certainly wish he had read (or re-read) his countryman Sir James Steuart. Perhaps he would have done so but for the depression caused by observing those acts of lawgivers touching money that filled the chief place in the public eye. Those acts, as they class themselves before me, were the debasement of metallic money, the issue of paper money, and the prohibition of the export of coin

---

* *Naturam expellas furcâ tamen usque recurret!*

and bullion. Of these, the first and the last were distinctly tainted with purely "mercantilist" origin. With reference to the latter I may mention, in passing, a curious fact, to which I have seen no allusion in regions where one would expect to find it, except in the statute book. It was not till Mill was in his teens that it became lawful to export guinea gold. The fifth century of this mercantilist law in England was closed in 1819. With such instances of vexatious or disastrous state interference before him it is not strange that monetary legislation exerted a certain repugnance in the thinker's mind.

What, then, is the natural effect, in the case of such men, of an unsympathetic attitude toward monetary jurisprudence? Evidently an incomplete, unsystematized handling of the subject. Where actual history is in sight to be appreciated by the experienced observer's eye, or where action is to be taken for which the counsel of the sagacious thinker is needed, we find the great excellency which the fame of such men justifies us in expecting. Once outside of that range, we are in strange country.

That I do not fail to appreciate that sagacity has already been shown. It remains to add evidence in continuation of what has been said of the place of money in the functions of government. The illustrations which I shall give under this head relate to the incompleteness and inconsistency of statements, the manner in which some of the great problems of Money are left outside the focus of attention, and the visionary character of some of the reasoning on the subject.

INCOMPLETE GRASP OF THE SUBJECT. 131

We have noted already the mode in which the action of the state—legislation and administration, creating, establishing, supporting a monetary system—is taken for granted. The great monetary questions of the day, chief among which is the regulation of Bank issues, are fully discussed. Properly speaking, for the sake of consistency, these subjects ought to be made to fit into a general system of monetary legislation. But this step seems not to have been attempted. Salient facts are recognized, but the scientific appreciation of them is incomplete, and there is no proper apportionment of them to their place in the system as a whole. For reasons already stated in what has been said of the general scope of the "Wealth of Nations," this remark applies far less to that great book than to the "Principles" set forth by Ricardo and by Mill.

The "sketchiness" of Ricardo's book in this regard is notably exhibited in a passage, which, in the days of a Royal Commission on Gold and Silver, wears a very strange air :

"It may perhaps be necessary," he observes, "to say a few words on the subject of the two metals, Gold and Silver." (p. 221.)

As if only a few words were necessary! Elaborate discussion is given of the modes of regulating money credit, of Paper Money and Bank-notes, all of which have an existence only relatively to Metallic Money. And yet the principles of regulation of Metallic Money are but lightly glanced at. As a matter of convenience Ricardo takes Gold to represent Metallic Money, and assumes Gold to be stable in value, and though he recognizes in the amplest manner that these are assumptions made purely for convenience and clearness, and without foundation in fact—still those chapters are wanting in which the relations of Gold and Silver and the question of the general level of prices should be dealt with. At the same time I cannot resist inquiring what would have happened if Ricardo had been led in some way, to put his Scheme of a Monetary System for England into his "Principles." Would not the necessity of cohesion have forced itself upon his mind? Could later economics have taken the tone we have witnessed, if he had treated *ex cathedrâ* of the Principles of Monetary Legislation with a high-pressure interference scheme to back them? The central idea of what I shall name Ricardo's Bullion Standard and Bullion Certificate Scheme, was parity maintained by all the force of law that was to be had. And I must also allow myself the daring statement that the same thing may be said of all orthodox plans for a convertible paper currency—if the philosophers only knew it!

The same incompleteness, with a touch of the visionary dogmatism of a mind possessed, as it were, with the idea of freedom, are visible in Mill. In his chapter *On the Value of Money as dependent on the Cost of Production*, he says:

"We are, however, to suppose a state, not of artificial regulation, but of freedom. In that state, and assuming no charge to be made for coinage, the value of money will conform to the value of the bullion of which it is made." (I, p. 24.)

With this passage we pass at once to the centre of Mill's system; we can at once proceed to judge of the correctness of his general ideas about money and the state.

We observe that he speaks of "a state, not of artificial regulation, but of freedom." We know he can only mean freedom *under the law*, for he is not speaking of savages, but of an organized society, and a purpose of his book is to afford counsel to rulers how to make wise laws. We at once ask, then, what is the principle of distinction between such "law" and "artificial regulation," so far as money is concerned. And then we find both principle and regulation brushed aside! The entire system breaks down through the one phrase "assuming no charge to be made for coinage." Mill actually assumes in his "state of freedom" the entire apparatus of "artificial regulation" under which he was born. He endows his "natural" state, by this brief but comprehensive assumption, not only with the general law of Money, but also with the Statute of the 18th year of Charles II, chapter 5, with the Tower Mint, and with a yearly appropriation for expenses. But even then he cannot reach the parity he speaks of between bullion and coin. Not merely free coinage and gratuitous coinage, but still another artificial regulation is wanted, namely, that statute which compels the Bank to buy gold bullion at a fixed price. And yet it is this which, in fact, really makes gold bullion stable in value in England! Is it necessary to add further evidence of the utter inadequacy of Mill's ideas of the relation of money and the state? I submit that this one passage makes good my charge.

Of course it is impossible to advance very far in political economy without treating of value; and when value is reached, money is not far off. Now it is no treason, in the year 1888, to say that money is a subject which presents some difficulties. It was convenient—very convenient— to treat of value directly without troubling one's self seriously about the " medium," money. But if one does not trouble one's self seriously about money, the principles of monetary legislation fade into thin air. It is quite in keeping with this mood to observe, as Mill does:

"There cannot, in short, be intrinsically a more insignificant thing in the economy of society than money."

Here, again, is an even more striking instance of dispraise of monetary legislation, than Ricardo's " few words." Of course, to us in this generation it is peculiarly easy to find such passages a ground of surprise. We live in a time of monetary discussions. Not to mention lesser proofs, we can recall in 1876 the Special Committee of the House of Commons on the Depreciation of Silver, and the Congressional Commission on Silver in the United States ; the International Monetary Conferences of 1878 and 1881, the Royal Commission on the Depression of Trade which closed its long labors in 1886, and the Royal Commission on Gold and Silver Currency, which followed, and is now * in session. After all such a profound stirring of opinion and effort of study, it seems to us very strange that a great economic teacher could say, " There cannot be intrinsically a more insignificant thing in the

---

* First printed in May, 1888.

economy of society than money." No doubt, in a certain sense, the statement is true, and the truth is an important truth ; but what is true in it is not a novelty, while the too vigorous statement, leading to an exaggeration of the truth, is new. The truth itself is of most venerable ancestry. Was it not early in Grecian fable that the legend arose of Midas, to whom the god gave his wish, that all he touched should turn to gold ? Midas starving in the midst of his gold,

> Rich beyond hope and wretched past despair,
> Loathing the wealth he cannot choose but coin,
> Cursing the boon that not an hour ago
> He prayed for,

as Ovid tells the story, offers a parallel, not too remote, both to the ideas of Dr. Smith about the Mercantile System and to analogous opinions as to the rôle of money. Taken, then, merely as a forcible statement of the purely ancillary relation of money to "real wealth"—to commodities and property and services which make up that sum of things desired, to attain which money is only a means—this phrase of Mill's commands assent. But it is more than this in effect; it is an indication of what I have spoken of, the disposition to ignore the nature, and the importance, of money and of monetary law.

This will appear more clearly upon examining the confusion between Money and Barter. Barter being an exchange of goods for goods *without money*, it is plain that to say that modern exchanges, which are in fact exchanges of goods for a price, and of a price for goods, are barter, is playing upon words. It is a metaphor, to be justified by rhetorical or poetic considerations, but not otherwise. In the mental process which its use implies, money sustains the rôle of a dissolving view. Always a "middle thing," μέσον, *tertium comparationis,* but sometimes viewed under the simile of an instrument, wheel, vehicle, etc., it becomes for some minds a "medium" and nothing else, and then as a mere "mode of exchanging," as Mill calls it, becomes quite diaphanous, as if it were thinned and expanded into an atmosphere, which, of course, is invisible. But these metaphors are serious affairs. The monetary question embraces a considerable range of interest. Extending from Indian taxation, or the solvency of France, to such a local domestic affair as the present abraded state of English gold coin, it is important enough to repay looking after. If you allow these metaphors full swing—and it lies in the power of the Royal Commission to do this—they will decide the questions before you off-hand. If trade is barter, of what use are standards, and statutes to watch over them? All that the "Precious" Metals have to do is to exist, and that they do by the help not of man, but of nature. No edicts are needed; the fulminations of Professors and of Princes are mere wasted powder. The way of Parliaments, Commissions, and Congresses of Monetary Unions is quite clear and perfectly simple. It is to do nothing!—but, of course, only *after repealing everything!*

The confusion of money and barter to which I allude finds root, I think, in one of those phrases for which

Ricardo's natural eloquence and cogency of statement are responsible. That he suffered some of the disabilities of the so-called "practical man" is an obvious remark when made, as I make it, fifty years after Senior said he was "the most incorrect writer who ever attained philosophical eminence." And in referring to money, he spoke as a dictator, especially after the Resumption of Cash Payments. It is one of his generalizations that seems to have obscured in the eyes of Mill some modest truths with which Adam Smith was quite content. I doubt if Ricardo realized the force of what he was saying. The evolution of doctrines amid the changes and chances of this world are not likely to have occupied his thoughts very seriously. And it is to one of his most brilliant generalizations that the error seems traceable. The truth conveyed was in fact so important and the metaphor so attractive, that it seems to have been impossible for his followers to make good those limitations of its field which should exclude serious error.

"Gold and Silver," says Ricardo, "having been chosen for the general medium of circulation, they are, by the competition of commerce, distributed in such proportions to the different countries of the world as to accommodate themselves to the natural traffic which would take place if no metals existed and the trade between countries were purely a trade of barter."

Here is, at the same time, a great truth, and a most prolific source of error. Of the truth it is needless for me to speak. I shall presently cite the opinion of Mill as to its originality. But what of the error?

Let us observe the hypothesis and dwell upon it a moment! "Natural traffic!" *Natura naturans!* If there were only no metals, that we might get back to a state of nature, of freedom! If we were in that happy state there would be the same traffic, we should buy freely, without money and without price, just as we do now. And it would be natural traffic, freed from the vexations that money brings.

It is a far-off echo of that devout wish with which the too-learned Pliny was, in his time, inspired by most famous authors of still elder days. *Utinamque posset e vita in totum abdicari,*—or, as the older translation gives it, "Oh that the use of Gold were cleane gone; would God it could possibly be quite abolished among men * * *. What a blessed world was that, and much more happier than this wherein wee live, at what time as in all the dealings betweene men, there was no coine handled, but their whole trafficke stood upon bartering and exchanging ware for ware, and one commoditie for another." What more attractive? And yet absolutely, hopelessly visionary! Is it in Plato's 'Republic,' or in Moore's 'Utopia,' or in 'The New Atlantis,' or in 'Oceana,' that this miracle of "natural traffic" can be imagined as taking place? Why this excursion into dreamland?

Now, I do not mean that it is possible that any good head could be so possessed with this dream as to vitiate all his thought. But is not a little unsteadiness of nerve enough when one is navigating, what Petty called two centuries ago, "the deep ocean of all the mysteries concerning money?"

Observe the effect this passage of Ricardo's had upon Mill. He says of it, after quoting it in full (v. ii, b. iii., c. xxi)—

"Of this principle, so fertile in consequences, previous to which the theory of foreign trade was an unintelligible chaos, Mr. Ricardo, though he did not pursue it into its ramifications, was the real originator. No writer who preceded him appears to have had a glimpse of it; and few are those who even since his time have had an adequate conception of its scientific value."

Observe also the sequel! "It is not with money," says Mill elsewhere, "that things are really purchased."

This, you will notice, is a statement which goes far beyond the idea which I have sought to express in the phrase "money is an order payable to bearer upon wealth in general;" and which, in various forms, is common to a great number of writers, among whom I may name Aristotle and Adam Smith. In Mill's mind this phase of money seems to grow in actuality. In another passage he observes—

"All interchange is in substance and effect barter; he who sells his productions for money, and with that money buys other goods, really buys those goods with his productions. And so of nations; their trade is a mere exchange of exports for imports; and whether money is employed or not, things are only in their permanent state when the exports and imports exactly pay for each other." (ii, 168.)

Let us analyze this with some care! "Things are only in their permanent state!" Precisely! There is the truth!

"Things" tend toward further exchanges, so as to rectify the balance. The order payable to bearer on wealth in general is a thing which the bearer naturally desires to "realize upon." It is true of individuals and it is true of nations. If a nation receives a mass of cash on balance of its foreign trade the tendency is (and should be) not "to use the most ferocious measures" (to quote a quotation of Herbert Spencer) "to keep it from going out again," but to circulate it. Of course the mercantilist would use the most ferocious measures to keep it back. Is it not evident that the anti-mercantilist crusader must wax a little warm in stoutly resisting, and was in no mood to mince matters of doctrine when he got the enemy within range of his mace?

Why was it that the great man did not calmly state the facts and omit the imaginary aggravating circumstances of rhetoric? Why say that exchanges with money are in substance and effect exchanges without money, or, in other words, that black is white? What but confusion can be gained by such tropes and figures? After this no wonder this same great treatise, that has done so much for the advancement of science, should offer matter so incongruous as speculations about a pound, which should "not express any real thing, but should be a mere unit of calculation?" (ii, 4.) In this latter case Mill seems to me to give more weight to a tale of Montesquieu's (and perhaps a dream of Sir James Steuart) than to the reasoned opinion of Ricardo. It is in such speculations that certain theories find their lofty source, which, when they show their importance in descending to practice, may take opposite directions, as if leaving a watershed. I should briefly describe two classes of them as the doctrine of the Printing Press, and the doctrine of the Banking House. Of the former, the Paper-Money school, little has been heard, I believe, by the Royal Commission, but the latter doctrine is certainly so strongly held in certain regions that I venture to say if Bacon were living he would call it "the idol of the Banking House."* It is the disposition to think that, for the monetary legislator, cash is unimportant because credit is colossal; which is not very remote from saying the trunk and branches of our tree are so enormous, that the roots are quite unimportant!

But enough has been said to show that as a systematized branch of knowledge Money lay outside the focus of Mill's attention.

---

* If to regard a metal as a standard of value carried with it no actual employment of pieces of that metal for the uses known in fact as monetary; that is to say, if the metal were purely a term of mental comparison and nothing more, as might be the case if one were to consider, as a matter of curiosity, what a horse "was worth" in platina or in gallium, the question might be treated in a different way.

There would, then, be no need of laws of Legal Tender, of Coinage, of Banking, there would be no Monetary Systems, there would be no money and no questions of currency, of monetary policy. But this is not the case. It is but a dreamland of the economic visionary to which this latter spiritual meaning of "standard of value" points. Money exists. The actual world of human society has always been, and is to-day, a world of payments as well as of price.—(See answer to Question VII of the Commission.)

With another illustration I close this letter. Mill remarks that:

"In order to understand the manifold functions of a Circulating Medium, there is no better way than to consider what are the principal inconveniences which we should experience if we had not such a medium?" * * *

What shall I say of this? If it were in a popular lecture there would be mere petulance and hypercriticism in noting what, from a higher point of view, will seem deficiencies. But it is not a popular lecture. It is in "Mill's Principles of Political Economy," and in the chapter where the completest scientific exposition of the rôle of money in society is to be looked for. Surely these are precincts that have no right to harbor metaphors and hypotheses which cannot give a satisfactory account of themselves! It is therefore quite germane to our object to observe that, taking the matter strictly, I find here a companion vision to Ricardo's.

This hypothesis of a world where there is no money at all, leads straight to dreamland. The reason of this is that the mind is invited to enter upon a supposition without going through to the end: it sees only certain features of the supposed case, but is not apprised concerning the existence of features it does not see, and no notice is given of the superficial and provisional character of any inferences which thus can be drawn. As Mill states it, the assumption is inevitably implied that "we" should be "we," that the modern world would be the modern world, or indeed (to go into particulars) that London could be London, and the English money-using community an economic body just as it is, if there were no English money. Is it not also implied that this would be true if there never had been any English money, or any money at all? Why not? To most readers certainly this would seem a natural conclusion. But this is absurd! Who can speak with certainty of detail upon a supposition which substitutes an imaginary history of civilization for the facts?

If once this full meaning of Mill's hypothesis is stated and accepted, its visionary character will presently stand revealed. We can assist the process by asking, Why not inquire how the world would get along if there never had been any division of labor, or any language? Or again, Why not attempt to characterize the family by the same method! The family is a very great subject of thought for philosophers of every school and specialty, although it is the most familiar thing there is—so familiar, indeed, that the word familiar is derived from the word family. But money is a great subject, too, in its humble way!

Let us make the attempt! In order, then, to understand the family, we should proceed upon the idea that there is no better way than to ask what would be our position if there were no sex and no children? Do you not agree with me that this is a fair parallel? Again, recalling the familiar analogy between the circulation of money and the circulation of the blood, let us imagine Harvey studying the circulation of the blood, and inquiring what would happen if there were a natural circulation where there was no blood at all.

How does this method strike you as a way of clearing the air, or, rather, of sending light into the nooks, corners, and recesses of the obscure labyrinth of money? Is it not an unpractical way of looking at the subject? And yet this is the century which appreciates Francis Bacon's method, which is getting itself trained to use the *novum organum!* Can it be said that money has here received its share of scientific treatment? Evidently not!

I submit that the views I have advanced are justified by the evidence I have presented. The natural result of the doctrine I have analyzed is evidently that unpractical fashion of thought, of which I spoke at first, that defect of sight or color-blindness in reference to monetary legislation, and a habit of mind which enlists the will to resist and to prevent the approach of knowledge. You will observe that there is a progression in the attitude toward money of these leading minds; a progression which may quite legimately have communicated a certain momentum to opinion in these last two or three decades. The progression is from apparent complacency and neutrality to indifference and finally disparagement. This course, as I say, tended to perpetuate itself, and its natural sequence is that in the higher walks of science money has, to an important extent, been ignored, and monetary legislation, as it were, "tabooed:"* language being used only consist-

---

*Among other curious results of this error is the fact that in some minds the practical monetary question of the day has, by a variety of

ent with the idea that the state ought not to have anything to do with it.

To remedy this condition of opinion it is necessary to change the fashion of thought throughout, and hence to begin at the source by a revision and correction of general ideas about money and the state, and to this work, as you are aware, I have sought to contribute. To the fact that such revision has not penetrated everywhere throughout the body of the learned is to be ascribed, as it seems to me, the unwillingness of some minds to accept, as conclusive, reasoning such as that which I briefly set forth at the outset of this letter. But for this fashion, the economic question as to the power of nations to maintain Parity between the Money-Metals would long ago, together with many other questions of moment, have been resolved in all minds conversant with economics.

If I am mistaken in this opinion, I shall be greatly indebted to you if you will set me right.

Believe me, Sir, with much respect,
Very sincerely yours,
S. DANA HORTON.

Athenæum Club,
London, May, 1888.

---

illogical links of association or analogy, been connected with a matter so foreign to it as the question of tariffs, of "protection" and "free-trade," and this, sometimes on one side, sometimes on the other, upon lines quite contradictory with each other.

MONEY AND THE STATE: OR, THE PLACE OF MONEY AMONG THE FUNCTIONS OF GOVERNMENT.

When, in the earlier stages of civil society, systematized government came into existence, there arose of necessity what I shall call an Institution of Obligatory Payment. This may be regarded as accompanying both the growth of rights and the differentiation or specialization of functions among the members of the community. Whether in public war or peace, or within the domestic sphere, in matters civil and in matters criminal, comes Obligatory Payment. Be it Tribute, or Tax, or Fine, or Damages, it is the agent, adjunct, and ally of those powers of the community to keep force and fraud in subjection, which are the very essence and life of the Civil State. The material of Obligatory Payment is money. It is the State which fixes upon the object with which payment can be made, and establishes the name of Money, or Units of Valuation.

But what of Voluntary Payment—the work of commerce with its medium of exchange—to relieve the individual from the manifold inconveniences of barter? Voluntary Payment is present and of equal date, if not, indeed, the elder. But not the stronger! The individual, one against all, cannot escape the controlling force of the corporate will, which, in prescribing how Tax and Fines and Damages are paid, shows him the most convenient medium for exchanges. Of course, the individuals form the State, governments are their representatives, and mere convenience in some measure leads the former to respect the will of the people. But the single corporate will is paramount. Whatever the play of interaction, the effective control is in the State. And the State cannot escape the duty of exerting a control, for that control is a condition of the State's existence. Without organization to restrain force and fraud the State ceases to exist. It must defend its existence against enemies; it must keep the peace within, and see that civil rights are respected in some measure; and for this it must have Obligatory Payments, Money, Accounts, Valuations. The tendency of economic writers has been to ignore this, and to start from the trader's medium of exchange, and to regard it alone.

In setting forth this view as my own I allow myself to cite the testimony to that effect of Professor De Laveleye, in an address before the French Institute (Acad. of Moral and Political Sciences), May 10, 1881.

A paper on 'The Parity of Bullion and Modes of Maintaining it,' which followed the above as first printed in London, June, 1888, is given on later pages in sequence to the chapter on 'Bullion or Coin?'

V.

FEDERATION FOR PARITY OF MONEYS AND THE ADVANCEMENT OF SCIENCE.

FEDERATION FOR PARITY OF MONEYS AND THE ADVANCEMENT OF SCIENCE.

An Address Answering the Question "What shall we do about Silver," before the American Association for the Advancement of Science.

ABSTRACT.

The persons addressed are the members of this Section. For them Silver represents a duty. It was Science turned politics that engendered that morbid condition of money which creates the Silver Question, and it is for the interpreters of Science to redeem this error by promoting a speedy settlement of the issues thus raised. What is to be taught by those who wish to advance Science? The true remedial policy was instituted by the United States in 1878, by proposing to nations controlling the majority of the money-metals the adoption of concordant laws assuring them legal equality. It is in supporting this lead that Science advances.

The basis of truth and fact sustaining this policy can be summarized on the following lines.

Note.—This subject was chosen by the Committee of Section I (Economic Science and Statistics) in 1888, and Professor Sumner and I were invited to represent the opposing sides of debate at Toronto, September 8, 1889. This paper was forwarded by me from Europe to the Secretary.

Affirmative Statement of the Federalist Position.

I.

That Gold and Silver are the Money-Metals, and that Gold is Money and Silver is Money to-day.

II.

That Parity of Moneys is desirable.

III.

That it is the law of each nation which determines what is Money in that nation.

IV.

That the preponderant employment—that is to say, economic "demand"—for Gold and Silver is an effect of the laws of nations.

V.

That Monetary Laws establish Parity.

VI.

That permanent Parity between Silver and Gold is producible by a proper regulation of their employment.

VII.

That concurrent laws for legal equality of the metals in an effective majority of nations will establish Parity outside as well as within their direct jurisdiction.

VIII.

That such Parity benefits each nation by assuring comparative stability to the valuations in which it is interested.

IX.

That Federation is a condition and a guarantee of such concurrent laws, replacing those which now maintain disparity.

X.

That the paramount monetary issue of the age is whether a settlement on this basis shall be made.

STATEMENT

OF

THE DIS-UNIONIST OR ANTI-FEDERALIST POSITION.

Scientific conservatism and dependence upon the example of England.

The opinion of Michel Chevalier in 1878.

FEDERATION FOR PARITY OF MONEYS AND THE ADVANCEMENT OF SCIENCE, OR " WHAT SHALL WE DO ABOUT SILVER?"

Who are "we" that are to do something about silver? What are the active forces of which I am to speak? Am I to set forth what I think we, the people of the United States, or of Canada, should do about silver? It is only at elections that the people can act, in the proper sense—act as one united force—and I am not aware that there is an election at hand. I may, however, say in passing, that if there were elections at hand, I should only need to repeat the substance of certain planks of political platforms about silver which have been actually adopted; for example, by the Republicans in the State of Ohio in 1877, by the National Republican Convention in 1884, and by the Republican and Democratic Conventions in New York State in 1885. The first mentioned is a recommendation, while the latter are a ratification, of the policy adopted by Congress in the second section of the Act of February 28, 1888. This is not the section compelling the compulsory coinage of silver dollars, it is that by which the United States inaugurated a policy of restoration of silver to its former equality with gold by joint action of nations.

This policy, which by its nature combines the elements of a domestic policy and a foreign policy, has remained since 1878 a settled policy of the United States. I venture to believe it is as firmly established as the Monroe Doctrine. So far, then, as the United States as a whole are concerned, I need not undertake the task of making suggestions about anything it may need to do with reference to silver.

Nor shall I ask what the several branches of the legislative 'powers that be', whether the Senate or the House, or this Committee thereof or that, have to do on this subject. Nor shall I venture to discuss the possibilities that lie before the President or his Ministers in this regard. No doubt there are essays to be written which might rightly hope to attain such an audience. But there is no need now to go beyond the limits of this room, or the list of the members who belong here, to find ample work to be done, good work, work of conversion, for the advancement of science, work that all the members are pledged to support.

The "we" of whom I speak, then, are the members of the section of Political Economy and Statistics of this Association. I conceive they have something to do for themselves and for their fellow-men in regard to this matter of silver. The silver question covers something more than a scientific generalization waiting to be proved, a compound waiting to be analyzed, a discovery waiting to be verified. All these can wait. But the silver question involves a duty to be performed, and to wait is to neglect that duty. It is a duty which the interpreters of science now living owe it to themselves—to the cause of learning—to perform without delay.

156 SCIENCE AND THE FEDERATION POLICY.

Be it known to all friends of science—and never forgotten—it was science which engendered the silver question with the dangers and anxieties that have come in its train. It was the mistaken learning of 1867, of 1871, and 1873, which did the damage that the settlement of the silver question is to check, and, as far as may be, to make good. It was upon the incital, and with the approval, of an overwhelming majority of the learned of all nations, that the statutes and decrees of silver outlawry in divers nations became fact. Americans must take to heart that for this general error of policy the United States have their share of responsibility, for in 1867* the influence of the American Union in the family of nations was militant in Paris, aiding and abetting the anti-silver movement then organizing. And all was done with the best intentions, and under the advice of counsel recognized as learned in the law.

What " we have to do about silver," then, is to educate

---

* This was shortly after the Latin countries had joined in a Monetary Treaty, forming the " Latin Union," which the United States was invited to join. Hon. Samuel B. Ruggles, of New York, was accredited to the Conference of 1867 by Mr. Seward, then Secretary of State. Among the monetary questions then debated was reducing the weight of the gold dollar, so as to coin (when specie payment should return) a five-dollar piece, which should equal either the English sovereign, or a proposed 25-franc piece, which was intended to replace the 20-franc piece, Louis d'or or Napoleon, in France.

In the Document of the Monetary Conference of 1878 are reprinted the various state-papers, which explain the situation in 1867. A *résumé* of the proceedings of the Conference, in the speech of Mr. de Parieu, is given in the Appendix.

public opinion and to advance science, to learn and to teach important truths relating to money—for silver is money, and has been since the economic world began— important truths, I say; truths that will assist the present generation of citizens or legislators to safeguard their higher interests by what they do or leave undone with reference to it.

What are these truths? The first truth of all, first because simplest and at the same time universal, *prima inter pares*, is that the policy of federation for equality of the metals before the law—which is the American policy, if our brothers of Canada* will permit us, *vis-a-vis* to Europe and Asia, to represent the Continent—is right.

The policy of federation to restore silver to its former legal position, the policy of establishing and maintaining parity between the two halves of the world's money, is right. The accord of an effective majority of nations to close a period of disastrous economic conflict and disturbance by a catholic measure of peace and order, is a good work. Once achieved, a nation may be proud of its share in it. There is enough of barbarism and dulness within sight in our time to serve as a foil to this enterprise of civilization; and individuals who contribute their little quota toward bringing about its success, need to have their labours

---

* I may add in parenthesis that they can the more willingly permit us to do this, since they are in some measure committed in favour of that policy. Such at least was the impression which the highly appreciated Canadian ally of the United States delegation, Sir Alexander Galt, conveyed to the members of the International Conference at Paris in 1881.

brightened if not lightened by appreciating the quality of it.

The project passes slowly towards achievement—slowly, for it must triumph over both the prejudices of men and the inertia of nations. But it is progressing, and progressing fast, now at length that the harvest of conversion in England is coming into sight—in England, which alone has blocked the way; for in 1881 the attitude of Germany promised her readiness to join in full with France and the United States when England should do so. The time, then, is approaching for realization of the project proposed in 1878, the time when civilization is to make a forward step to reach a *united standard*.

What the members of this section " have to do about silver" is to accelerate this advance; to recognize, and upon occasion to teach, the basis of truth and fact upon which is reared this policy of federation to secure legal equality between silver and gold.*

I shall try to characterize briefly this basis of truth and fact by a rough sketch-map, political rather than economic, giving practical generalizations rather than their scientific sub-structure.

---

* As has long been my custom I give notice to any one seeking information touching the measure proposed in 1878, that the Document of the Conference of 1878 is still gratuitously distributed from the Department of State at Washington, by mail, upon application to the Chief Clerk.

AFFIRMATIVE STATEMENT OF THE FEDERALIST POSITION.

I.

That Silver and Gold are the Money-Metals, and that Gold is Money and Silver is Money to-day.

Of the above affirmation I select as the only probable object of denial which calls for encounter, the statement that *silver is money to-day*. Are all the members of this section fully aware of this? I hope they are, but I fear they are not; I fear there are exceptions. I have had the opportunity of meeting, in books or in conversation, the minds of most of the learned of our century who have dealt with monetary questions, and I have found in all that goodly company few who entirely realized—in the subtle yet most important sense in which the phrase is now to be used—that silver is money. This sense or meaning of the phrase springs from the internationality of money; the solidarity of interest, the effective contiguity, or the continuity of the various systems of money (which make up the total money of the world), whereby each has an interest in all, enjoys the lateral support of all, and each serves in part as a means of business communication with the other. There is here a truth which is far from having completed its struggle for recognition. Indeed the concepts in use to-day in monetary discussion are curiously adapted to veil it from the understanding. What with "Single Standard"* and "Double Standard" and "Bimetallism" and "Monometallism," it is singularly easy to ignore the internationality of money. Then again there is the word "demonetize." What have we not heard of eloquence about the demonetization of silver, and yet—in spite of the demonetizing devil and all his works—silver is money. So likewise, one might say, for generations men have heard of the conquest

---

* In connection with my criticism of the verbal fallacies prevalent among the partisans of gold, and especially the application to money of the word "Standard" in the sense of the exact sciences, to which space is given in pages 45 and 47, I may justly add a *pendant* touching the silver side of this protracted controversy; for there are verbal sins on our side that are highly regrettable. What, with *metallisms mono* and *bi*, a subject already difficult and obscure, has been befogged and bemuddled; in fact, if one were to say bimetallism = be-muddle-ism he would not be far wrong.

No doubt, special study is required that one may realize, as, for example, Bacon did, the "difference it makes what a thing is called," how "words, as a Tartar's bow, do shoot back upon the understanding of the wisest, and mightily entangle and pervert the judgment"—how "the ill and unfit choice of words wonderfully obstructs the understanding"—how "words plainly force and overrule the understanding, and throw all into confusion, and lead men away into numberless empty controversies and idle fancies."

I doubt if any one has used either of these muddle-isms—mono or bi—, much without being, in appreciable measure, "thrown all into confusion" by them, with "obstruction of the understanding," and so led away "into numberless empty controversies and idle fancies."

If the object were talk and not action, confusion and not clearness, what better reinforcement could be found?

Whoever assists, as I have tried to do, to disinfect such words, gives

of Russia by the great Napoleon—the remarkable thing about which was that it never occurred.

There have been local Acts, and partial Acts, of outlawry against silver, Acts which have done more harm to the erring constituency of gold than to the constituency of silver. But that is all. It is ten years since Germany gave up trying to "make soup out of hot water alone," as Bismarck described it, and abandoned her sale of bullion made of melted thalers.

In closing, a word of definition rather than argument concerning the supply of silver. Silver is a money-metal, imperishable and rare. The annual find of new metal has never been more than a minute fraction of the existing stock. In spite of silver mares' nests, whether in Australia or in the Americas, there is no valid ground for expecting any real revolution in the conditions of new supply, nor even that the fluctuations of silver output will equal those of gold in the past. Hence the stock in existence—that is to say the economic "supply"—is a limited supply; a monopoly of nature not to be broken down.

---

succor in spite of themselves to the Romeos of reform, who take the poetic view, and find a less misleading name not needed for a rose so sweet as this, thereby most innocently forgetting that while it is true "A rose under any other name *would* smell as sweet," the sweetness of it is not within their jurisdiction. Their humble, prosaic, and practical object is merely to persuade people in this busy world to take their cause on its merits and not believe it is what its enemies say it is, nor what their words assist in making it appear.

The point has been settled by the English-speaking race in saying, 'Give a dog a bad name and hang him.'

II.

That Parity of Money is desirable.

This affirmation is not unnecessary, as an unbiased mind might suppose. There are most serious obstacles to logical thinking on this head. The mental vision of our time suffers largely from what I will imagine an oculist calling " atrophy of the apparatus of accommodation." Or perhaps one may say that there is normal sight, but it is only in spots.

A criss-cross of premium or discount between the moneys of different centres of business is recognized as an abomination to the economic mind in every professor's study in the world, provided the places are near each other, as for example New York and Philadelphia, or London and Manchester, or Paris and Marseilles. The same truth has vogue when applied to Paris, London, New York, and San Francisco. The negation of such common basis, the crisscross of premium and discount, a kind of organized disorder or Babel of valuations—a financial St. Vitus' dance—is recognized as a grave malady by all regular physicians. It is plain to all they need a common and stable basis for the valuations through which their business proceeds. Here there is no help but in parity. But beyond this range, distance seems to bring confusion to the view. How is it with parity between Asia, Europe, and the Americas? Here, for old-school professors, the light grows dim and all signs seem to fail. Their lapse of logic is as great as if the regular pharmacopœia should allow its prescriptions to be used only for people engaged in retail trade.

III.

That it is the Law of each Nation which determines what is Money in that Nation.

To a public which has passed from state bank notes to silver certificates it is unnecessary to expand this thesis.

IV.

That the Preponderant Employment—that is to say, economic "Demand"—for Silver and Gold is an effect of the Laws of Nations.

This is a simple corollary of the preceding. To one who is disturbed by the contrast between use in the arts, and monetary use, and attracted by the subtleties of causation and of motive, I can briefly suggest two queries. Do legislatures make certain material legal tender because individuals like certain kinds of ornament? Do not individuals choose ornament in part because of the costliness of the material, and of its immediate convertibility into money?

V.

That Monetary Laws establish Parity.

In establishing money of different kinds or denominations, such laws invariably seek to determine the relation of these kinds or denominations. If they are wise laws they succeed. A law which makes twenty-dollar notes and one-dollar notes equally legal tender, effects an equation between twenty ones and one twenty. If one denomination were made convertible and legal tender, while the other is neither convertible nor legal tender, the nominal equation is likely to be falsified by a discount on the one or a premium on the other.

VI.

That permanent Parity between Silver and Gold is producible by a proper Regulation of their Employment.

As has been stated, the stock-in-existence—that is to say, the economic "supply"—is limited by nature. To regulate the relative "demand" is to regulate their relative value.

VII.

That concurrent Laws for legal Equality of the Metals in an effective Majority of Nations will establish Parity outside as well as within their direct Jurisdiction.

It is the "law of supply and demand" which operates as a guarantee of the equation.

If the great Powers and their probable allies give legal equality to silver and gold (of course at the same ratio) their parity at points outside of the direct jurisdiction of these nations cannot be prevented, except by an alteration of human nature, leading men to prefer loss to gain. There may be fluctuations of "exchange," but that does not affect parity.

Ample experience also justifies the averment. In late centuries the fluctuations of relative value were fluctuations within the range of effective legal ratios. In this century, so long as the Mint of Paris was open (before 1873) there has been substantially parity at Paris, and the local fluctuations elsewhere were chargeable, substantially, to "exchange" on Paris. I say "substantially" to make room for dealing fully with misapprehensions current in relation to this point. Without entering into detail I will briefly mention that I have discovered the proof that standard gold bullion has fluctuated in London in this century as against standard gold coin.

VIII.

That such Parity benefits each Nation by assuring comparative stability to the valuations in which it is interested.

The benefit applies in various directions and degrees in different nations, but there is something like equality in the shares of the nations in this benefit, because of an equality in the ratio of such benefit to the total economic interests of the nation.

IX.

That Federation is a condition and a guarantee of such concurrent laws replacing those which now maintain disparity.

This natural view, which guided the Government of the United States, and afterwards that of France, in approaching other nations on the subject, is supported by the subsequent inaction of nations. Each is unwilling to move without the other, and it is only accord which will make it safe to break the vicious circle.

X.

That the paramount monetary issue of the age is whether a settlement on this basis should be made.

There is no alternative to this settlement, which under the guarantees of federation gives parity through concurrence of laws, other than the perpetuation of the evils of that instability in the foundations of business and investment whereof mankind has had ampler experience since 1871 than at any period since the Thirty Years War. The mere delay fostered by opposition to settlement creates new obstacles to settlement. The opponents of the federation policy are in a double sense friends of disorder.

The Dis-Unionist or Anti-Federalist Position.

Those who oppose the growth of opinion in favor of Federation may be conveniently classified as follows :

First Grouping.

Those who have learned only a part of the truths hitherto set forth.

Those who have refused to learn any of these truths.

Second Grouping.

Those who think the federation project will never be adopted, chiefly because of the expected continuance of England's refusal to co-operate.

Those who think the federation would not maintain parity between the two metals even if England were to co-operate, with free coinage of an English Silver Dollar.

I hope that my friends in the dis-unionist camp will find nothing to offend them in this classification. One who has been militant, as I have for so many years, naturally attains what I may call a certain perspective in regarding the position of his "friends the enemy;" and their Parthian campaign of retreat has been full of instruction. In fairness I may confess that the key-note of what I have been saying was given me by one of the highest names in the camp of the opposition and in the literature of money, for

Michel Chevalier is among the prophets for all who have a monetary faith. It was by another anti-silver champion, I should add, by Esquirou de Parieu,* the economic adviser of Napoleon III. and father of the Latin Union, that I was introduced to Chevalier. The distinguished author of the first great Treatise on Money said to me, "*You will never succeed in converting England.*" The prophesy was made in the Institute, at the close of a meeting of the Academy of Moral and Political Sciences, at which he had presided. I did not, however, relax my labors amid the foundations of monetary science.

On other pages the reader will find material bearing upon Chevalier's forecast: in the references to the various stages of growth of the Silver movement in England, and an account of its strength in 1889.

---

* MARIE LOUIS PIERRE FELIX ESQUIROU DE PARIEU (b. 1815), member of the Institute of France, Deputy in 1848, Minister in President Napoleon's Cabinet (1849-'51), head of the Council of State (1855-'70), member of the Ollivier Cabinet (1870), Senator (1876). His principal work is a *Treatise on Taxation* (Paris, 5 vols., 1862).

His numerous contributions to monetary discussion gave impulse to the movement for the unification of coinages in connection with the metric system, and are among the main forces which led to the anti-silver decisions of the International Monetary Conference of 1867, of which he was the guiding spirit and virtual President.

Had the Latin Union, or had France, gone on in the path he marked out, the mintage of silver would have been stopped *before the war* with Prussia or Germany. An interesting field of surmise is opened by the query, how this measure would have affected Germany.

His Report summing up before the Conference the results of its proceedings is reprinted in full in the Appendix.

VI.

BULLION OR COIN?

BULLION OR COIN?

It has been brought to my attention that certain English journals (December, 1889), in discussing Mr. Windom's proposals to substitute Bullion for Coin as the basis of our increasing paper issues, assume a lofty tone of criticism, and this fact has suggested to me that pages from my portfolio might assist in covering a certain deficit in the stock of learning available for the general public.

In this country there are symptoms in some quarters of a sense of dread, growing out of the novelty of the measures proposed to Congress, while in other quarters objection and opposition announce themselves, which can perhaps be fairly described as arising from a sense of injured pride, as if the national silver dollar were threatened with disrespectful treatment. The examination which I propose may therefore naturally take form in the query: *How is the "future of the silver dollar" to be affected by ceasing to coin it and using bullion in its place?*

This form of query will, perhaps, most simply indicate the standpoint which people in this country generally will take in looking at the subject. The silver dollar is a rallying point, a watchword, a formula of faith, for many minds, notably in the Mississippi Valley and in the Mountain States, and any apparent attack upon it must undergo most jealous scrutiny.

I shall make no attempt to anticipate the various lines of criticism, on matters of detail, of the Bill to be discussed by Congress, which would serve as response to the above query. Indeed, I pass by important subjects of discussion which suggest themselves, and restrict myself to the bare general issue which makes the title of this paper.

My effort is to set forth general truths, in view of which it is well that the discussion should proceed.

(1.) *It is futile to treat the silver dollar independently of silver itself.*

I am aware of the temptation this subject exerts upon subtle minds, offering a field of distinction as delicate as the law, if not indeed as fine as old-time metaphysics. I shall say naught in disparagement of the process of abstraction, which peels down concepts by gradations as fine as the outer skin of an onion ; for it may be as useful to a thinker, as to a microscopist, to—

> Distinguish and divide,
> A hair twixt south and southwest side.

But there are regions of discussion where such niceties are out of place, and seriously impede the understanding. The hotspur partisan of silver denies the "depreciation" of silver, and is justified, so far as a part of what the gold fanatic *means* by depreciation, is concerned. There is a factitious 'appreciation' of gold. Yet it is a fact. To explain how it was brought about does not abolish the why and the wherefore of its continuance as fact.

I have in other pages told my story of the course of

'fructifying causation,' whereof the present condition of monetary systems is the outcome ; how enthusiasm for metrical reform found no scholarship nor statesmanlike grasp of the teachings of experience to restrain the effort to unify the 'world's measure of values' by abolishing what seemed a mere disturbing element, the silver unit. In the gradual recognition of the suicidal character of this effort, reformers, scholars, statesmen, have since found occupation. But however unfortunate the error proved—for Europe as well as for this country—still these European laws which made the silver question were passed.

The esteem in which silver was held relatively diminished; the esteem in which gold was held increased. Whatever distinctions are made with *ap*- and *de*-preciation, there is no doubt that it was silver which went down relatively, and gold which went up. To refuse this fact a recognition of any share of its importance is to repeat the error of the panegyrist who too zealously based the praise of his hero upon battles which he would have won if he had not been prevented by the enemy. In such an undertaking a keen sense of humor assists in sharpening the perception of facts.

So far as the future of the silver dollar of Hamilton and Gallatin is involved in the broader question of the relative monetary rank which silver has in fact lost, but which will be restored to it when the agitation and education in Europe elsewhere referred to in this volume shall have done their work—this point will be briefly touched in other pages.

I now turn to another vital fact which bears directly upon the question here at issue.

(2.) *The people of the United States do not take to the silver dollar very kindly.* They do not seem to want more than one apiece, *per capita,* for their pockets, their tills, and their strong-boxes. They persist in "*treating Silver as a commodity,*" to borrow a very vague term for a very plain use.

However inconvenient this fact may be, it can only be dealt with as a fact. It is futile to try to explain it away. The fact is fact. Silver certificates are not silver dollars, and can no more be made into silver dollars than orange-peel water can be made into wine by stress of imagination. Silver dollars have been within reach for eleven years. Halves and quarters have been within reach still longer. Yet there are twenty-two millions of silver change that have been losing interest for many years as a "dead asset" in the Treasury; a melancholy monument of the days of callowness and inadvertence when the United States Congress was assisting the demonetization of German silver. I have never heard that the Treasury has interposed any obstacles in the way of a demand for silver dollars, as compared with other current money. We must accept the books of the Treasury as a record of the people's will. In the last four years there have been about sixty millions of silver dollars in the hands of the people. I know of no indication that a change of habit is to enlarge the use of them.

I am glad to believe, however, that such an increase is possible. It can hardly be affirmed with certainty that we have reached the saturation point in reference to silver coin, or that measures may not be devised to promote the further popular use of coin. The subject merits attention greater than it appears to have received. In referring to it I take occasion to make my reservations, and disclaim any opinion adverse to extending the use of coin. Whether the greater use of coin (both gold and silver) in Germany and in France stands in connection with the thriftiness of Germans or Frenchmen is a subject that will bear study. It appears probable that the use of coin, and to some extent the hoarding of coin, especially by that vast majority of the population that lives by manual labor, tends to promote thrift in the individual, as well as to support sound finance in the government.

In dealing, however, with the monetary use of silver coin it is important to recognize the marked peculiarities of our system in reference to gold. The gold in the Treasury as stated for July 1, 1889, consisted of 186 millions belonging to the Treasury, and 117 millions warehoused therein for the benefit of those who use gold certificates; and 65 millions of the total sum were in bullion.

Why not leave silver unminted as well as gold?

For any possible change of habit in the direction of extended use of silver dollars, the existing stock of them is already a superabundant provision. If we take the extreme supposition of a change in the habit of the people which should double their absorption of these coins, there would still be left in existence, beyond its requirement, over two hundred millions of them.

Why should the people be taxed to pay for minting more dollars? The minting has cost some millions of dollars, and it certainly seems probable that money could be expended in some other way to better advantage.

The terms of Mr. Windom's proposition and the facts just referred to seem to narrow the issue to the query: *Is it not worth while to omit minting coin which, when minted, will be used as bullion?*

This apparent confusion of the two ideas which we have hitherto kept separate, will be useful if it serves as an occasion for defining them. It is perhaps very easy to ignore or forget that coin may be bullion, though bullion is not coin. The difference of meaning here is but one degree removed from that which constitutes a mare a horse, though a horse is not a mare. Coin is, in fact, subdivided bullion—bullion of legal fineness duly certified. If it lie in a vault, the bullion use of it predominates. If it pass from hand to hand, the coin use is in the ascendant.

Passing now to another distinction, I observe that while coin is money by tale, and bullion is potential money by weight, bullion may also be really money, effectively money, if the law so provide. The law provides for turning bullion into coin, for its purchase or its exchangeability, and it can also give it directly the power of paying debts. I am not aware that it has ever been done, but it is possible to make ingots full legal tender under proper regulations.

The advantages of paper.

So far as the safety and security of the proposed paper representatives of the deposited bullion are concerned, it is a notable fact that in this country, by favor of the confidence which the manifold guarantees of our financial system inspire, the element "credit" seems to disappear. Confidence is so complete that it is easy to forget that it exists. The acceptance of a Government receipt for warehousing money-metal, resembles accepting a valid transfer of title to immovable property in the place of manual appropriation and possession. So strong is this confidence that the analogy of "livery of seisin" suggests itself; an illustration which the layman will find no difficulty in following when he reflects how the *deed* that was *done* when John Doe handed to Richard Roe a clod from the field he was selling him, is the predecessor of the paper *deed* which in these days is made to "do"—much to the relief of the modern John and Richard.

Of the advantages which the use of paper offers, when thus made a plenipotentiary representative of money-metal, some are sufficiently obvious, others are less likely to be known, and some, indeed, can hardly be said to be always appreciated even by those regarded as conversant with such matters.

So far as the objections to the use of paper are concerned (including the expense) it should be very clearly understood that the issue at present under consideration does not, strictly speaking, involve that side of the question, for the contrast to be drawn is merely between certificates based upon coin and certificates or notes based upon bullion.

Of the advantages of paper, I mark under the first head above referred to, the ease of carriage, and the relief given from the necessity of counting or weighing. An advantage less likely to attract attention is the ease of identification of ownership. These several advantages belong equally to the two kinds of paper under consideration.

Paper based on bullion.

Beside these is to be noted in favor of the use of bullion, the saving of expense by not minting.

If we inquire for objections here we shall find that under prudent management no inconvenience can arise, for the source from which danger could come, under existing circumstances, is the improbable event of sudden and extreme panic, in which the timid would seek possession of their money-metal and would be embarrassed in their efforts to use it for payments.

The friction of coin against coin, making wear and tear which goes on till the coin has to be reminted, may occur when coin is in transit, when it is moved in a bag, as well as when it is handled or carried in the pocket. Bullion can be shipped not only with more convenience but with less abrasion than coin.

Again, bullion is used by weight. The scales are better adjusted than in the case of coin. Here we touch the source of subtleties, to which no doubt in all the centuries of man's experience money has given rise ; one of the 'mysteries of money.' Indeed, how can the mystery be penetrated when we realize that 'coin is something that always ought to be, yet rarely or never is, but at the same time is taken as if it were what it ought to be,' and that this puzzle is fact in all monetary systems by force of enactment, whether it be decree of autocratic, or statute of representative government!

There is an ideal fineness of metal, or proportion between the precious metal and the alloy, and an ideal weight of metal of the proper fineness. But the processes of mintage do not often attain the desired ideal perfection, and the law gives tolerance for error within certain limits, which in the quaint language of the coiner's art are termed the "remedy;" remedy above and remedy below, within which limits the coin is accepted as if it were of the true weight and fineness. To this slight variation is added the reduction of weight which normal wear and tear or artificial processes can produce. And for this, laws and custom also give a limited tolerance. Thus is offered a field for little speculations which, when multiplied, may play a greater part in the business world than economists find it easy to trace or measure.

In the use of bullion the scales, as I said, can be more consistently applied, and so at least a part of the uncertainties and difficulties of the use of coin be avoided.

It may be not without interest to enter upon a brief examination of past experience relating to preferences of policy as between bullion and coin. Suggestive lines of contrast between earlier times and ours in this regard, will be found, as it were, to cross each other.

Bullion in banks.

In the early history of banking, developed as it was to meet the need of trade beyond the local jurisdiction, a trade which we should now call 'international,' bullion value was necessarily looked to as security rather than the currency of coin for which the guarantee was local and limited. This would apply as a general statement to the various precursors of our modern banks in the Italian Republics, in the Free Cities of Germany and the Low Countries, and to the English goldsmith, of whose notes the English bank-note is the successor. When a new departure was taken at the close of the XVIIth century, by the founding of a national "Bank of England," which has, in some measure, served as a model for banking systems in other countries, its charter, which prohibited dealing in all other goods, made gold and silver bullion, as well as bills of exchange, the staple of the enterprise. Gold and silver bullion still remain the lawful basis of the notes which modern English legislation has made legal tender between citizens, so long as they remain convertible.*

The policy of Seigniorage.

The familiar antithesis between popular rights and privilege maintained by arbitrary power, finds its parallel in

---

* The act of 1844 limited the amount of silver in the Issue Department to one-fourth the gold--one part of silver to four parts of gold. Since the Gold Discoveries no use has been made of this privilege.

the contrast between the seigniorial system and free mintage. The right of a citizen to have his bullion turned into coin without denial or delay was established by the English Parliament in 1666, along with the principle of gratuitous mintage, to which I shall presently allude. The policy of Princes, however, operated in the main in the same direction under the seigniorial system, as freedom of mintage under the popular system. It was the interest of Princes to coin as much as possible, in order to recruit their finances by seigniorage. The percentage of bullion thus gained meant not only pocket-money for the seignior, the Lord of the Mint, but the means of carrying on the State.

The confusion and injury thus imposed upon business interests will be recognized when it is seen that coins thereby acquired a local currency value far beyond the value of the metal they contained, while the bullion value remained of necessity preponderant in the calculations of international trade. Thus the power of turning bullion into cash could be used as an instrument of oppression as well as of speculation by the favored courtier to whose hands it fell.

Gratuitous Mintage.

The principle of gratuitous mintage, though not yet generally accepted, tends to impose itself in our time. It has a curious history. While the motive for adopting it in England in 1666, the time of its first appearance in modern law, seems to have been to promote an enlargement of the circulation by inducing citizens to bring their bullion to the mint, yet the underlying theory of it is a subtle truth intimately interwoven with the very nature and purpose of the venerable institution of money.

It is this : that money should be good wherever it goes, and equally good in all places; worth as much in one place as another. But if coin is to be worth as much in one place as another, its value should be its bullion value, the value of the metal of which it is made. To accomplish this result, the coining must be done gratuitously : for if there be a charge paid for the coining, the coin is worth more than the metal, at least at the place of minting. Hence the state which maintains the mint must assume the burden of minting without charge ; the taxpayer thus assuming a burden which " naturally " would fall upon the bullion-owner.

My remark that gratuitous mintage has a curious history will be justified when the reader learns that this simple statement with which I venture to think he will find it not very difficult to concur, is but an amplification of the dicta of leading jurists of the Middle Ages. I I have traced this doctrine to them;[*] and far beyond them I found its source in the Roman law. If I put the Roman's theory into the language of to-day, I may say it means " the internationality of coin."

---

[*] The statement of this discovery is set forth in " Monetary History and Monetary Jurisprudence," an address before the British Association for the Advancement of Science, at Manchester, September, 1887.

The principle is now generally accepted to the limited extent of abolishing seigniorage, but the cost of coinage is still very generally charged to the depositor. France has reduced her charge several times in this century, but still charges for coining gold, and when she coined silver, charged more *ad valorem* than for gold. In India there is a heavy charge for coining rupees, a part of which should perhaps be really counted as seigniorage. In this country we maintained a coinage charge for a limited period.

Free Sale of Bullion.

It will be seen upon reflection that a system of obligatory purchase of bullion, which I shall name " Free Sale of Bullion," in which the full value is given in current money, is the fullest possible application of the principle that underlies both free mintage and gratuitous mintage. There is no time lost in mobilizing bullion into current money. The system introduced by the statute of 1666 leaves a little loss of interest to be borne by the depositor, namely, interest for the time taken in manufacturing the coin, the length of which must depend upon the convenience of the operation of the mint. This loss is fixed by a modern English statute, for gold, at three half pence per sovereign. The Bank is compelled to pay £3 17s. 9d., for the ounce of gold which is worth £3 17s. 10½d. Our statute of 1792 charged half a cent per dollar, if both the depositor and mint director desired; which suggests the query whether the Treasury of those days had the cash on hand for its "Bullion Fund."

Free Mintage, Gratuitous Mintage, and Free Sale of Bullion.

We are now prepared to mark the relation and distinctions between free mintage, gratuitous mintage, and free sale of bullion.

Free Mintage is of the first importance. The right of the owner of bullion to have it turned into coin is a right of primary and fundamental import as establishing the legal status of money-metal. Gratuitous Mintage is of subordinate rank; for mintage may be free and bullion thus become potential money, in the full sense of the phrase, whether the cost of minting it be paid by the owner or by the State. As I have indicated, Gratuitous Mintage is a practice still foreign to important monetary systems, while Free Mintage is generally established.*

It will, I think, be recognized that a right of Free Sale of Bullion, as I have called it, is entitled to a distinct place in our classification, though I do not recall ever having heard of it, or read of it in monetary books.

---

* Here I may properly explain that the adjective "free" has been applied in authoritative works, as including Gratuitous Mintage as well as Free Mintage in the sense above defined, and that I have done what I could to promote clear thinking by seeking to naturalize the above distinctions in the language of money. It is evident that the two ideas are distinct in their nature, and that nothing but confusion can be gained by fusing them under one word.

MONETARY POLICY IN THE FUTURE. 185

Free Sale of Bullion has existed in various countries in a special form, as a concomitant or arrangement of convenience incidental to a system of Free Mintage, as for example, when the Mint (or a Bank) is bound to pay for the bullion at once upon accepting it for mintage. In the instances lately referred to, a fixed charge was deducted to cover the advantage in time and convenience thus given the bullion owner at the expense of the Mint. The Free Sale of Bullion produced in this country, which is now proposed for the action of Congress, is free from this deduction.

Monetary Policy in the future.

These several lines of historical development seem to converge toward the following policy :

The establishment (by enactment and not merely by favor of administrative discretion), of the right of free mintage, and of gratuitous mintage ; the actual amount of mintage performed by Government in obedience to this rule being limited by—

The establishment of the right of free sale of bullion ; the monetary use of this bullion being secured by—

The establishment of a system of paper representatives, which circulate as money, transferring the title to the bullion deposited.

I state the idea in general terms which are applicable to such various forms of paper issue and conditions of redemption as may suit the respective convenience of the several monetary systems in which the principles above stated might be adopted. I also withhold any statement of detail as to amounts and price—which in presence of the existing general outlawry of silver are vital questions, so far as that metal is concerned—and likewise the conditions to be fixed under which bullion would be received; as for example, the place of receipt, or the composition of the metal, whether it is already ascertained, or to be ascertained, or of coinable fineness, or of fineness held to be, in various degrees, "suitable to the operations of the mint."

It seems apparent that speaking generally, the trend of habit in the Western World is toward the policy I have outlined.*

There is, as I have indicated, no full acceptance of such policy on the part of any nation to-day. Habits and institutions change slowly, and it would be bold prophecy to aver that the general adoption of this policy is near at hand. I merely aver that the tendency is in that direction.

Is there good ground for solicitude on this account, or any general ground for opposition to this tendency? I see none.

---

* I say nothing here of the expanding use of coin in a community that has not known it before; as for example, Africa, or the Pacific Islands; nor do I propose to speak of Asia, nor venture on the great "Chinese puzzle" of money—the puzzle of Chinese money—sycee, 'cash,' and foreign dollars, and the tael, and a mint under the banner of the Green Dragon.

Bullion and the General Remonetization of Silver.

The question now arises whether the movement for joint action of nations to restore silver to its former equality with gold offers any conflict of principle with the tendency which I have above ascertained.

As I have borne some share in that movement in various countries since its inception, I may not inappropriately give my testimony on that issue.

I see no conflict between the two, no objection to a forward step in the direction above indicated. It is true that the idea of minting, of coin, as distinguished from bullion, has all along been kept in the foreground in the advocacy of such restoration of silver to its former place. It was natural and proper that this should be so. The central feature of monetary systems has been, is, and is likely to remain—a unit of valuation embodied in coin. This being the case, free mintage is the natural and proper objective point for the advocates of the reform proposed.

But the fundamental object is equality of legal status for the two metals. As the greater includes the less it is plain that this implies no opposition to an enlarged employment of metal in the form of bullion as compared with coin. Indeed I have, for many years, been of the opinion that the adoption of the proposed measures for legal equalization of the metals would tend to reduce for both of them the now exaggerated need of spending and of losing so much in the minting and use of coin.

These views may now conveniently be tested by reference to the formal proposals made in the Conference of

1878, and by a further examination of the bearing of Mr. Windom's plan upon the policy of the Conferences.

The policy established by the Allison Amendments to the Bland Bill.

Under the authority of the act of February 28, 1878, calling the Conference of 1878, the following propositions were presented by the American Commissioners, in August, 1878, to the representatives of the various Powers in Paris, the form being that of a draft resolution :

I. It is the opinion of this Assembly that it is not to be desired that Silver should be excluded from Free Coinage in Europe and the United States of America. On the contrary, the Assembly believes that it is desirable that the Unrestricted Coinage of Silver, and its use as Money of Unlimited Legal Tender, should be retained where they exist, and, as far as practicable, restored where they have ceased to exist :

II. The use of both Gold and Silver as Unlimited Legal-Tender Money may be safely adopted.

First.—By equalizing them at a relation to be fixed by international agreement ; and

Secondly.—By granting to each metal, at the relation fixed, equal terms of Coinage, making no discrimination between them.

The following third proposition was prepared and held in reserve, awaiting the development of the views of the Conference :

III. The Delegates here present agree to recommend

to their respective governments that, by the free coinage of silver at a relation to be agreed upon, or provisionally, through *extended coinage upon government account* and the *accumulation of silver bullion in Public Treasuries*, they make a concerted effort to restore silver to its function as money of full power.

In the absence of co-operation in Europe, the course of the United States was thus definitely marked. We maintained the attitude of favoring Concurrent Free Mintage, ready to establish it as soon as Europe should be ready; and in the years which have passed, Congress has carried out alone the proposition, which the Commission of 1878 formulated and placed in the second rank.

An *extended coinage on Government account* has been kept up, and a notable *accumulation* made *in the Public Treasury of silver bullion*, but subdivided, in the form of coin. The proposition now made is to leave bullion unminted.

The novelty of Mr. Windom's plan.

The proposal of the Secretary of the Treasury is that holders of native* silver bullion shall have the right to sell it to the Government at the market price for new "Treasury notes" (expressed in dollars) which are legal

---

* The product of the mines of the United States or of ores here smelted and refined.

tender to the Government and also convertible in certain ways.*

This is proposed as a substitute for the present law under which the Government is compelled to purchase and coin two million (*gold*) dollars' worth of silver bullion per month, and has the liberty to purchase up to four millions' worth.

The plan is presented in view of a very general sense of dissatisfaction with the present law of compulsory coinage, which is shared by the Secretary. At the same time the plan is conceived in the spirit of entire accord with the policy of the Conferences, which its author puts in view in his Report as directed toward the true goal, the final and satisfactory solution of the silver difficulty.

It will appear, from what has gone before, that while the proposed law, regarded as a whole, is without precedent, yet the novelty of it, so far as the issue between bullion and coin is concerned, lies in the frankness and fullness of its adaptation to facts. This is a rare merit.

How unwieldy a monetary system is, how difficult it is

---

* The further details are as follows: The notes are to be redeemable on demand at the Government's option, either in gold coin or in silver bullion of equal value to the notes on the day of demand, or in silver dollars at the holder's option. The Government in effect becomes the owner of the bullion although compelled to hold the deposit, but has the right to dispose of bullion at the market price to the limited extent of any demand for redemption made by holders who are unwilling to take silver dollars in return for notes, and it has the right to coin bullion and issue the coin to make good any gold or silver coin issued for redemption of notes. Mr. Windom's Bill was presented to Congress January 20, 1890.

for nations to mould and modify their monetary policy by reference to changing facts which affect its soundness, is shown by ample experience throughout the past.

Perhaps the following illustration will commend itself to the reader, quite independently of any bias touching matters of controversy.

The surplus in the Treasury, long the source of political pre-occupations, offered in the late electoral contest a very apple of discord, as an evil which the opposing champions of High and Low Tariff charged each upon the other. Yet so far as I am informed, in the whole year of debate which began with Mr. Cleveland's Message of December, 1887, and ended with General Harrison's election in November, 1888, no word was said in public concerning an undisputable source of the surplus with which neither customs nor excise, neither protective duties nor the tax on spirits and tobacco, etc., had aught to do.

I refer to the item of Seigniorage, as the language of the Treasury calls it (on full Legal-Tender money), which has reappeared on the books of an English-writing National Treasury for the first time since early in the reign of Charles II. We have taken to the modern representative of "His Majesty's rate," so naturally that orators and newspapers now take it quite for granted! If bullion or cash had been held in the Treasury to make good in specie the face value of the Silver Coin outstanding, dollars and change, which would have taken a hundred millions, there would have been no surplus at all to speak of! Even now I do not recall seeing anything in print as to the effect of

Mr. Windom's plan in checking the surplus. If his proposal to repeal the present compulsory coinage law be not adopted, the sum of near nine millions is given in the Treasury estimates for the coming years as the expected revenue from Seigniorage on Silver Dollars.

Contemporary movements in England are of analogous effect. The Bank of England still neglects its legal privilege of issuing notes on Silver Bullion, presumably because silver is not regarded as 'good enough.' Yet the Treasury has been buying silver at 22 and coining it at 14.30! This 50 per cent. in Seigniorage on change, issued at a time when gold half-sovereigns are being withdrawn, is a welcome *pendant* to our Dollars!

In both countries a rise in silver would turn into real profit this nominal profit in the past, but check it in the future.

In view of the peculiar courses into which the practice of nations as to silver has fallen, it is doubly important for monetary thinkers to recur to first principles; to ascertain, as it were, the points of the compass, and get a rudimentary notion of sailing directions, which should be available for the fleet of ships of State.

I therefore, with whatever emphasis I can command, present the following averments:

Acts of silver outlawry adopted between the First International Monetary Conference (1867) and the Second (1878), the chief of which was the closing of the Paris Mint, created for the money-using world a transition state

THE PROJECT OF FEDERATION. 193

of unstable equilibrium, the only escape from which is by that return to concurrence in maintaining equality of the two money metals which was proposed to the nations in 1878. No arrangement for silver money in the period which elapses before the solution proposed through the Conference of 1878 is attained, can have the prospect of stability and the certainty of effect which gold money enjoys. The chief test of new measures is whether or no they advance the desired return to concurrent laws equalizing the metals; and the general criterion is, whether or no they adapt themselves to the facts as they are, rather than to visionary theories, which may be conceived with a view to what the facts ought to have been, what they ought to be now, or what they should be in the future.

Legal equality of the metals.

I now pursue further the inquiry touching the plan of concurrent action of nations for the restoration of silver. I submit that in such a plan, the question how much each member of the proposed Union may prefer to economize in its minting, and in its use of coin, may advantageously be left to the intelligent self-interest of the nations respectively. They can safely do what they please with the bullion they receive. It is a matter in which other nations are not concerned.

In so far, however, as *equality of legal status* between the two metals is involved, all nations are interested, and hence in any complete scheme of joint action, the conditions under which bullion can be exchanged for current money come necessarily into view. While the desired equality can be substantially secured through the right of free mintage, it can be perfected only by equalizing, as between the two metals, the conditions which may exist as to the right of sale of bullion. Whatever right is given to one metal should also be given to the other. The question whether the Government shall hold the bullion uncoined is another matter. So are the questions whether it shall make a charge for minting coin or no, and whether it shall make a deduction for time, like the three half-pence to the pound which the Bank of England retains. I do not mean that these are not important subjects. I mean that they are of subordinate rank, as compared with equality of treatment for the two metals within the borders of the several nations.

As will appear more fully in the sequel, the point here raised of equal rights for silver and gold bullion has not entirely lacked attention. The object aimed at would naturally be obligatory purchase (Free Sale) of gold and silver bullion in each country, at identical relative rates for either metal in the various respective currencies. I reprint below an extract from earlier publications which contains matter bearing upon this point.

On referring to this extract it will perhaps be found to sustain the view which has been foreshadowed in the observations already made in this paper, that the new departure proposed by Mr. Windom, while conceived in its details with a view to the determining conditions of the present state of affairs in one country, is capable of extension and of application in all countries as an element of a general amendment of monetary systems.

THE PARITY OF BULLION, AND MODES OF MANTAINING IT.

(First printed with 'The Parity of Moneys, as regarded by Adam Smith, Ricardo, and Mill,' which forms chapter IV of this volume.)

In advocating the Reinstatement of Silver as Money the chief practical measure recommended has been Free Coinage, that is to say, the duty of the Mint to coin for all comers, either *gratis* or with a charge, according to the laws of the country. This would leave the door open to those little inequalities of value from which a Gold Coinage System has not always protected *gold* bullion,* even when its position was the most favorable—while it lay between the Tower and the Bank of England.

A suggestion touching this important point of detail in the plan for joint action of nations, was made in the Conference of 1881 by Mr. N. G. Pierson, a delegate of Holland (now Governor of the Bank of Holland), namely, that Banks of Issue could be charged with a duty, which would remedy this difficulty, namely, the duty of buying bullion from all comers at a fixed price for each metal. There are also other grounds in favor of such a measure, which I will not enter upon here.

---

* Evidence on this subject is given in 'The Silver Pound,' page 60.

Some years later, being invited to deliver an address before the American Bankers' Association (at its meeting in Boston, August, 1886), I chose the Parity of Bullion as my subject, and made my address an argument for the adoption of a resolution which I caused to be presented, and which was adopted.

The resolution is as follows:

WHEREAS, The question of proper measures to be taken in concert by the commercial nations, in order to regulate metallic money has, since the International Monetary Conferences of 1878 and 1881, received earnest and increasing consideration, while the growing divergence between the precious metals has caused cumulative disturbance of values, and has injuriously affected business relations in all parts of the world, and threatens further evil for the future, and,

WHEREAS, The policy proposed to the nations by the United States in 1878, and by France and the United States in 1881, of restoring silver to free coinage by a union composing the chief monetary Powers, deserves universal support; and,

WHEREAS, It is important, in order to prevent inequality between different nations, in the operation of the monetary system so proposed, that silver bullion and gold bullion should enjoy equality, as well as silver coin and gold coin; and,

WHEREAS, Experience has shown that the provision of the law of Great Britain, whereby it is the duty of the Bank of England to buy all gold offered to it at a fixed price per ounce, tends to establish a fixed price for gold bullion universally, and that analogous provisions of law in the several nations of the European continent tend further to relieve gold bullion from local fluctuations of price; and it is evident that similar provisions applied to silver bullion, in support of its use as money, would give it similar protection from fluctuation; and,

WHEREAS, Such provisions must become an important part of any plan of international action, and hence deserve thorough and thoughtful consideration; therefore, be it

RESOLVED, That a committee be appointed by the President to take into consideration this whole question in every particular and report to the Executive Council of this Association at such early date as shall be found convenient.

The Resolution was supported by Mr. George S. Coe, of New York, a founder and former President of the Association, and was moved by Mr. Deshler, of Ohio, and seconded by Mr. Moss, of Ohio. The Committee was afterwards appointed. I am not informed concerning any report.

The Bank Charter Bill, which was laid before the Second Chamber of the States-General of Holland in April, 1887, contains (according to my translation) the following proposed amendment of the existing Act, calculated to give effect to the plan mentioned:

"The State, in the event of its entering a Monetary Union founded on the system of the double standard, and in case the obligation shall have been laid upon the chief Banks of Issue in the countries that form this Union, to buy at the mint-price all the money-metal offered them for sale, of which the coinage has been made free to all by law, retains the privilege of imposing the same duty upon the Bank of the Netherlands."

VII.

RICARDO

ON

BULLION NOTES AND SILVER.

RICARDO ON BULLION NOTES AND SILVER.

In the wide circle who respect the authority of leaders of thought in the past a peculiar interest will be attached to the views of David Ricardo upon monetary subjects, for his prestige in the broader field of economic thought attaches peculiarly to his labors on currency. His memory is still—and well it is that it should be so—"the shadow of a great name." Dying in his prime, at the close of a long struggle of financial politics in which he had been militant, and leaving works which are a landmark in science, his public career fortified his reputation and influence in later days as a thinker, by the authority which belongs to conspicuous service in action.

In examining some years ago into the factors of the then general conviction among learned men in England, that the exclusion of silver from English money (except as change) was a sound and wise measure, I was led to examine closely into the opinions of this notable man about silver and gold. The result was very different from what would have been expected, judging from the attitude on that subject lately assumed by his disciples, for the impression seemed universal among them that the law and the prophets against silver are fortified by Ricardo's name.

I shall, therefore, in indicating his opinions upon bullion and coin, set forth what he thought on the broader issue of the "battle of the standards."

Ricardo's literary activity began in 1808, when he put himself in the van of the movement to reform the paper money regime,* two years in advance of the famous Bullion Committee. It was not long after that he brought forward a scheme of paper notes based on bullion. In 1816 he printed full " proposals for an economical and secure currency and on the profits of the Bank of England." The greater part of this pamphlet deals with the internal regulation of the Bank and with its relation to the Government and the public. I reprint in the Appendix the scheme which he describes as " an expedient to bring the English currency as near as possible to perfection." The central point of interest here is that this perfection consisted, in his mind, in making the notes redeemable in uncoined gold (or silver), at the mint standard or price, instead of by delivery of coin.

With reference to Ricardo's attitude in relation to the respective claims of silver and of gold to be the "standard" or chief money of England, there is this to be said. It plainly did not lie in his plan to complicate the main issue and weaken his own position as an apostle of convertibility and "Hard Money," as we should say, by attaching himself as a partisan to the claims of either silver or gold, or of the two together, as the unit of coinage.

I call attention to the phrase unit of coinage, because I find that Ricardo used the word "standard" in a sense quite different from that which we attach to it commonly

---

* The suspension of cash payments had begun in 1797. Resumption was ordered by the act of 1819, and was completed in 1823.

to-day. It is a very malarious word and needs constant disinfecting by definition to be used with safety. I find Ricardo was in favor of the "silver standard," and yet I do not believe that he meant by that the demonetization of gold.

Without taking ground rigidly in favor of either of the three proposed or possible local "standards" or units of value (the single gold unit, the single silver unit, and the dual silver and gold unit), Ricardo declares his preference for silver, and gives his reasons. At the same time an impartial recognition of the availability of the two metals which is natural to a time when, as I have shown, the idea of abolishing one of them had not been conceived, is presented in his writings in a manner which is not a little confusing to the modern reader. He often, apparently for the sake of convenience, speaks of "gold," when another writer—whom experience had warned that precision was vital— and would have said "metallic money," or "the money-metals."

This practice, while harmless at the outset, has naturally, under the changed conditions which have obtained for a later generation, become so misleading in its effect as to require these special words of caution to one who shall cite Ricardo on monetary subjects. An example of this nature may be found in the naive account given of Ricardo's position by the late Mr. J. R. McCulloch, who became for a later generation a representative of "gold orthodoxy," and who, in his reference to Ricardo in the account of his life and writings, prefixed to the collected Works, of which he was the editor, *entirely ignores the existence of silver*. This falsification of most important testimony is the more dangerous because of its innocence.

Ricardo's plans* were not adopted in full. The Act of 1816 made gold the "Standard Measure of Value," imposed a heavy Seigniorage on Silver Coin, and left the exercise of the right of Free Coinage (which it re-enacted) subject to the issuance of a Proclamation of the Crown.

Peel's Bill, as it was called, the Resumption Act of 1819, which closed the paper money period that began in 1797, applied the idea of redemption in bullion to the following extent: It provided that the Bank must deliver on demand in exchange for bank notes, gold bullion of standard fineness not less than sixty ounces at one time, first, at £4 1s. per ounce for a certain period; then at any rate between that figure and £3 19s. 6d. per ounce; then at the latter figure; then at any rate between £3 19s. 6d. and £3 17s. 10½d.; then from May 1, 1821, to May 1, 1823, at the

---

* The following comment may prove of interest:

"I cannot resist inquiring what would have happened if Ricardo had been led in some way to put his Scheme of a Monetary System for England into his 'Principles.' Would not the necessity of cohesion have forced itself upon his mind? Could later economics have taken the tone we have witnessed, if he had treated *ex cathedrâ* of the Principles of Monetary Legislation with a high-pressure interference scheme to back them? The central idea of what I shall name Ricardo's Bullion Standard and Bullion Certificate Scheme was parity maintained by all the force of law that was to be had. And I must also allow myself the daring statement that the same thing may be said of all orthodox plans for a convertible paper currency—if the philosophers only knew it!"—*See above, page* 132.

latter figure, which was the mint price of gold; and from
May 1, 1823, in gold coin if required. The Bank had the
option of paying in coin after May 1, 1822.

In fact, however, the Bank anticipated this date, and
began paying in coin May 1, 1821, so that the experiment
of bullion redemption was not fully tried.

Ricardo's comment on this action of the Bank is interesting. It was made in Parliament during the debate of
1822. He maintained that the inconveniences of the return to a metallic standard had been infinitely increased
by large premature purchases of gold. They ought not
to have paid in specie until 1823. Mr. Peel's bill *was intended to try whether a bank could not be advantageously
carried on upon the principle of paying the notes in bullion.*
If the bank had gone on wisely in their preliminary arrangement, the bullion part of the plan would have worked
for a number of years beyond the time stipulated.

Without going into the pros and cons of Ricardo's
measure, I may allude to two elements of conviction then
in force, which probably had exerted a decisive influence
in defeating the bullion redemption feature.

Though curiously diverse and disparate, the two lines
of opinion lead to the same conclusion.

First was the confidence inspired by the book of
Lord Liverpool, whose death occurred just as Ricardo
came upon the monetary stage, and whose prestige as a
lifelong counsellor of George the Third was fortified
by his measures to maintain a coinage system of "legal
tender, by weight as well as by tale," which were first

adopted in 1774, and the principles of which were supposed to be impregnably established by his "Treatise on the Coins of the Realm in a Letter to the King" in 1805.

The second element to which I refer was the abhorrence felt toward one-pound notes, as a temptation to forgery. Ricardo's plan involved their maintenance. To those who prayed "Lead us not into temptation," it seemed a wrong thus to facilitate forgery, " a dreadful wound to the morality of the people," to quote a phrase from the *Edinburgh Review*. The notes seemed stained with blood, not quite innocent, but blood that need not have been shed. These notes of small denominations came in with the suspension of cash payments— the statute prohibited them before that—and it is said that between 1797 and 1818 three hundred and thirteen forgers died on the scaffold.

In connection with the fact of Ricardo's preference in favor of the silver standard for England, it is well to remember that there was nothing phenomenal in this piece of good sense, for the anti-silver sentiment which is known to this generation is very modern. I have elsewhere set forth ample evidence on this subject. It was the metrical reform movement, at its height after 1850, in which the prepossessions of the physical scientist and of the accountant put to sleep the judgment of the economist and the prudence of the statesman, that inspired the attack against silver. The history of bullion in English law affords a curious bit of corroboration to this statement.

When the Bank Charter Act came before Parliament for

renewal in 1833, the monetary reformers, with Mr. Lloyd, better known as Lord Overstone, at their head, succeeded in making it obligatory upon the Bank to publish regularly a statement of its condition. Now, in that statement *gold and silver bullion were fused together*. They appeared in print as "bullion"—a collocation plainly abhorrent to later generations when gold orthodoxy had come into the ascendant. Coming from Lord Overstone, the admission is singularly strong evidence of the general opinion—that one money-metal was "as good as the other."

The Bank Charter Act of 1844, by restricting the proportion of silver to be held as a deposit to one-fifth of the total amount, made it necessary to report silver bullion by itself, and a provision was enacted to that effect.

An interesting instance also occurs to me of the reappearance of the idea of Bullion Certificates in a form which satisfied in full the theory of Sir Robert Peel as to the true standard of Great Britain being a definite quantity of bullion.

In 1847, Mr. Haggard, a respected official of the Bank of England, published a pamphlet, entitled "Observations on the Standard of Value and the Circulating Medium of this country," in which he set forth a plan for the reformation of the English Monetary System, which I present here in brief, stating it entirely in my own words:

> The Standard of Value to be Silver Bullion; four ounces (thirty-seven-fortieths fine) being the substratum of a Paper Pound Sterling.

The Full Legal Tender circulation to consist of paper representing that Bullion; the Paper (Bank notes, so called) being Legal Tender from the Bank, as well as between individuals.

The coin to consist of Gold and Silver at $15\frac{1}{2}$ to 1; Gold Legal-Tender for £200; Silver Legal-Tender for £2; both kinds charged with 'seigniorage.'

VIII.

A PAN-AMERICAN DOLLAR AND THE POLICY OF UNION.

A PAN-AMERICAN DOLLAR AND THE POLICY OF UNION.

Until the status of Silver as a money-metal is restored it is futile to fix a weight for an international dollar.

No doubt it would be a convenience to have coins of different nations of the same weight or of weights bearing very simple numerical relations to each other; but to give such coins legal-tender power outside the country that mints them is another matter altogether.

The United States invited England, France, and Germany to join in settling the status of Silver, but never proposed to accept their coins as legal tender in the United States.

In the greatest work* ever composed by a minister of Foreign Affairs while minister, John Quincy Adams observed that "to despair of human improvement is not more congenial to the judgment of sound philosophy than to the temper of brotherly kindness;" and it was to improvement by assimilating the weights and measures of different countries that his thought and work were directed.

The analogies of such a reform with the assimilation of the weight of national coins suggest the application of this

---

* His Report upon Weights and Measures prepared in obedience to a resolution of the Senate of March 3, 1817. Philadelphia, 1821.

remark to the present theme. Unfortunately the three score years and ten which have passed since philosophy and brotherly kindness were thus seen to bid men hope, afford material I will not say to encourage despair nor to discourage effort, but at least to fortify patience.

"Uniformity of weights and measures," said Mr. Adams, "is and has been for ages the common anxious and earnest pursuit of France, of Great Britain, and, since their independent existence, of the United States." And yet, to-day, in 1890, the Anglo-cosmopolitan world still counts in feet, pounds, and gallons; albeit, at the same time, side by side with them, the unified French system has been slowly enlarging its sphere. But in the domain of coinage no such orderly progression, still less a steady march toward uniformity appears. To say volcanic upheaval, is to give a better description of the fact. It is true that there have been achievements in the line of uniformity. Notable among these is the unification of German coinage systems, which came with an analogous rectification of the political map of Europe; but its effect was to perpetuate diversity while reducing the extent of existing diversity. The new "gold mark" of 1871–'3 bears no simple relation to dollar, franc, sovereign, guilder, ruble, or rupee. It is also true that within this period a cosmopolitan silver dollar has, step by step, won its way to adoption by a goodly part of Christendom. If my count is correct a hundred and twenty millions of population now accept a silver piece which began its career as the Hercules crown, the five-franc piece of the French Revolution. From Finland to

Cadiz, by way of the Danube and Greece, from Paris to Patagonia, by way of Hayti and Cuba, that weight of silver is money for the nation or league that coins it. But not at the same rate! There is a nominal value and a bullion value, and for seventeen years the two values have been divorced. Coins struck at different mints, of the same weight of silver, some are worth many per cent. more than others, according to the gold price of Silver. Uniformity or even identity is thus defeated in favor of something which is at the same time nominal and intrinsic, and to which the lore of the scales, the thermometer, and the microscope gives no clue. It is in the presence of such facts and of the broad considerations arising from them that the proposal of a Pan-American silver dollar must be assigned to its place.

To complete our survey of them I shall ask the reader the frank question whether he ever, before reading this paper, had heard of the five-franc piece as a coin of semi-universal currency—whether he ever was informed of this assimilation of coinage systems, extending from Finland to Patagonia?

Now I venture to believe he never heard of it before. No doubt he has heard of the five-franc piece, perhaps handled it—indeed, it was once a dollar of the United States, full legal tender at $93\frac{1}{3}$ and at 93 cents—and he has probably heard of the Latin Union, perhaps been a tourist within its borders, in France, Italy, Belgium, Switzerland. But my question relates to that far greater range of unification, which touches at one extremity the ancient Grand Duchy of Finland and covers a goodly part of the ancient American Empire of the Spanish dollar on the other. It is of this I venture to believe the reader has never heard before.

This affirmation I make in order to elicit an important lesson which bears directly on our theme, namely: the narrow range of interest actually engaged in this matter of uniformity of the weight (and alloy) of coins. Without being trivial when regarded alone, the subject is relatively trivial when brought, as it generally is, into competition with the really vital issues involved in coinage policy. Side by side with these its insignificance can be described only by a figure; as, for example, the insignificance of smart uniforms or well-burnished musket-barrels as compared with a successful campaign.

Of course there is great difficulty in recognizing the true perspective in monetary matters, by reason of the subtlety of the distinctions of which careful account must be made. Thus, as we have observed, there is uniformity apparent and uniformity real, which may change places under the operation of various causes; there is identity which is real and yet nominal at the same time. In dealing with coins we are engaged with the problems of evanescent value, with the 'mysteries of money.' The mind must accustom itself to pass with ease from point to point of such a sequence of ideas as identity, uniformity, parity, exchangeability, convertibility, redemption. Starting with a bit of stamped metal, which is a simple thing to describe, or weigh, or analyze, one must review, or be prepared to review, the conflicting financial policies of nations. It is like the difference between standing on the shore and navigating the ocean.

We return to consider a universal American dollar as a practical measure to-day. We have seen that the advantage of such a coin is not likely to be very great under any circumstances. We now advance to the observation that as matters now stand it is impracticable to attain this advantage, whatever it may be.

If Mexico should diminish the weight of her dollar to equal the dollar of Hamilton, of the Fathers of our Republic, there would be the same difficulty as to its value, the same contrast which has so often been observed at the two ends of the bridge at the boundary at El Paso, the bullion value for one and the higher face value for the other, the latter appearing the more real because of its relation to the majority of existing exchanges and valuations in which Americans are interested. If Brazil should undertake to establish her paper-money in some stable relation to a new silver piece equal to our dollar, in the place of gold milreis, it could make no change in the fact that the Anglo-American silver dollar is at par with gold, and the Latin-American dollars are not. So if the other Latin countries should abandon the Hercules crown, with its associations of historical continuity going back beyond the pound of Charlemagne, there would still be that fatal bar of premium or discount to bring uniformity to naught.

Thus far we have spoken merely of assimilation, of uniformity in the weight of a silver dollar to be issued by the several American States; but there is another and radically different proposition involved in the plan as it is usually entertained. Moreover the distinction to which I here give emphasis is not as often apprehended as it should be, even in quarters where thorough acquaintance with the subject is looked for.

I refer to the plan of making such a coin legal tender in a nation other than that under whose authority it was minted. There is a constantly active disposition to fuse this idea and the idea of uniformity together, suppressing the vital distinction which I vindicate.

In considering this plan of reciprocal legal tender we will leave at one side the facts as they are, to which we have already directed our attention. We will imagine for the moment that silver occupies the same monetary rank in all of the several American countries; and upon this supposition we will proceed to the inquiry *why* the proposed coin should be legal tender in each, *why* it should have compulsory currency in countries other than that in which respectively it was coined?

If the coins are good, if they are of full weight and purity, they will pass on their merits when exported to other countries where similar dollars are coined. They there come into the hands of the class of men who are familiar with coins, and know whether they are good or not. Thus they would serve in the payment of commercial balances between countries as international money, as gold does now. They would be taken on their merits just as gold eagles are taken in Paris and London, or napoleons

CURRENCY OF FOREIGN COINS. 217

in London and New York, or sovereigns in New York and Paris. The eagle, the napoleon, the sovereign, are not legal tender except in the country that coins them. Why should the silver dollar receive a greater privilege?

The coins of the different states of the Latin Union are, it is true, receivable in the public offices of each state, and under the system of internal revenue there prevailing the practice of these offices is potent in establishing the currency of coins. But this arrangement grows out of the semi-political and social causes which have led to a thorough-going uniformity of coinage (embracing multiples and fractions of the franc), established with centralized and concurrent control—a system made practicable by the close vicinity of these nations and the entire ease and great extent of communication between them. And even under these circumstances the law does not enforce that compulsory legal tender between individuals which we are now considering.

Such compulsory currency, conferred merely by favor of a foreign stamp upon a coin, seems plainly to be a statutory arrangement, by help of which, although contrary to the intent of the legislator, fraud may be assisted to find its victim. It is not difficult for a citizen to understand what are the coins of his own country and the merits or demerits of the several pieces which may come to him in his business transactions. But imagine people in the various country neighborhoods scattered over the continental domains of the United States called upon to deal with coins of any and all American Republics, Haytian, Dominican, Mexican, Nicarauguan, Guatemalan, Honduran, Salvadorian, Costa Rican, Venezuelan, Colombian, Bolivian, Ecuadorian, Peruvian, Chilian, Brazilian, and Argentine! An opportunity for undiscoverable frauds of which the defenceless poor must be the chief victim! Even leaving the question of counterfeiting out of sight, the facility of finding a market for light coins in the country districts would be a continual temptation. And neither local nor international control would avail wholly to neutralize this temptation.

It is also to be considered that so far as governments should under such a system become responsible for making good the defects of the circulation, the scheme would tend to make the greatest monetary Power a guarantee for all. And as fate seems to have marked out the United States for that position, the burden, whatever it is, would fall here.

Now, if there were any great advantage to be gained by a system of reciprocity so very far-reaching it would be necessary to enter into the details of debit and credit, *pro* and *con*, in this behalf.

But there are none! There is no close political and social inter-relation, nor is there close neighborhood between the Anglo-American Republic and the Latin-American Republics such as could, by mere iteration of the effort, enlarge into the range of practical importance the trivial convenience to importers and tourists of not having to exchange one kind of cash for another. When the steamers at New York for South America are as many and as crowded as those now sailing for Europe, and when the trains carry more passengers across the Mexican than across the Canadian border, it will be time to take into favorable consideration a reciprocity of legal tender or a fusion of currencies, which we have not thought seriously of offering to the pound sterling or to the Canadian dollar.

This reference to our policy in Europe brings in view the fact that such reciprocity or fusion formed no part of the plan of monetary federation proposed to the European nations in the Conference in Paris in 1878. That proposal referred not to the weight nor to the extra-territorial currency of coin, but to the material of money. It dealt with the substance, not with the form. The question of form was excluded.

This was not done without opposition.

The issue was raised and was decided. The utterances of the American delegates at both Conferences will be found in harmony with the aims of the agitation which preceded the decision of Congress to call the Conference, and with reference to which the words of the statute would naturally be construed. In the Document of the Conference of 1878, I took pains to bring into prominence the distinction between our proposal and earlier plans of monetary union. I reprint extracts bearing on that subject in the Appendix. I may also refer to late remarks on the same subject on page 39.

It will be seen that in formulating the policy of the United States as we did, we not only disengaged the important from an entanglement with the trivial, but removed from a plan that is practical and practicable an extraneous element, both impracticable and impolitic.

And now what shall we say of the Act of Congress approved March, 1888, which put among the objects to be deliberated upon in a Conference of the Delegates of American Nations in Washington,

> *the adoption of a common silver coin to be issued by each government, the same to be legal tender in all commercial transactions between the citizens of all the American states?*

Here we have bound in one phrase, for all American republics,

> assimilation of weight and value,
> reciprocity of legal tender,

the first of which—at least at present—is quite impossible, and the second objectionable in a high degree under any circumstances.

One may well wonder how such a bill could become law. It must be admitted with regret that this legal-tender clause gives a striking instance of the lack of adequate arrangements for the revision of the language of bills before Congress; a lack which has been often remarked, and will, no doubt, in due time be supplied. The evil genius that inspires legislative 'slips of the pen' could hardly have chosen a more shining page than that which bears an invitation from this country to the Latin-American Republics to a Conference in Washington, intended to promote brotherhood throughout the Americas.

The sequel, as thus far developed, is, in brief, the following:

The International American Conference which was convened in October, 1889, appointed a Committee on Monetary Federation, from which final reports were made at the close of March, 1890.

Hon. T. Jefferson Coolidge (United States) presented a minority report, the recommendation of which was to the effect that the Delegates to the Conference advise their respective governments that it was inexpedient to adopt a common silver coin, to be either a partial or full legal tender in the several countries, until the efforts of the United States to re-establish the former status of silver by concurrent action with European nations shall have been successful.

In closing his address Mr. Coolidge added: "I desire it distinctly understood that I approve entirely of all the Republics of the Americas adopting a currency of uniform fineness and weight. My objection is to the legal-tender clause."

In the final Report of the Committee the following resolution was proposed:

The International American Conference is of opinion that great advantages would accrue to commerce between the nations of this continent by the use of a coin or coins that would be current, at the same value, in all the countries represented in this Conference, and therefore recommends—

1. That an International American Monetary Union be established.

2. That as a basis for this Union an international coin or coins be issued, which shall be uniform in weight and fineness and which may be used in all the countries represented in this Conference.

3. That to give full effect to this recommendation there shall meet in Washington a commission composed of one delegate, or more, from each nation represented in this Conference, which shall consider the quantity, the kind of currency, the uses it shall have, and the value and proportion of the international silver coin or coins and their relations to gold.

4. That the Government of the United States shall invite the commission to meet in Washington within a year, to be counted from the date of the adjournment of this Conference.

The report is signed by the Hon[s.] E. A. Mexia (Mexico), Morris M. Estee (United States), José Alfonso (Chile), Jeronimo Zelaya (Honduras), Juan Francisco Velarde (Bolivia), and Carlos Martinez Silva (Colombia).

The resolution was adopted.

IX.

ON MEASURES IN AID OF DEMONETIZATION.

ON MEASURES IN AID OF DEMONETIZATION.

Repugnant as demonetization is to the friends of silver, it is not unlikely that some of the interesting incidents of that erroneous policy may have escaped attention; and hence it may be profitable to analyze the situation with a view to possibilities in that direction. The reader will observe that I am not attempting to prophesy. I am merely suggesting certain elements for a seaman-like forecast bearing upon the navigation of a ship of state.

The friend of silver desires to enlarge the range of its monetary use; the demonetizer to reduce that use by closing his territory against it. Now, it will become apparent upon examination that so far as the general position of silver is concerned it makes little difference in what particular place this monetary use exists. To increase the use of silver in one place and thereby diminish it in another is futile.

The practical absurdity of this course is duplicated when the measure proves a political blunder. And this would be the case if *re*monetization in the United States facilitates *de*monetization abroad. Not only will it do no good to silver, so far as the dollars *re*monetized are balanced by dollars *de*monetized, but wherever it happens it weakens the silver party and its prospects by withdrawing from their side the political interest in a general restoration of silver to its place as money, that grew out of the former ownership of this silver, which we suppose to be demonetized.

For example, there is the case of Austria-Hungary. According to report, efforts are on foot there to establish the gold standard. Suppose that circumstances are provided by pro-silver action here which enable Austria-Hungary to sell out her silver stock for gold. That stock is not a very great sum, yet as far as it goes it would neutralize that amount of 'monetization' here. But beyond all that is the political effect of shutting the doors of that Empire to silver in the future. And that effect does not stop at the border. It must bear upon the future policy about money of the growing Danubian States, of Russia, of Germany, and so of Italy. To produce such a result tends to darken the future of silver.

Let us for a moment consider what *might* be done in other countries in the way of demonetizing silver and what loss, if any, would accrue to them from such act.

Demonetization or a reduction of monetary employment may be said to occur wherever the character of money is, in law or fact, withdrawn from silver.

These conditions I find to be fulfilled by the following acts:

(1.) Any step toward closing the mints now open to silver.

(2.) Any step withdrawing legal tender privileges from silver.

(3.) The retirement and melting down of silver coin, now circulating at a nominal rate. (Europe.)

(4.) The accumulation of gold stocks in the place of silver stocks, where silver coin circulates at its normal value. (Asia, South America, and Mexico.)

Of these acts, a decrial of coin (3) and a change of legal tender law (2) need be public. The practice of a Treasury as to the receipt of coin may, *de facto*, reduce as well as enlarge the legal tender privilege without attracting general attention.

Below the range of such public acts, the monetary employment of silver may be diminished, privately as well as openly,

by Governments, by Banks, etc., by individuals.

What direct and immediate losses are likely to accrue to the actors, through such acts of demonetization?

The direct and immediate loss is, in any case, very slight, provided the act does not immediately produce an actual fall of silver relatively to gold. I emphasize the words "direct and immediate," for experience amply teaches that such losses exert a deterrent effect out of all proportion greater than their importance (as compared with the losses which are remote or indirect) would warrant. And the visible or obvious remote and indirect loss will be very slight, provided the act does not clearly promise to produce an actual fall of silver at a later period. To an enlightened eye there is a real loss in the tendency of such acts to defeat, or at least postpone, the future settlement of the relations of money-metals, which, remaining unsettled, must continue to maintain unrest in various degrees throughout the various regions of the economic world. But this objection does not appeal to the partisan of gold, and hence would not avail to check the supposed efforts of a gold party to get rid of silver.

Moreover, if the United States undertakes to 'take care of silver,' it is easy for a European to belittle these evils and dangers. So, too, of the danger referred to in the proviso that the act of demonetization shall not produce an actual fall of silver. It is easy for a European who wishes to do so to think he can transform his little stock from white to yellow, without disturbing the market, so long as a great Power like the United States is monopolizing as a purchaser.

With reference to (3) the melting down of coins circulating above their normal value relatively to gold, it is important to mark the prevalence of an exaggerated estimate of the losses which would arise from such acts. I say exaggerated, but I must add that there are notable instances where even a preposterous estimate has been recommended to the public in good faith by highly reputable authorities.

For example, the two hundred and fifty million dollars in the Bank of France have been talked and written of as if the sale of them, supposing the present price maintained, would mean a *loss* of sixty millions. The same reasoning is applied to other Banks, and to the Government of France, and other States.

The use made of such erroneous estimate is to support the proposed wholesale acceptance of silver here, without limit of amount (or source), not upon trial, not as an experiment, not as a measure to induce European nations to come forward and join us in a settlement, but as a permanent establishment based on unilateral faith, a final committal quite independent of anything Europe may in the future actually do to disappoint the confidence, so widely professed, in what Europe is going to do.

Now in this matter a mistake would mean mischief. For these States together could, if the United States made it profitable for them, quietly absorb all the gold now in the United States, leaving us on a silver basis and without hope of a permanent ratio.

We will, therefore, examine the supposition and endeavor to ascertain what inference is warranted in the premises.

I aver that the Government that issued such coins, and by its laws maintains them at a fictitious value, relatively to gold, finds in them no real guarantee beyond their metal value, present or prospective. That is all they are really " worth " to the Government. For the difference between their metal value and their face value, they have a credit value. This the Government can destroy or maintain. The Government maintains that credit. Thus full legal tender silver coin to the face value of near a thousand million dollars is kept at par, at this nominal value, in the Latin Union, Holland, and Germany.

But suppose the way to be opened to these Governments to sell out their silver stock at an advance, or at the present price. As matters stand they cannot sell without lowering the price. But the supposition we are analyzing is, that the situation is changed so that they can sell out. And the object of the inquiry and of the conclusion which I have stated to be preposterous, is to show their loss would be enormous, and therefore there is not even a possibility that it would be incurred. It would in fact appear, from such reasoning, that no inducements America can offer will draw European silver across the sea!

Now I find such a sale could be made, in the supposed case mentioned, without any true pecuniary loss at all, except a slight percentage for expenses—freight, insurance, etc., between Europe and New York.

Taking the case of the Bank of France, this supposition implies that she would receive 190 million dollars of gold instead of 190 millions' worth of silver, coined at a face value of 250 millions.

This coin is in use as a deposit for bank notes. How large an issue could be based on gold, which is the chief standard metal, the only international money of the Western Hemisphere? Evidently, if the Government so wished, the convenience or advantage of maintaining the existing figures of monetary stock could be attained with gold as well as silver, and thus indemnity for any apparent loss be easily given to the Bank. The actual value of the gold would serve as security for not less an amount than the nominal value of the silver.

Where, then, is the loss? It does not exist.

With caution which in some cases may be superfluous, I again remind the reader that this supposition with which the advocate of "unlimited and unconditional silver" seeks to disarm objection is merely supposition, or rather a series of suppositions; supposed cases, however, which every business man must fairly face if he wishes to deal competently with the subject.

Now the supposition that a great demonetization or sale could take place without depressing the gold price of silver is one which demands extreme effort in order to be realized, and only the extreme measures proposed to Congress could for a time compass the result of maintaining silver at its price in such event. Here then is the strength of the case against demonetization. And here is shown the radical difference between extreme pro-silver measures and moderate pro-silver measures, to be adopted by Congress.

Europeans can be depended upon to recognize that such cashiering of silver coin, if undertaken in Europe on a large scale (as it was, for example, by Germany), in the absence of extreme measures here, would defeat the object in view to the extent of not keeping up the gold price of silver.

At the same time it is a plausible view that if other countries are buying up silver, demonetization might be proceeded with so gradually as to make the substitution of gold for silver productive of no immediate loss.

It may be taken for granted, gold being the accredited "standard" of the western nations, that there is an anti-silver party in each important country of Europe, excepting perhaps Holland and Spain. Of such a party in its dormant state it may be said, they would like, if they could, to see the work of demonetizing silver completed, each in its own country, but not in other countries. Opposed to them there is in each country a silver party, with its various respective degrees of strength, and such party would endeavor to defeat any further acts of demonetization, and, on the contrary, to promote joint action of nations to restore silver, so that existing laws excluding silver may be repealed.

We are investigating the anti-silver side, the gold party's side of an account of the effect of a pro-silver measure adopted at this time by one nation alone. Such a measure facilitates demonetization in other countries:

so far as it enlarges the employment for silver,
or raises the price of silver.

If its upward 'push' be slight, it tends to enable demonetization to proceed gradually without loss, because the supposed pro-silver measure will prevent a fall in the price of silver. If its upward push be great, it makes it more profitable to demonetize. For those who insist upon regarding a mere liquidation or closing out of an account as a loss, it is cheaper or less expensive. This estimate

EFFECT IN THE FUTURE. 233

thus supposed to be made of what is profitable, or cheap, refers to the past.

To illustrate: Silver being at, let us say, 72 cents to the dollar, America takes measures which bring it where it fluctuates from 85 to 90. That enables a Treasury to melt and put on the London market, and export to Asia and Africa, say, 20 millions a year of 5-franc pieces, at an advance of, say, 20 per cent. on what the silver in them was worth before. Now, these 20 millions are only $1\tfrac{1}{3}$ per cent. of the silver money of Europe (counting change), and only 8 per cent. of the silver stock regularly held by the Bank of France as deposit to secure its notes. This sale would be very profitable, looking merely to the past.

How is it as to the future? If silver is going higher, this sale will not seem so profitable. It will seem a loss, not of actual property, but of possible profit.

I now give a brief glance to the forces which prevent acts of demonetization.

As I have abundantly set forth on other pages the interest of each nation in Europe is that stable parity be established between the money-metals, and hence in the true account-keeping of national interests acts of demonetization are injurious to the State. The policy proposed in the Conference of 1878 was right—right for each nation. The gold party are wrong in each nation. The silver party are right.

But this was true in 1873, 1876, 1878, 1881, and has been true ever since. And yet the Silver Question is still the Silver Question! Error once in the saddle is slow to dislodge. Prejudice, dogmatism, and the inertia of nations make a mighty combination. The silver party are not yet in control so as to bring Germany and England to meet the requirements of other nations. And monetary policy is exposed to all the hazards of politics.

At the same time there is a peculiarity of monetary politics which has its favorable as well as its unfavorable side. With such a risky subject the odds are in favor of doing nothing. And Europe has done nothing important in the way of demonetization since May 16, 1879, when the sale of the German stock of thaler-bullion was stopped.

It may be of interest to refer in postscript to a peculiar effect of the *extent* of the rise of silver supposed to be produced by a measure taken by one nation without guarantees from others. There is a maximum price here for silver, that is, 100 cents on the gold dollar (at 15.98 to 1). It cannot go beyond that. This maximum is fixed by the existence of our silver dollars, which would bear down any influences which might tend to make the silver worth more than the gold dollar. As silver approaches the maximum, the profit of demonetization becomes greater, but the motive for delaying such action becomes weaker.

For example, let us suppose that Europeans think there is a good chance that America will raise silver from 72 cents to 1 dollar (15.98 to 1). They would naturally wait for a rise before selling. To induce them to wait till the rise reaches 90 there is the gain of 18 points on 72, or 25 per cent. For the balance of the possible rise, the "pull," the argument in favor of waiting, is only 10 points on 90, or 11 per cent. So the inducement to wait after silver reaches 90 is less than half what it was at the start.

APPENDIX.

THE ANTI-SILVER MOVEMENT AND ITS REVERSAL.

THE ANTI-SILVER MOVEMENT AND ITS REVERSAL.

A DOCUMENTARY CHRONICLE.

I.

INTRODUCTORY.

The documents of proof and justification hereinafter reprinted should be regarded in perspective as connected with the events now to be stated in brief; for if thus seen they assume their true positions relatively to each other. They will also be found in harmony with these fundamental truths—

That the joint acts of nations in breaking up an established parity between the two parts of the world's money owed their origin to mistake, to the mis-education of public opinion, rather than to the self-interest of any class. With error everywhere prevalent among the learned, the actual adoption of anti-silver measures came as a product of organized agitation and of political management. It is upon these same lines that the concurrent repeal of anti-silver laws in various nations is to be attained: first, education—the conversion of proficient advisers of public opinion in the several countries—and in aid of this, agitation, organized agitation, and all the political management that can be brought to bear. Of such management 'international strategy' is the highest form.

The Successive Steps in the Outlawry of Silver.

The Conference of 1867 at its seventh session adopted unanimously the following resolutions:

The Conference expresses the hope that the measures taken by the governments of the different states to modify their monetary system, in conformity with the basis laid down by the Conference, may end in diplomatic conventions.

As soon as answers shall be received from the different states to the communication officially made to them of the labors of the Conference by the French government, that government, in accordance with the answers that may be received, will call a new Conference, if necessary.

The following paragraph was also adopted, except as to the date, the United States voting for the date May 15 and Great Britain for June 1, 1868:

It is desirable that answers should be received before the 15th of February next.

The first overt act of Government following upon these recommendations was a Franco-Austrian Preliminary Treaty of July 3, 1867, as to the 8-florin piece. In the Scandinavian countries a movement was at once set on foot, which finally culminated in the Report of the Swedish Monetary Commission (published in 1871), and in the several successive steps taken to reduce the legal position of silver in the Scandinavian Union, definitively established by the Treaty of Sweden and Denmark, of December 18, 1872. The Treaty of Accession of Norway was of date October 16, 1875.

No action of great moment followed in other countries until after the Franco-Prussian war, when, by the Act of December 4, 1871, the new German Empire assumed the sovereign right of coinage, established a gold unit (the "mark") at $15\frac{1}{2}$ to 1, and stopped the mintage of silver. The act of July 9, 1873, completed the provision for the new Imperial gold money with silver change, and provided for the retirement, melting, and sale of the existing silver coin of the German States. The German silver sales reached a total of about 140 millions of dollars' worth. They were stopped on May 16, 1879, leaving about 150 million thalers full legal tender in Germany.

In France a Treasury Order of September 6, 1873, limited the amount of silver to be accepted by the Mint, and thereafter a limited coinage of *quotas* was agreed upon, from time to time, by the States of the Latin Union. In France silver mintage was stopped in 1876.

In Holland the Act of June 6, 1875, suspended the mintage of silver for private account, and established a gold coinage.

In the United States a Bill to 'discontinue the silver dollar' was presented in Congress in January, 1868. It was also proposed to reduce the gold coins, one Bill making the half eagle of equal weight with the 25-franc piece, another with the sovereign. These subjects, however, were then doubly removed from actuality, the money of the country being chiefly paper, in which gold was at a premium, while silver again was at a premium above gold. Two years later a measure discontinuing the silver dollar, which had been maturely prepared by Treasury officials, was recommended to Congress by the Secretary. The Act was finally passed and approved February 12, 1873.

The Ratio Since 1870.

The annual average ratio of Silver Bullion to Gold Money in London is given by various authorities as follows:

	Silver to Gold.		Silver to Gold.
1869-'70	15.60 to 1.	1880	18.00 to 1.
1871	15.50	1881	18.24
1872	15.64	1882	18.27
1873	15.93	1883	18.65
1874	16.13	1884	18.63
1875	16.63	1885	19.39
1876	17.80	1886	20.78
1877	17.19	1887	21.10
1878	17.96	1888	21.98
1879	18.39	1889	about 21.50

The lowest figure in—

	Silver to Gold.		Silver to Gold.
1876	20.17 to 1.	1888	22.65 to 1.

The Silver Dollar of the United States stands at the ratio to gold of 15.98 * to 1. Its bullion value was 70½ cents (0.70574), at the lowest figure yet reached—41⅜ pence to the ounce "standard" in London in 1888, equivalent to a ratio of 22.65 to 1.

---

* Or rather, 15.988372095023093023, but usually called 16.

II.

THE WORK OF THE CONFERENCE OF 1867.

Report of Mr. De Parieu.

At the eighth and last session, Saturday, July 6, 1867, on invitation from His Imperial Highness, Prince Jerome Bonaparte, the President of the Conference, M. de Parieu, the Vice-President, read the following report: *

Monseigneur and Gentlemen:

In the month of December last, when the French government communicated the International Convention of the 23d December, 1865, to the States here represented, and called their attention to the grand idea of monetary uniformity, those communications were at first received with a certain hesitation in some particulars. We have been, perhaps, too long accustomed to consign many generous ideas, sustained only by common sense, to the region of dreams, leaving them to be buried by prejudice and the blind consideration of the immutability of existing facts. We all know that every enterprise of general interest requires a spirit of unity in its aims and principal means of accomplishment.

There were many points in the monetary question so difficult that they caused divisions in the doctrines and the views of the past.

The idea of monetary uniformity long languished in the aspirations of poets and economists. The members of

---
*As given in translation accompanying Mr. Ruggles's Report.

the Convention of the 23d of December, 1865, encouraged by the success of their labors, warmly welcomed the practical idea of their extension ; and on witnessing the success of the monetary union concluded between France, Belgium, Switzerland, and Italy, notwithstanding the false situation caused by the forced circulation of paper in one of the States, it was hard for the government that had presided over the Conference of 1865 to refrain from asking the support of the world for a more extended monetary uniformity.

The Minister of Foreign Affairs has told you how much the imperial government was pleased at the eagerness of all the sovereign States of Europe and of the government at Washington in sending delegates to the Conference proposed to them. In giving to the assembly a president whose great name, exalted position, manifest impartiality, and decided sympathy for monetary uniformity have given our discussions a brilliancy and importance that we could not expect from our own resources, it has complimented you more highly than could be done by words, and has thanked you all, men distinguished for diplomatic merits, economical science, or technical experience in the monetary art, for the earnest welcome you have given to the ideas you were called together to examine.

What was the precise object of your Conference, the nature of the questions it was to expound ?

This, gentlemen, was the first object of your reflections, and upon it the success of your meeting depended. The government of the Emperor might prepare the studies, but it could not fix the terms.

Monetary science is vast; many of its problems are debated by philosophers. Not one could be avoided. Appeals were to be made to reality, the only solvent of such problems, and the one of particular importance in the subject now before us for consideration.

At the Trade Conference of 1864, in Frankfort, it was truly said, "monetary questions are more practical than all others."

The chief question for examination was the monetary standard.

On this subject you are aware that the world is divided between three different systems—the gold standard, the silver standard, and the double standard. It was indispensable to know which of these forms would furnish the most desirable and permanent basis for a monetary unity.

Governed by these considerations, you have agreed upon a series of questions as the basis of your labors, on the report of a committee of seven members, in the formation of which all the systems had been equitably represented.

This 'questionnaire,' to adopt a neologism of our administrative language, you unanimously adopted in the following terms:

"1st. What is the best way to realize monetary unity—by the creation of an entirely new system independent of existing systems, and in that case what should be the basis of that system; or, by the combination of present systems, taking into consideration the scientific advantages of certain types, and the number of nations that have already adopted them ? In the latter case, what monetary system ought to be chiefly considered, with the reserve of any improvement that might be made in it?

"2d. Can identities or partial assimilations of monetary types be now constituted on a large scale by adopting the silver standard exclusively ?

"3d. On the other hand, can that result be reached by adopting a gold standard exclusively ?

"4th. Could a similar result be obtained by adopting the double standard, and fixing in all the nations the relative value of gold and silver?

"5th. In case of a negative response to the preceding questions, is it possible or expedient to establish identity or partial assimilation of monetary types on a large scale with a silver standard, leaving each state the liberty of preserving its gold standard?

"6th. Is it possible and useful to establish identity or partial assimilation of monetary types on a gold basis, leaving each state the liberty of preserving its silver standard?

"7th. In case of affirming one of the two preceding questions, would the internationality of the coin adopted as a common standard be a sufficient assurance of its continued circulation in each state, or would it be necessary to stipulate a certain limit in the relation between the value of gold and silver, or to provide for the case in which international coins would run the risk of being expelled from circulation in any of the contracting states?

"8th. For the success of monetary unity is it necessary to constitute an identical unity of metallic composition everywhere with similarity of weight and denomination, and what basis is to be adopted; or is it enough to constitute common types of a common denominator as high as multiples of 5 francs for gold?

"9th. In case gold is adopted as an international metal, would it be useful for the types of that coin adopted by the Monetary Convention of the 23d of December, 1865, to be completed by new types of 15 and 25 francs for the sake of unity and in the spirit of reciprocity? In this case what should be their dimensions?

"10th. In case of affirmative to questions three or six,

would it be useful to regulate silver or copper coins by common obligations as to their composition or standard, their limit in payment, or the amount of their issue?

"11th. Would it be proper to fix certain means of control to insure the exact coinage of the common types of the international money?

"12th. Besides the immediate practical possibilities already discussed, would further discussions of general principles be desirable to spread over Europe the assimilations already effected or hereafter to be realized in respect to money?"

Although no idea of exclusion has entered into this "questionnaire," it is remarkable that its discussion during five sittings has suggested no serious addition; on the contrary, the 10th and 11th questions you have put off, although the principle of measures of control has been judged indispensable to the success of the monetary conventions, and the 12th question was left undecided.

The decisions of the Conference, as a whole, have been regulated by the dominant desire that any future monetary legislation shall result, as far as practicable, in diplomatic conventions between different states, to secure them against their own inconstancy. It is the evident interest of the states to secure the political advantages of the assimilation of their monetary types by the reciprocal circulation of their coins.

You did not think the reciprocal circulation in public banks, as resolved upon in 1865, completely answered the aspirations for a monetary uniformity; and, contrary to some reserves found in your minutes, you thought legal currency ought to be considered the last word in the tendencies to unity.

The nine first questions of your sittings are comprised

in three formulas too abstract to be discussed, and I will reduce them to their simplest form of expression.

The whole world agreeing upon the benefits to be derived from monetary unity, but the difficulties and delays of effecting it being very apparent, the question is, How can it be effected? By the creation of a new monetary system established *a priori*, or by strict adhesion to existing systems, or simply by bending them, so to speak, and perfecting them hereafter?

Such was the triple problem proposed for your solution.

All of your states, except Belgium, have agreed not to propose a new system, lest such an undertaking might indefinitely delay the desired monetary assimilation.

A new system would have probably been founded upon the adoption of a decimal gold piece of a certain weight as a unity. You do not say that such a regularity could be attained without difficulty, however beautiful it might be in theory, and without disturbing inveterate habits found in the attachment to the silver franc, almost a copy of the old French *livre tournois*.

Instead of seeking a system new in all its parts, you have preferred to adopt that of the Monetary Convention signed at Paris on the 23d of December, 1865, and which, being now adopted by Rome and Athens, seems by a fortunate coincidence to reunite the greater portion of the countries in which, at the close of ancient history, civilization by various modes had marked out the perimeter of its first empire.

The close union of this system, in its silver coins, with the metrical weights, whether the coins be considered as a distinct standard or as small change, and the 72,000,000 of people that use it and are attached to it, have made you regard it as a centre of assimilation around which the efforts of other nations might cluster with probabilities of success. But you did not look upon the system as fixed and perfect.

You rightly thought it capable of contraction or extension ; that, though the unit was called a *franc* here, a *lira* there, and a *drachma* elsewhere, still a greater latitude was possible, particularly in regard to the unit value.

Most of the civilized nations have a monetary unity above a franc in value, the piastre, the thaler, the ruble, and the dollar, four pieces similar in origin and name, are nearly, the quadruple or quintuple of the unit adopted in the convention of 1865.

If the German and Dutch florins and the Spanish crowns differ less from the franc, on the other hand the wealthy British civilization places its monetary unit much higher in value.

Though the small Roman state has converted its *scudo*, similar to the piastre and dollar, into francs, we can hardly hope that larger and more populous states will immediately adopt all the monetary unities we have reported in the convention of the 23d of December, 1865. You have, therefore, thought proper to suggest a single unit as a common denominator, borrowed, from the system of the convention, around which the other unities should circulate.

If silver had been adopted for the unitary basis, all other systems might have been assimilated to the franc as a common denominator. But could the silver franc have been the pivot of equations, commensurabilities and coincidences desired in the monetary systems we would like to make universal for the benefit of exchange, trade, travel, financial, statistical, and scientific operations? To a certain extent, this was the chief question for your deliberations.

Here the laws that brought the precious metals into contact with the wealth of communities, and which have twice given a monetary system to the universe, came into consideration. The rule of these laws was broken by the great historic catastrophe that separated ancient from modern civilization by an intermediate period of poverty and barbarism, but now strikingly reproduced after a lapse of nearly eighteen centuries.

In the time of Augustus, when gold had gained the ascendancy in money circulation, the Roman poet exclaimed:

> Æra dabant olim ; melius nunc omen in auro est,
> Victaque concedit prisca moneta novæ.

From the middle ages to our day, the revolution that Ovid mentions incompletely, for he omits silver, has lain quiet, till it breaks out now with renewed strength and peculiar mineralogical, industrial, and commercial circumstances. No new invasion of barbarism can reverse its course in Europe, where silver first took the place of iron and copper, and where silver is now displaced by gold.

In most of the civilized nations of Europe and America the latter metal has become the principal instrument of circulation, because its portability and density particularly recommend it as the material for monetary unity. When the convention of the 23d September, 1865, closed, three of the associate states wished gold to be the choice of the convention. Even in the last century, a learned man of Germany, where so many grand ideas originate, declared that gold was destined to become the bond of the monetary systems of the universe.

By a most singular coincidence, when only two out of

twenty states had gold for a standard, your conference decided upon it for the standard, with silver as a transitory companion; and this was done because the double standard was necessary in certain states that were used to it, or where silver was the exclusive standard.

This valuable unanimity on a question so important, tending to perfect the monetary system of the convention of 1865, will certainly influence public opinion, and certain men in the interior of states who may have retained any doubt on the question.

In thus adopting gold as a basis for the desired union, it was only in a common denominator above the franc that it was possible to realize the useful equations and frequent coincidences in the systems to be brought together; for, in gold coins, the very minute differences could not be distinguished with precision by the process of coinage, and already the mere distance of five francs may be sometimes difficult to express sufficiently in the external form of the monetary disks.

The weight of five francs in gold of nine-tenths fineness, the standard which was unanimously approved, and also one of the conditions of the convention of 1865, then appeared to be the proper denominator for the basis of the desired assimilation between the monetary systems of the twenty states represented.

You are aware that the coins of the union of 1865 are already grouped around this denominator.

For example, it was shown how near the type of 25 francs came to the pound sterling, the half-eagle of 5 dollars, and a piece adopted by the Vienna conference to represent the value of ten florins. This type of 25 francs, especially recommended in the conference by the representatives of Austria and of the United States, has been unanimously accepted by the states that voted in the discussion of question nine, but on optional conditions.

Your opinions were more divided, in fact equally, in regard to the utility of recommending at present a gold piece of 15 francs, the approximate equation of 7 florins of the Netherlands and South Germany, and of 4 thalers of North Germany. But, without recommending this type, as you did that of 25 francs, you nevertheless agreed that, if circumstances rendered it proper, it would be open to no serious objection in itself, unless it might be in the delicacy of the process for coining it distinctly.

The eventual extension of the types of gold coins would necessitate, *a fortiori*, for the states that desired it, correlative latitude in the forms of their silver coins, the internationality of which is of less importance.

Such, gentlemen, are the simple but instructive and plain bases that you have thought proper to accept as a sort of siege to the citadel of monetary diversity, the fall of which you would like to behold, or, at least, to gradually destroy its walls, for the benefit of the daily increasing commerce and exchanges of every description among the different members of the human family.

The desire of not detaining you longer, gentlemen, after a session of three weeks, is my apology for the imperfection of this hastily written digest, which is made in the hope that some decision may be reached by the middle of February, 1868, or at least some instructive steps taken by the governments that have sent you to this Conference.

If the germs of our collective, enlightened, and benevolent aspirations, freed from the unpleasant compensations that sometimes attend the most seductive reforms, in which we are all animated by the true spirit of civilization and modern progress, shall come to fructify around you, I hope, gentlemen, you will pleasurably recall the honorable memories of the part you have taken in these delicate scientific discussions, with the satisfaction of their joint pursuit, under a presidency so memorable, and with a facility and harmony as perfect as that of delegates from a single nation in its ordinary deliberations.

E. DE PARIEU,
Vice-President of the International Monetary Conference.

III.

THE GERMAN COMMERCIAL CONVENTION OF 1868.

One hundred and nineteen German cities were represented in this Convention. The organization of the earlier *Handelstag* has been kept up by a Permanent Committee of fifteen, of which Dr. Adolf Soetbeer, of Hamburg, whose literary activity in monetary matters began in 1846, was a prominent member. The following resolution was presented by him as Official Reporter on the question of the Standard at the first session, and was debated at length and adopted at the following session. It will be apparent upon consideration of the resolutions, that that basis of public favor which made it possible for the German Parliament in 1871 and 1873 to establish the Gold Standard, was largely the artificial product of an ably-directed, perseveringly-pursued, literary agitation which disseminated among the business men throughout Germany an enthusiasm for the principles identified with the name of Dr. Soetbeer and with the Conference of 1867.

Resolution Adopted.

Inasmuch as the measures recommended by the First German Commercial Convention, in Heidelberg, May, 1861, and by the Third Commercial Convention, in Frank-

---

Extract from the Report of the Proceedings of the Fourth German Commercial Convention (*Handelstag*) held at Berlin between the 20th and 23d October, 1868. Reprinted from the Document of the Conference of 1878.

fort-on-the-Main, September, 1865, for the purpose of securing monetary unity in Germany, have not met with earnest attention or practical acceptance at the hands of the German Government, and as there are no signs that such attention or acceptance will be accorded to them; and inasmuch as a plan of a Universal International Monetary Union on the basis of the Gold Standard has been elsewhere adopted with zeal, and is being pursued with perseverance; and especially inasmuch as the proceedings of the International Monetary Conference which met in Paris in the year 1867, in which also the Plenipotentiaries of Prussia and of other German States took part, have now been made known, the German Commercial Convention in its present fourth assembly pronounces itself to the following effect:

1. The speedy attainment of a practicable monetary unity in all German States is now, as formerly, regarded as exceedingly important and desirable.

2. As far as the special scheme of the future unified German monetary system is concerned the propositions for a unified reckoning by marks (thirds of a thaler), the Silver Standard being retained, which was abandoned by the Conventions of 1861 and 1865, are withdrawn, and, on the contrary, the following recommendations are made:

3. Monetary unity, and at the same time such a general monetary reform as befits the age, can be brought about by the adoption, at the same time, by all the German States of the *Single Standard with full application of the Decimal System*, in pursuance of the principles recommended by the International Monetary Conference of Paris in its report of the 6th July, 1867.

4. As far as relates to the future German monetary system after the adoption of the Gold Standard, special notice

is directed to the proposition to introduce unit of value and of account equivalent to the *Gold five-franc piece* with its decimal multiples and its division into 100 shillings, or to adopt for a unit of account the gulden as the tenth part of a principal Gold Coin identical with the 25-franc piece, and divided into 100 kreuzers.

The Commercial Convention, in presenting a collection of written opinions concerning the transition to the Gold Standard, and the proceedings of the present meeting, petitions the August Presidency of the North German Confederation, as well as the August Governments of Bavaria, Württemberg, Baden, and Hessen, without delay to take appropriate measures in order that a uniform monetary system of the kind before mentioned may be agreed upon, and as soon as possible be laid before the North German Diet and before the Legislatures of the South German States for their acceptance in constitutional form, in order that, if by any means it be practicable, the monetary reform may take effect, at the latest, on January 1, 1872, at the same time with the new System of Weights and Measures, which already has been published as law in the States of the North German Confederation, the early adoption of which in the South German States is also strongly to be desired.

The Permanent Committee is herewith authorized to adopt such measures as may be necessary to further the object of the pending resolution.

IV.

THE PROPOSALS OF THE UNITED STATES BEFORE THE CONFERENCE OF 1878.

At the second session, on the 16th of August, the Commissioners of the United States submitted the two following propositions:

I.

It is the opinion of this Assembly that it is not to be desired that Silver should be excluded from Free Coinage in Europe and the United States of America. On the contrary, the Assembly believes that it is desirable that the Unrestricted Coinage of Silver, and its use as Money of Unlimited Legal Tender, should be retained where they exist, and, as far as practicable, restored where they have ceased to exist:

II.

The use of both Gold and Silver as Unlimited Legal-Tender Money may be safely adopted.

First.—By equalizing them at a relation to be fixed by international agreement; and

Secondly.—By granting to each metal, at the relation fixed, equal terms of Coinage, making no discrimination between them.

The following third proposition was prepared and held

Extract from the Report of the American Commission. (Page 213.)

in reserve, awaiting the development of the views of the Conference:

III.

"The Delegations here present agree to recommend to their respective governments that, by the free coinage of silver at a relation to be agreed upon, or provisionally, through extended coinage upon government account and the accumulation of silver bullion in public treasuries, they make a concerted effort to restore silver to its function as money of full power."

At no time during the further proceedings did the interest of our mission appear to require the presentation of this proposition.

At the seventh and concluding session, on the 29th of August, the following reply to the propositions submitted by the Delegates of the United States was offered on behalf of the majority of the European Delegates:

The Delegates of the European States represented in Conference wish to express their sincere thanks to the Government of the United States of America for having procured an international exchange of opinion upon a subject of so much importance as the monetary question.

Having maturely considered the proposals of the representatives of the United States, they recognize:

I.

That it is necessary to maintain in the world the monetary functions of Silver as well as those of Gold, but that the selection for use of one or the other of the two metals, or of both, simultaneously, should be governed by the special position of each State, or group of States.

II.

That the question of the restriction of the Coinage of Silver should equally be left to the discretion of each State, or group of States, according to the particular circumstances in which they may find themselves placed, and the more so, in that the disturbance produced during the recent years in the Silver market has variously affected the monetary situation of the several countries.

III.

That the differences of opinion which have appeared, and the fact that even some of the States which have the Double Standard find it impossible to enter into a mutual engagement with regard to the free coinage of Silver, exclude the discussion of the adoption of a common ratio between the two metals.

Contemporaneously with the presentation of this paper, individual expressions of opinion were offered by several of the Delegations, which may be seen in the journal accompanying this report.

To this declaration of the European Delegates, the Delegates of the United States rejoined with the following statement of their views, with which the formal proceedings of the Conference terminated:

In response to the address of the representatives of the European States, the representatives of the United States desire, on their part, to express their thanks to the European States for accepting their invitation and consulting with them upon a subject of so much importance.

The representatives of the United States regret that they cannot entirely concur in all that has been submitted to them by a majority of the representatives of the European States.

They fully concur in a part of the first proposition, viz., that "It is necessary to maintain in the world the monetary functions of silver as well as those of Gold," and they desire that ere long there may be adequate co-operation to obtain that result.

They cannot object to the statement that "the selection for use of one or other of these two metals, or of both simultaneously, should be governed by the special position of each State;" but if it be necessary to maintain the monetary functions of the two metals as previously declared, they respectfully submit that special positions of States may become of secondary importance.

From so much of the second proposition as assigns as a special reason for at present restricting the Coinage of Silver "that the disturbance produced during the recent years in the silver market has differently affected the monetary situation of the several countries," they respectfully dissent, believing that a policy of action would remove the disturbance that produced these inequalities.

In regard to the third and last proposition, they admit that "some of the States which have the Double Standard," or, as they prefer to say, use both metals, "find it impossible to enter into a mutual engagement for the free Coinage of Silver."

They as representatives of the United States, have come here expressly to enter into such an engagement. The difficulty is not with them, and, wherever it may be, they trust it may be soon removed. They entirely concur in the conclusion drawn from this state of the case that it "excludes the discussion of the adoption of a common ratio between the two metals " if the nations are not ready to adopt a policy to uphold it. We remain upon ours; the European States upon theirs.

R. E. FENTON.
W. S. GROESBECK.
FRANCIS A. WALKER.
S. DANA HORTON.

V.

THE CONFERENCE OF 1881.

DECLARATIONS OF FRANCE AND THE UNITED STATES.

Mr. EVARTS, on behalf of the Delegates of France (Magnin, Dumas, De Normandie, and Cernuschi), and of the United States of America (Evarts, Thurman, Howe, and Horton), read the following Declaration:

The Delegates of France and of the United States, in the name of their respective Governments, make the following Declarations:

1. The depreciation and great fluctuations in the value of silver relatively to gold, which of late years have shown themselves, and which continue to exist, have been, and are, injurious to commerce and to the general prosperity, and the establishment and maintenance of a fixed relation of value between silver and gold would produce most important benefits to the commerce of the world.

2. A convention entered into by an important group of States, by which they should agree to open their mints to free and unlimited coinage of both silver and gold, at a fixed proportion of weight between the gold and silver

From the Document of the Conference, page 502.

contained in the monetary unit of each metal, and with full legal tender faculty to the money thus issued, would cause and maintain a stability in the relative value of the two metals suitable to the interests and requirements of the commerce of the world.

3. Any ratio, now or of late in use by any commercial nation, if adopted by such important group of States, could be maintained; but the adoption of the ratio of $15\frac{1}{2}$ to 1, would accomplish the principal object with less disturbance in the monetary systems to be affected by it than by any other ratio.

4. Without considering the effect which might be produced toward the desired object by a lesser combination of States, a convention which would include England, France, Germany, and the United States, with the concurrence of other States, both in Europe and on the American continent, which this combination would assure, would be adequate to produce and maintain throughout the commercial world the relation between the two metals that such convention should adopt.

RESOLUTION FOR ADJOURNED MEETING IN 1882.

The Conference, considering that in the course of its two sessions it has heard the speeches, declarations and observations of the delegates of the States hereinafter enumerated;

Germany, Austria-Hungary, Belgium, Denmark, Spain, The United States, France, Great Britain, British India, Canada, Greece, Italy, The Netherlands, Portugal, Russia, Sweden, Norway, and Switzerland;

Considering that the declarations made by several of the delegates have been in the name of their governments;

That these declarations all admit the expediency of

taking various measures in concert, under reservation of the entire freedom of action of the different governments;

That there is ground for believing that an understanding may be established between the States which have taken part in the Conference;

But that it is expedient to suspend its meetings;

That, in fact, the monetary situation may, as regards some States, call for the intervention of their governments, and that there is reason for giving an opportunity at present for diplomatic negotiations;

Adjourns to Wednesday, 12th April, 1882.

VI.

THE PROPOSED CONFERENCE OF 1882.

COPY OF AN IDENTICAL NOTE SENT TO THE VARIOUS POWERS BY THE GOVERNMENTS OF FRANCE AND OF THE UNITED STATES, MARCH 31, 1882.

PARIS, *March* 31, 1882.

The International Monetary Conference which was convened at Paris last year, upon the invitation of France and of the United States, and in which the Government of   was represented, adjourned to meet the 12th of April, 1882.

In making this decision at the session of July 8, 1881, the Delegates anticipated that, before the date thus fixed, the Governments represented in the Conference would be able to prepare solutions of the questions involved, with a view to the conclusion of an international convention, the terms of which should be discussed and determined by the Conference.

This anticipation has been, in part, realized. From all the information which has been received, it appears that in a large number of States the question has continued to be the subject of earnest consideration and that various plans have been under discussion, with the object either of re-establishing the free coinage of silver money, or of restoring to the metal silver its proper international value by enlarging its use as coin. Up to the present time, however, these investigations do not appear to have produced conclusions sufficiently positive to serve as a basis for formal deliberations of the Conference.

Hence, in the opinion of the Government of the United States, in conformity with the view entertained by various other Governments, notably by those of Germany, Holland, and Italy, there would be no sufficient advantage in reopening the discussions of the Conference at present.

In this situation, the Governments of the United States and of France are of the opinion that it would be desirable to defer the convocation of the Conference, subject to a determination, on the part of the States interested, of the date for its reassembling, the same to take place within the present year.

VII.

FOREIGN COINS AS LEGAL TENDER AND THE POLICY OF UNION.

In all cases where communities which have maintained independent Coinage Systems have come into union with each other, or into subjection one to another, a conflict of coinages must naturally ensue, and the settlement of such conflict must naturally offer analogies both with the jarring of the money systems of independent nations and with that monetary pacification which is the aim of international contract.

For instance, the monetary arrangements arising out of the consolidation of the Roman Empire, or, later, out of that of the royal power of France, and that of the United Kingdom of Great Britain, must offer such analogies, while the partial and desultory coinage legislation of the Holy Roman Empire of the German Nation in past centuries, and in its turn the speedy monetary unification of the new German Empire of to-day, would offer similar points of resemblance and of instruction.

In the Document of the Monetary Conference of 1878 is given a list of Coinage Treaties, the result of researches which enabled me effectively to characterize the policy I had so long sought to promote.

The possible future monetary treaty of the chief Western Powers, contemplated by the advocates of the policy adopted by the United States in the law of February 28, 1878, under which the Conference was convoked, differs

---

NOTE.—From the Document of the Monetary Conference of 1878.

in an essential point from treaties of which history offers an example. Such treaties have, it is believed, invariably had for their object a Fusion of Currencies or Mutuality of Legal Tender; the coins struck in one country were to receive legal currency in another; and this interchangeability of coins was the main object of the treaty.

This general object may have implied the purpose, or carried with it the result, that a certain metal or certain metals should become or remain material of coinage in the contracting countries, and may have included the obligation of each party to maintain by appropriate laws the legal-tender character of such coined metal.

But it was the coining and not the metal: it was the subdivision and the stamping of the material, and not the material itself, that offered the motive of the contract. Indeed, until the middle of this century, it appears to have been taken for granted—perhaps unconsciously, but in any case by general consent—that the two metals would remain Money; that they would retain an international currency as material for Money sufficient to guarantee their general status. Gold might be excluded here from formal rights of legal tender, and there silver might seem ostracised, but there was no combined effort to exclude silver, and the nations which would not admit gold as compulsory legal tender furthered its use as a trade coin.

With the outlawry of silver in Europe comes a new order of events, and to that new order of events the proposed amendments of law were adapted. The advocates of the policy adopted by Congress dealt with the material, not with the stamping of its subdivisions.

The object of this policy would be fully met by a treaty which should merely guarantee the equality of the metals before the law. Under such a treaty the contracting parties might each retain undisturbed their national coins; their mutual engagement would relate merely to the use of the two metals as full legal-tender at the same ratio. This implies that in making such coins, uniform freedom should be granted to the private individual to have such metal coined; and that the same charge, or absence of charge, for mintage, should obtain in the contracting nations; and that at the same time full legal-tender power should be appropriately secured by each contracting country to its *own coins* thus struck.

An examination of the history of Coinage Confederations, will reveal that their disadvantages or deficiencies arose either, 1st, from this extra-national legal currency of coins, which was their primary object; or, 2d (when they contemplated the concurrent use of the two metals), from an extra-federal demand for gold at a silver price higher than that assigned to the metal in the federal Coinage System.

These disadvantages which inhered in all European Monetary Unions actually formed are believed to be excluded from that which the United States has proposed to the nations for discussion. It is not essential, nor is it an important practical object of this policy that extra-national legal currency of coins should be included in the contract; while the union contemplated is so large that, so far as probabilities can be calculated, its tranquillity could not, under any circumstances which this generation is warranted in anticipating, be disturbed by an extra-federal demand for gold.

VIII.

THE ROYAL COMMISSION ON GOLD AND SILVER, 1886–1888.

EXTRACTS FROM THE FINAL REPORT, NOV. 6, 1888.

PART I. *Signed by all the members of the Commission.*—Lord HERSCHELL, Sir JOHN LUBBOCK, Bart., M. P.; Mr. J. W. BIRCH, Hon. C. W. FREEMANTLE, C. B.; Sir T. H. FARRER, Bart.; Rt. Hon. LEONARD H. COURTNEY, M. P.; Rt. Hon. Sir LOUIS MALLET, C. B.; Rt. Hon. A. J. BALFOUR, M. P.; Rt. Hon. HENRY CHAPLIN, M. P.; Sir D. BALFOUR, K. C. S. I.; Sir W. H. HOULDSWORTH, Bart., M. P.; Mr. SAMUEL MONTAGU, M. P.

SEC. 186. "It must be borne in mind that in the case of other commodities the effect of changes in the supply and demand is both more marked and more immediate. These commodities are generally produced for the purpose of consumption at an early date or within a comparatively short period. The supply at any time available for the market, or capable of being placed on it at short notice, is therefore a very important element in the process by which its value is fixed.

"The precious metals on the other hand are but to a slight extent consumed, and the available supply consists of the accumulations of previous years.

"It follows, therefore, that in their case a diminution or an increase in the new supply is of less importance than in the case of consumable articles, and that an increase or diminution in demand has also a smaller effect. The important consideration with regard to them at any one

---

NOTE.—From a circular of the Bimetallic League.

moment is rather the relation between the total stock then in existence and the then existing demands upon it."

SEC. 189. "Looking, then, to the vast changes which occurred prior to 1873 in the relative production of the two metals without any corresponding disturbance in their market value, it appears to us difficult to resist the conclusion that some influence was then at work tending to steady the price of silver, and to keep the ratio which it bore to gold approximately stable."

SEC. 190. "Prior to 1873 the fluctuations in the price of silver were gradual in their character, and ranged within very narrow limits. The maximum variation in 1872 was $\frac{5}{8}$d., and the average not quite $\frac{5}{16}$d., while in 1886 the maximum was $2\frac{9}{16}$d., and the average nearly $1\frac{1}{8}$d. It has not been, and indeed hardly could be, suggested that this difference can be accounted for by changes in the relative production or actual use of the two metals."

SEC. 191. "The explanation commonly offered of these constant variations in the silver market is that the rise or depression of the price of silver depends upon the briskness or slackness of the demand for the purpose of remittance to silver-using countries, and that the price is largely affected by the amount of the bills sold from time to time by the Secretary of State for India in Council.

"But these causes were, as far as can be seen, operating prior to 1873, as well as subsequent to that date, and yet the silver market did not display the sensitiveness to these influences from day to day and month to month which it now does."

SEC. 192. "These considerations seem to suggest the existence of some steadying influence in former periods, which has now been removed, and which has left the silver market subject to the free influence of causes, the full effect of which was previously kept in check. The question, therefore, forces itself upon us:—Is there any other circumstance calculated to affect the relation of silver to gold which distinguishes the latter period from the earlier?

"Now undoubtedly, the date which forms the dividing line between an epoch of approximate fixity in the relative value of gold and silver and one of marked instability, is the year when the bimetallic system which had previously been in force in the Latin Union ceased to be in full operation; and we are irresistibly led to the conclusion that the operation of that system, established as it was in countries the population and commerce of which were considerable, exerted a material influence upon the relative value of the two metals.

"So long as that system was in force we think that, notwithstanding the changes in the production and use of the precious metals, it kept the market price of silver approximately steady at the ratio fixed by law between them, namely 15½ to 1.

SEC. 193. "Nor does it appear to us *a priori* unreasonable to suppose that the existence in the Latin Union of a bimetallic system with a ratio of 15½ to 1 fixed between the two metals should have been capable of keeping the market price of silver steady at approximately that ratio.

"The view that it could only affect the market price to the extent to which there was a demand for it for currency purposes in the Latin Union, or to which it was actually taken to the mints of those countries is, we think, fallacious.

"The fact that the owner of silver could, in the last resort, take it to those mints and have it converted into coin which would purchase commodities at the ratio of

15½ of silver to one of gold, would, in our opinion, be likely to affect the price of silver in the market generally, whoever the purchaser and for whatever country it was destined. It would enable the seller to stand out for a price approximating to the legal coin and would tend to keep the market steady at about that point."

PART II. *Signed by six members of the Commission.*—Lord HERSCHELL, Sir JOHN LUBBOCK, Bart., M. P.; Mr. J. W. BIRCH, Hon. C. W. FREEMANTLE, C. B.; Sir T. H. FARRER, Bart.; Rt. Hon. LEONARD H. COURTNEY. M. P.

SEC. 9. "However much opinions may differ as to the extent of the evil arising from the increased difficulty which a fluctuating exchange interposes, we do not think its reality is open to question."

SEC. 101. "There cannot be two opinions as to the very serious effect which the continued fall in the gold price of silver has had on the finances of the Government of India."

SEC. 102. "We are fully impressed with a sense of the difficulties which surround the Indian Government, and of the serious questions to which any proposed additional tax must give rise. It is not only the embarrassment which has already been caused to the Government of India that has to be borne in mind, but the impossibility of foreseeing to what extent those embarrassments may be increased, and their difficulty augmented, by a further depression in the value of silver."

SEC. 107. "We think that in any conditions fairly to be contemplated in the future, so far as we can forecast them from the experience of the past, a stable ratio might be maintained if the nations we have alluded to* were to ac-

---

* The United Kingdom, Germany, the United States, and the Latin Union.

cept and strictly adhere to bimetallism, at the suggested ratio. We think that if in all these countries gold and silver could be freely coined, and thus become exchangeable against commodities at the fixed ratio, the market value of silver as measured by gold would conform to that ratio, and not vary to any material extent."

Sec. 119. "Apprehensions have been expressed that if a bimetallic system were adopted gold would gradually disappear from circulation. If, however, the arrangement included all the principal commercial nations, we do not think there would be any serious danger of such a result.

"Such a danger, if it existed at all, must be remote. It is said indeed, by some, that if it were to happen, and all nations were to be driven to a system of silver monometallism, the result might be regarded without dissatisfaction.

"We are not prepared to go this length, but at the same time we are fully sensible of the benefits which would accrue from the adoption of a common monetary standard by all the commercial nations of the world, and we are quite alive to the advantage of the adoption by these nations of an uniform bimetallic standard as a step in that direction."

PART III. *Signed by the other six members of the Commission.*—Rt. Hon. Sir LOUIS MALLET, C. B.; Rt. Hon. A. J. BALFOUR, M. P.; Rt. Hon. HENRY CHAPLIN, M. P.; Sir D. BARBOUR, K. C. S. I.; Sir W. H. HOULDSWORTH, Bart., M. P.; Mr. SAMUEL MONTAGU, M. P.

Sec. 28. "We think that the above remarks upon the evils affecting both the United Kingdom and India, if taken in connection with the more detailed statement in Part I of the Report, will sufficiently indicate our view as to their nature and gravity; and that they are largely due to the currency changes which have taken place in the years immediately preceding and following 1873.

"We think that too much stress cannot be laid upon the novelty of the experiment which has been attempted as the result of the above changes. That experiment consists in the independent and unregulated use of both gold and silver as standards of value by the different nations of the world.

"We are strongly of opinion that both Metals must continue to be used as standard money; the results of using them separately and independently since 1873 have been most unsatisfactory, and may be positively disastrous in the future.

"It cannot be questioned that until 1873 gold and silver were always effectively linked by a legal ratio in one or more countries.

"It is equally indisputable that the relative value of the two metals has been subject to greater divergence since 1874 than during the whole of the 200 years preceding that date, notwithstanding the occurrence of variations in their relative production more intense and more prolonged than those which have been experienced in recent years."

Sec. 29. "In 1873-74 the connecting link disappeared, and for the first time the system of rating the two metals ceased to form a subject of legislation in any country in the world.

"The law of supply and demand was for the first time left to operate independently upon the value of each metal; and simultaneously the ratio which had been maintained, with scarcely any perceptible variation, for 200 years, gave place to a marked and rapid divergence in the relative value of gold and silver, which has culminated in a change from $15\frac{1}{2}$ to 1 to 22 to 1."

Proposed Remedy.

Sec. 30. "It appears to us impossible to attribute the concurrence of these two events to a merely fortuitous coincidence. They must, in our opinion, be regarded as standing to each other in the relation of cause and effect.

"We cannot, therefore, doubt that if the system which prevailed before 1873 were replaced in its integrity, most of the evils which we have above described would be removed; and the remedy which we have to suggest is simply the reversion to a system which existed before the changes above referred to were brought about; a system, namely, under which both metals were freely coined into legal tender money at a fixed ratio over a sufficiently large area.

"The effects of that system, though it was nominally in force only within a limited area, were felt in all commercial countries, whatever their individual systems of currency might be; and the relative value of the two metals in all the markets of the world was practically identical with that fixed by the legislation of the countries forming the Latin Union.

"As regards the possibility of maintaining such a system in the future, we need only refer to the conclusion at which our colleagues have arrived in Sec. 107, Part II. (see above), and with which we entirely agree."

Sec. 34. "No settlement of the difficulty is, however, in our opinion, possible without international action.

"The remedy which we suggest is essentially international in its character, and its details must be settled in concert with the other Powers concerned.

"It will be sufficient for us to indicate the essential features of the agreement to be arrived at, namely—

(1) Free coinage of both metals into legal-tender money; and

(2) The fixing of a ratio at which the coins of either metal shall be available for the payment of all debts at the option of the debtor."

Sec. 35. "The particular ratio to be adopted is not, in our opinion, a necessary preliminary to the opening of negotiations for the establishment of such an agreement, and can, with other matters of detail, be left for further discussion and settlement between the parties interested.

"We, therefore, submit that the chief commercial nations of the world, such as the United States, Germany, and the States forming the Latin Union, should in the first place be consulted as to their readiness to join with the United Kingdom in a conference, at which India and any of the British Colonies which may desire to attend should be represented, with a view to arrive, if possible, at a common agreement on the basis above indicated."

Sec. 36. "We have indicated what appears to us to be the only permanent solution of the difficulties arising from the recent changes in the relative value of the precious metals, and the only solution which will protect this and other countries against the risks of the future."

Certain remedial suggestions of the authors of Part II are reprinted on page 26.

IX.

THE STRENGTH OF THE ENGLISH SILVER PARTY.

The gist of the report presented in Paris lies in the following :

BIMETALLIC LEAGUE.

"The object of the League is to urge upon the British Government the necessity of co-operating with other leading nations for the establishment, by international agreement, of the free coinage of gold and silver at a fixed ratio."

President, HENRY H. GIBBS.
Chairman of General Council, H. R. GRENFELL.

Vice Presidents:

The list of nearly 200 Vice Presidents is not reprinted here, as their names will be found among the prominent names in the Deputation of May 30.

Trustees of Guarantee Fund, HENRY H. GIBBS, S. SMITH, M.P., ABRAHAM HAWORTH, ROBERT BARCLAY, GILBERT BEITH.

Executive Council:
Chairman, ROBERT BARCLAY, Manchester.

John A. Beith, Manchester.
Thomas Bell, Whickham (Co. Durham).
Rt. Hon. Henry Chaplin, M.P.
Henry Coke, Liverpool.
Geo. B. Dewhurst, Manchester.
Geo. Handasyde Dick, Glasgow.
John S. Dods, Manchester.
R. L. Everett, Ipswich.
Frederick J. Faraday, Manchester.
J. C. Fielden, Manchester.

F. B. Forbes, London.
H. T. Gaddum, Manchester.
Robert Gladstone, Liverpool.
C. W. Gray, M.P.
Edward H. Greg, Manchester.
H. R. Grenfell, London.
J. H. Gwyther, London.
E. A. Hague, Manchester.
Frank Hardcastle, M.P., Bolton.
Ralph Heaton, Birmingham.
John Holliday, Manchester.

BIMETALLIC LEAGUE. 275

Sir W. H. Houldsworth, Bart., M.P.
Isaac Hoyle, M.P., Manchester.
Henry Lathbury, Manchester.
Samson S. Lloyd, London.
Capt. F. C. Loder-Symonds, Faringdon.
Charles Macdonald, Manchester.
Sir H. M. Meysey-Thompson, Bart.
Samuel Montagu, M.P., London.
John Muir, Glasgow.
Samuel Ogden, Manchester.
James Parlane, Manchester.
A. D. Provand, M.P., Manchester.
J. F. S. Rolleston, Leicester.
Edward Sassoon, London.
I. Seligman, London.
T. H. Sidebottom, M.P., Manchester.
T. C. Taylor, Batley.
John Thomson, Manchester.
William Westgarth, London.
Thomas Willson, Ryde, Isle of Wight.

Hon. Treasurer, ABRAHAM HAWORTH, Manchester.

Bankers: BANK OF ENGLAND, Manchester; CHARTERED BANK OF INDIA, AUSTRALIA, AND CHINA, Hatton Court, London, E. C.

Secretary, HENRY MCNEIL, F.S.S., Haworth's Buildings; 5 Cross street, Manchester.

Central Agricultural Committee: Offices, 2 Princes street, Great George street, Westminster, S. W.; Hon. Secs., RICHARD DAWSON and A. WESTON JARVIS, M.P.

Hon. Secretaries:

London, Carl Von Buch, M.A., 11 Queen Victoria street, E. C.
Glasgow, Wm. Ewing, 7 Royal Bank Place.
Bradford, J. M. McLaren, Canal Road.
Bolton, Lewis Haslam, Ravenswood.
Blackburn, John Hargreaves, Higher Bank.
Batley, T. C. Taylor, Sunny Bank.
Ipswich, R. L. Everett, Rushmere.
Brecon, W. S. Miller, Forest Lodge.
Chorley, A. C. Smethurst, Charnock House.
Newcastle-on-Tyne and District (Industrial Organizations), J. J. Harris, 83 Northbourne street, Newcastle-on-Tyne.
Oxfordshire and Berkshire, Captain F. C. Loder-Symonds, Hinton Manor, Faringdon, Berks.
Walsall, W. H. Duignan.
Southport, S. Hardman, 191 Lord street.
Congleton, A. C. Conder, Bath Vale Mill.
Birmingham, Frederick Ash, Snow Hill.
Bristol, J. H. Howell, Castle Green.
Swansea, Frederic S. Bishop, Glanrafon.

THE SILVER DEPUTATION
TO
THE MARQUIS OF SALISBURY, K.G.,
PRIME MINISTER,
AND TO
THE RIGHT HON. G. J. GOSCHEN, M.P.,
CHANCELLOR OF THE EXCHEQUER,
May 30, 1889.

The Right Hon. HENRY CHAPLIN, M.P., introduced the deputation.

Duke of Richmond and Gordon, K.G.
Duke of Portland.
Duke of Manchester, K.P.
Duke of Abercorn.
Marquis of Abergavenny, K.G.
Earl of Crawford and Balcarres.
Earl of Coventry.
Earl of Radnor.
Earl of Londesborough.
Lord Basing.
Lord Burton.
Lord Hindlip.
Lord Castletown.
Rt. Hon. Sir H. J. Selwyn Ibbetson, Bart., M.P.
Sir John Puleston, M.P.
J. Addison, Q.C., M.P.
R. G. Webster, M.P.
G. W. Balfour, M.P.
Sir Robert Jardine, Bart., M.P.
W. J. Beadel, M.P.
G. H. Bond, M.P.
Samuel Smith, M.P.
Isaac Hoyle, M.P.
Col. The Hon. F. C. Bridgman, M.P.
G. H. Finch, M.P.
Sir W. H. Houldsworth, Bart., M.P.
Sir Rainald Knightley, Bart., M.P.
Sir E. A. H. Lechmere, Bart., M.P.
Sir Lewis Pelly, K.C.B., K.C.S.I., M.P.

Earl of Erne, K.P.
Earl Stanhope.
Earl Manvers.
Earl Amherst.
Earl of Yarborough.
Earl Fortescue.
Lord Willoughby de Broke.
Lord Walsingham.
Lord Cheylesmore.
Lord Rowton.
S. Williamson, M.P.
Lt.-Col. Sandys, M.P.
T. Milvain, M.P.
T. Fielden, M.P.
J. Corbett, M.P.
W. Pomfret Pomfret, M.P.
Leonard Lyell, M.P.
Lord Henry Bruce, M.P.
Sir R. H. Paget, Bart., M.P.
H. Seton-Karr, M.P.
E. P. Mulhallen Marum, M.P.
Samuel Montagu, M.P.
Rt. Hon. E. Heneage, M.P.
Frank Hardcastle, M.P.
Wm. G. Mount, M.P.
A. Weston Jarvis, M.P.
Hon. J. S. Gathorne Hardy, M.P.
W. W. B. Beach, M.P.
Admiral R. C. Mayne, M.P.
A. D. Provand, M.P.
Ed. Hardcastle, M.P.
H. H. Howorth, M.P.
T. Roe, M.P.
Marquis of Granby, M.P

THE SILVER DEPUTATION. 277

Sir Roper Lethbridge, K.C.S.I., M.P.
Marquis of Carmarthen, M.P.
F. Seager Hunt, M.P.
H. Knatchbull-Hugessen, M.P.
Sir E. Birkbeck, Bart., M.P.
J. Pinkerton, M.P.
T. H. Sidebottom, M.P.
Hon. G. N. Curzon, M.P.
M. J. Stewart, M.P.
W. E. M. Tomlinson, M.P.
Col. Cornwallis West, M.P.
P. A. Muntz, M.P.
W. Sidebottom, M.P.
T. K. Tapling, M.P.

J. W. Maclure, M.P.
Sir J. E. Dorington, Bart., M.P.
Col. Saunderson, M.P.
J. Rankin, M.P.
George Howell, M.P.
C. W. Gray, M.P. (Chairman Central Chamber of Agriculture).
Major Rasch, M.P.
J. C. Lawrance, Q.C., M.P.
A. R. Heath, M.P.
Colonel Eyre, C.B., M.P.
Baron Dimsdale, M.P.
J. Bazley-White, M.P.
F. S. W. Cornwallis, M.P.

DELEGATES FROM CHAMBERS OF AGRICULTURE.

Banbury, W. J. Warner.
Berks and Ox, Wm. G. Mount, M.P. (Chairman).
Capt. Loder Symonds.
J. Thursby.
Thos. Wells.
Geo. Adams.
Arthur Harvey Thursby.
Bucks, Baron F. de Rothschild, M.P
Viscount Curzon, M.P.
Col. Liebert Goodall.
Col. R. Purefoy Fitzgerald.
Hon. Egerton Hubbard, M.P.
W. J. Whitehouse Griffin.
W. H. Grenfell.
Canterbury, W. Nethersole.
Cirencester, H. J. Marshall.
Cowbridge, J. S. Gibbon.
Gloucestershire, B. St. John Ackers.
J. P. Sargeant.
W. Priday.
Hertfordshire, Baron Dimsdale, M.P.
Kendal, W. H. Wakefield.
Leicestershire, J. F. L. Rollestone (President).

Sir F. F. Fowke, Bart.
George Stratton, J.P.
Alderman T. Wright.
Thomas Nuttall.
R. F. Martin, J.P.
H. Clough Taylor.
W. Thorpe.
Lincolnshire, Earl of Yarborough.
A. R. Heath, M.P.
Col. Eyre, C.B., M.P.
J. C. Lawrance, M.P.
J. M. Richardson.
R. H. Ellis.
Theodore Trotter.
Maidstone, J. Bazley-White, M.P.
F. S. W. Cornwallis, M.P.
R. A. Hamilton Seymour.
Thomas Powell.
Capt. J. R. Isherwood.
Herbert Ellis.
Frank Woodham.
W. S. Forster.
Monmouthshire, Henry Williams.
Norfolk H. M. Upcher.
M. P. Squirrell.
Notts, W. N. Nicholson.

278   APPENDIX.

Sevenoaks, W. H. Crouk (Chairman).
Shropshire, W. T. Topham.
Somersetshire, G. Troyte Bullock.
Suffolk (East), Roger Kerrison.
R. L. Everett.
Rev. J. F. A. Hervey.
A. Harwood.
Suffolk (West), Duncan Parker (Chairman).
Swindon, Howard Horsell.

Tunbridge Wells, W. Roper.
Worcestershire, T. B. Woodward (President).
T. H. Crane.
Yorkshire (West Riding), W. Lipscomb (President).
Charles Clay (Vice-President).
Percy Tew, J.P.
George Newton.

CHAMBERS OF COMMERCE.

Liverpool.—Henry Coke (of David Sassoon & Co.), President of the Liverpool Chamber of Commerce and Director of the Mersey Docks and Harbor Board. Robert Gladstone (of Ogilvy, Gillanders & Co., Liverpool, London, Calcutta, and Rangoon), Director of the Liverpool Chamber of Commerce and Chairman of East India and China Trade Section. Hugh Lyle Smyth (of Ross, T. Smyth & Co., Corn Merchants).

Birmingham.—P. Albert Muntz, M.P., President of the Birmingham Chamber of Commerce. Henry W. Elliott (of Elliott's Metal Coy., Lt.), Chairman. J. William Tonks (of T. & J. Bragg, Australian and Indian Trade), Vice-Chairman. Ralph Heaton (of the Mint), Birmingham. Fredk. Ash (of Sutton & Ash, Iron Merchants). T. B. Chantrill (of Chantrill & Co., Russian Trade). W. Wyley Lord (of J. C. & W. Lord, Indian and South American Trade). Fredk. Blood (of Fredk. Blood & Co.).

Bolton.—Frank Hardcastle, M.P. James Booth, J.P., Vice-President. Fredk. W. Briscoe, Secretary.

Leith.—R. C. Munro Ferguson, M.P. (at the special request of the Chamber).

LABOR ORGANIZATIONS.

United Textile Factory Workers' Association.
Northern Counties' Amalgamated Association of Weavers.

Weavers' Association, Preston . .
Blackburn and District Power Loom Weavers' Association.
Bury Operative Weavers' Association and also the Bury Trades Council.

James Mawdsley, Chairman.
Thomas Birtwistle, Gen. Sec.
David Holmes, President.
W. H. Wilkinson, Secretary.
Joshua Barrows, Organizing Sec.
Luke Park, Secretary.
A. H. Cottam, President.
George Barker, Secretary.
Samuel Hardman, Secretary.

Amalgamated Association of Operative Cotton Spinners.	Wright Wood. James Robinson.
Do. Bolton Provincial.	J. T. Fielding, Secretary.
Do. Oldham Provincial	E. Mellor, President. Thos. Ashton, Secretary.
Oldham Provincial Card and Blowing Room Operatives.	George Silk, Secretary.
Manchester and Salford Trades Council.	M. Arrandale, President. C. Scholes, Treasurer. George D. Kelly, Secretary.
Newcastle and Gateshead Trades Council.	E. Girling, President. J. J. Harris, Secretary.
Bradford Trades Council.	R. Bower, President. S. Shaftoe, Secretary.
Wolverhampton Trades Council.	W. F. Mee, Secretary. W. Day.
Hyde and District Trades Council.	Samuel Fildes, President. W. Bancroft, Secretary.
Stalybridge Trades Council.	W. H. Carr, President. S. Sidebottom, Secretary.
Southport Trades Council . . .	W. Morland.
Preston Trades Council	J. Naylor, President. T. W. Carlisle, Secretary.

GENERAL.

Lord Alwyn Compton; Lord Algernon Lennox; Hon. Algernon Egerton; Sir Henry Hoare, Bart.; Lt.-Gen. R. H. Keatinge, V.C., C.S.I.; Lt.-Gen. Sir Andrew Clarke, G.C.M.G., C.B., C.I.E.; Sir Leppel H. Griffin, K.C.S.I.; Sir Hector M. Hay; Sir Henry Halford, Bart.; Sir T. C. Hope, K.C.S.I., C.I.E. (late Public Works Member of Viceroy's Council in India); Sir James Allport; Sir G. K. Rickards, K.C.B.; Rt. Hon. Sir Louis Mallet, C.B.; Sir Rivers Thompson, K.C.S.I. (late Lt.-Gov. Bengal); Sir Seymore Blane; Sir H. Meysey-Thompson, Bart.; Sir George Sitwell, Bart.; Sir Edward Sladen; Col. Sir W. D. Davies, K.C.S.I. (late Financial Com., Punjab); Hon. Sydney Greville; Henry H. Gibbs; H. R. Grenfell; Hon. G. Cuthbertson; Professor Foxwell, M.A.; Jacob Wilson; H. E. Busted, C.I.E. (late Assay Master, the Mint, Calcutta); J. Burnaby Atkins; Rev. H. F. Burnaby; G. Beaumont; Major Craigie (Sec. Central Chamber of Agriculture); Moreton Frewen; E. P. Squarey (President of the Institute of Surveyors); E. A. Cazalet; Col. Morland Hutton; J. H. Jefferies; John Musgrave (Chairman Whitehaven Joint Stock Bank, Chairman Whitehaven Harbour Trustees, Chairman Solway Junction Railway), Whitehaven; J. Henderson; Capt. Loder Symonds; H. Maule; H. J. Marshall; Rev. E. Penwarne-Wellings (Sinclairs); H.

Frost; Agnew Pope (Proprietor *British Trade Journal*); W. J. Moore; Donald Nicol, Argyllshire; C. D. Field (late Judge of the High Court, India); George Hollings; Herbert B. Praed (Banker, 189 Fleet Street, E.C.); W. J. Topham; R. H. Pinhey; George Stratton; Major-General Trevor; G. S. Sutherland; W. H. Grenfell (High Sheriff of Bucks); G. W. Allen, C.I.E.; George Cadell; S. B. L. Druce; J. Longworth; J. D. Rees; J. D. Ward; Henry Hoare; A. P. Sinnett; Major-General Sir W. Moore; A. C. Tupp (Bengal Civil Service); J. H. Manners Sutton, Newark; Geo. Handasyde Dick (of Geo. Handasyde Dick & Co., Glasgow, Manchester, and Bombay); Geo. Bull, Burton-on-Trent; Jas. T. Calvert, Sunderland; Colonel E. Bond, Chepstow; Jas. Hy. Howell (of Llewellyn & James), Bristol; Edward Langley, Bath; Ben. Elmy (of Elmy & Co.), Congleton, Cheshire; W. J. Humfreys, Hereford; C. M. Hutton Riddell (of Samuel Smith & Co., Bankers), Newark; W. H. Duignan (of Duignan & Elliott, Chairman of the Cannock Agricultural Co., Limited), Walsall; Ely Andrew (Chairman of J. Andrew & Sons, Limited), Ashton-upon-Lyne; Richard Dawson (late M.P., Leeds); H. Mallaby Deeley, Chester; Richard Shaw; Joseph Lees (of Lees Brothers, Limited, Cotton Spinners). Oldham; Wm. Green, Birmingham; Councillor J. C. Laird, New-Castle-upon-Tyne; R. W. Granville Smith; Edwd. W. Wrigley (of Lees & Wrigley, Cotton Spinners), Oldham; Richard Williamson (of Williamson & Sons, Ship-owners), Maryport; H. Watson (of Rt. Watson & Sons, Limited, Manufacturers), Oswaldtwistle; A. W. Byron, Chesterfield; Alfred Hickman (Ironmaster and Colliery Owner), Wolverhampton; T. F. Firth, Heckmondwike (Vice-President of the Associated Chambers of Commerce); W. J. Cuthbertson, Annan, N.B.; Stephen Cocker (of Welch & Cocker, Cotton Manufacturers), Preston; Lewis Halsam (of John Halsam & Co., Bolton and Manchester, Cotton Manufacturers); W. R. Moss (Director of Crosses & Winkworth, Ltd.), Bolton; John P. Halliwell (Cotton Manufacturer), Darwen; James Eckersley (of Davies & Eckersley, Bleachers, Adlington, Lancashire); W. S. Miller (Alderman of Breconshire), Brecon; George Whittaker (Cotton Manufacturer), Accrington; James Pertwee, Chelmsford; James Christy, Chelmsford; William H. Goodwin, The Ferns, Lugwardine, Hereford; Francis C. Clark, Winchester.

LONDON.

Edward Sassoon (of David Sassoon & Co.); James Greig (of A. Blockey, Greig & Co., Discount Brokers); Hermann Schmidt (Discount Broker); Henry C. Hayter (of Hayter & Hayter, Woollen Manufacturers); Wm. Westgarth (of W. Westgarth & Co.), Chairman of Australian Trade Section of the London Chamber of Commerce; Oscar von Ernsthausen (formerly of Ernsthausen & Co., London and Calcutta); F. Eisenlohr (of Ernsthausen & Co., London and Calcutta); E. Howley Palmer (of Dent

THE SILVER DEPUTATION. 281

Palmer & Co.), Director of the Bank of England; Reuben Sassoon; Alfred L. Cohen; Ernest Noel; J. V. L. Wells (of J. W. Laud & Co.); Thomas Hanbury (late Bower, Hanbury & Co., Shanghai); Neptune Blood, Stock Exchange; R. S. Gundry; W. Stewart Young, and at Hong-Kong; J. T. Denniston, Secretary Mexican Railway Company; Wm. Paterson (of Paterson & Simons, and at Singapore), Chairman of the Chartered Bank of India, and of the London, Paris, and American Bank, Vice-Chairman of the India and China Section of the London Chamber of Commerce; J. Howard Gwyther (Managing Director, Chartered Bank of India, Australia, and China); W. W. Cargill, Director of New Oriental Bank Corporation; L. R. C. Boyle, ditto; G. H. Tod-Heatly, ditto; R. T. Rohde (New Oriental Bank Corporation); E. De Wael (of G. Allard, Banker); Ernest Seyd; S. Ezekiel (of Messrs. David Sassoon & Co.); C. von Buch; A. L. Capput; W. G. Cuthbertson; J. R. Tennant; Wm. Barclay; Col. C. H. T. Marshall; Henry May; Hon. G. T. Maitland.

MANCHESTER.

John A. Beith (of Beith, Stevenson & Co., Manchester and Glasgow, Director, Manchester Chamber of Commerce, and Director of the Mersey Docks and Harbor Board); Wm. Thos. Rothwell; H. T. Gaddum (of H. T. Gaddum & Co., Silk Merchants, &c.); H. Lathbury (of Lathbury & Co.); John Holliday (of Farbridge, Holliday & Co., of Manchester, Glasgow, Hong Kong, Shanghai and Manila, Director of the Manchester and County Bank); J. S. Dods (of Dods, Ker & Co., and Calcutta); F. J. Faraday; Samuel Ogden (of S. Ogden & Co., Chairman of the Old Silkstone and Dodworth Coal and Iron Co., Director Manchester Chamber of Commerce); James Whitehead; Chas. Macdonald (of Macdonald, Miller & Co., and late President of the Bombay Chamber of Commerce); Ed. H. Greg (of Robt. Greg & Co., Cotton Spinners and Manufacturers); A. C. Smethurst; Alexander C. Carus; Henry McNiel.

BLACKBURN.

L. Wilkinson, of Wilkinson & Son, Cotton Manufacturers; Richard Shaw, of R. & J. Shaw, Cotton Manufacturers; E. J. Ainsworth, of J. Ainsworth & Sons, Cotton Manufacturers; Thos. Longworth, of Solomon Longworth & Sons, Cotton Spinners and Manufacturers; Arthur Longworth, ditto; John Hargreaves, Cotton Manufacturer; Jonas Hindle, of Edw. Briggs & Co., Cotton Spinners, of Blackburn and Padiham; J. H. Hartley, of Hartley Bros., Cotton Spinners, Blackburn and Preston; Robert Clayton, of H. & T. Clayton, Cotton Manufacturers; Rich. Greenwood, of Greenwood Bros., Cotton Manufacturers; Wm. Kay, of Wm. Kay, Sons, Cotton Waste Dealers; and others.

X.

THE MONETARY CONGRESS OF THE FRENCH EXPOSITION (1889).

Official Delegates.

ENGLAND.—Delegates of the British Government : Hon. C. W. Frementle, C. B., Deputy Master of the Mint, and G. H. Murray, Esq., of the Treasury.

ARGENTINE REPUBLIC.—Delegate Extraordinary of the Argentine Republic: M. Pellegrini, Vice-President of the Republic; and Delegate of the Argentine Commission, M. Leon Walls.

BELGIUM.—Delegate of the Belgium Commission: M. Georges de Laveleye, Editor of the *Moniteur des interests materiels*.

BOLIVIA.—Delegate of the Bolivian Government : M. Felix Avelino Aramayo.

BRAZIL.—Delegate of the General Brazilian Commission at the Exposition : M. Eduardo da Silva Prado.

CHILI.—Delegate of the Government of Chili : M. Carlos Morla Vicuna, Secretary to the Legation of Chili in France.

DENMARK.—Delegate of the Government: M. Levy, Director of the National Bank of Copenhagen.

DOMINICAN REPUBLIC.—Delegate of the Government: M. Isidore Mendel, Ex-President of the Chamber of Commerce of Santo Domingo, and Ex-President of the Commercial Bank of Santo Domingo.

SPAIN.—Delegate of the Spanish Commission at the Exposition : Don Juan Navarro Reverter, Engineer, Deputy in the Cortez, and M. Joaquin Lopez Puygcerver, Ex-Minister, the Deputy in the Cortez.

GREECE.—Delegate of the Greek Commission at the Exposition : M. Antoine Vlasto.

HOLLAND.—Delegate of The Netherlands Commission : M. J. Freiwald, President of the Executive Netherlands Committee at Paris.

ITALY.—Delegates of the National Italian Committee : MM. L. Luzzatti, Deputy of the Italian Parliament, and Gentili di Giuseppe, Count of Fantoni.

JAPAN.—Delegate of the Government of Japan : M. Count Tanaka, Minister Plenipotentiary of Japan to Paris.

MEXICO.—Delegates of the Government of Mexico : MM. Antonio del Castillo, Engineer, and Gilberto Crespo.

MONACO (Principality).—Delegate of the Government : M. Jolivot, Member of the Council of State.

SALVADOR (Republic.)—Delegate : M. S. Badel.

About 175 names were on the list of members of the Congress.

LIST OF CONGRESSES,

Held under the auspices of the Ministry of Commerce, Industry, and Colonies, at the Universal Exposition of 1889, with date and duration.

Accidents to Workmen, Sept. 9-14.
Æronautics, July 31 to Aug. 3.
Agriculture, July 3-11.
Alcoholism (study of questions relative to), July 29-31.
Anthropology, Criminal, Aug. 10-17.
Anthropology and Archæology, Prehistoric, Aug. 19-26.
Architects, June 17-22.
Baking and Bread Making, June 28 to July 2.

Bibliography of Mathematical Sciences, July 16-26.
Blind, for the Amelioration of the Condition of, Aug. 5-8.
Carrier-Pigeon Fanciers, July 31 to Aug. 3.
Celestial Photography, ———.
Chemistry, July 29 to Aug. 3.
Chronometry, Sept. 2-9.
Colonies (study of questions relating to), ———.

Commerce and Industry, Sept. 22-28.
Dentistry, Sept. 1-7.
Dermatology and Syphilography, Aug. 5-10.
Dwellings (Cheap), June 26-28.
Electricians, Aug. 24-31.
Ethnographical Science, ———.
For the Protection of Works of Art and Monuments, June 24-29.
Geographical Sciences, Aug. 6-12.
Homœopathy, Aug. 21-23.
Horticulture, Aug. 16-21.
Hydrology and Climatology, Oct. 3-10.
Hygiene and Demography, Aug. 4-11.
Instruction, Primary, Aug. 11-19.
Instruction, Secondary and Higher, Aug. 5-10.
Instruction, Technical, Commercial, and Industrial, July 8-10.
Intervention of the State in Contracts of Labor, July 1-4.
Intervention of the State in Emigration and Immigration, ———.
Intervention of the State in the Price of Food, July 5-10.
Irrigation, Sept. 22-27.
Joint Stock Companies, June 12-19.
Life-Saving, June 12-15.
Mechanical Appliances, Sept. 16-21.
Medical Jurisprudence, ———.
Medicine, Mental, Aug. 5-10.
Medicine, Veterinary, Sept. 19-24.
Methods of Construction, Sept. 9-14.
Metrology, Sept. 19-25.
Mines and Metallurgy, Sept. 2-11.
Monetary, Sept. 11-14.
Officers and Non-Commissioned Officers of Fire Brigade, Aug. 27-28.
Otology and Laryngology, Sept. 16-21.
Peace, ———.
Photography, Aug. 6-17.
Physical Exercise in Education (for the encouragement of), —— 15 to ——.
Popular Traditions, ———.
Profit-Sharing, July 16-19.
Property, Industrial, Aug. 3- —.
Property, Real, Study of the Transfer of, Aug. 8-14.
Property, Rights of, in Works of Art, July 25-31.
Psychology, Physiological, Aug. 5-10.
Public Charities, July 28 to Aug. 4.
Relief Work in Time of War, July 28 to Aug. 4.
River and Harbor, Oct. 7- —.
Sabbath Observance, ———.
Society of Literary Men, June 17-27.
Statistics, ———.
Stenography, Aug. 4-11.
Stores, Co-operative, Sept. 8-12.
Therapeutics, Aug. 1-5.
Trades Unions, July 11-13.
Unification of Time, ———.
Women (Works and Institutions of) ———.
Zoölogy, Aug. 5- —.

APPENDIX TO CHAPTER VII.

CURRENCY PROPOSALS OF D. RICARDO.

From " OBSERVATIONS on some passages in an article in the *Edinburgh Review*, on the depreciation of paper currency; also suggestions for securing to the public a currency as invariable as gold, with a very moderate supply of that metal." (1808.)

For the reader's convenience I have italicized passages which state the author's views about silver.

I will also give an outline of the system of money then in force.

The legal ratio was 15.21 to 1. Gold and silver coin were unlimited legal tender, but above 25£ silver was legal tender, not by tale but by weight. The stock had long consisted of gold—which, at that ratio, was the "cheaper money"—with a small amount of worn and defaced change. As a provisional measure, the coinage of silver had been stopped by act of Parliament in 1798, just after the suspension of specie payments.

" Let the Bank of England be required by Parliament to pay (if demanded), all notes above 20£, and no other, at their option, either in specie, in gold standard bars, or in foreign coin (allowance being made for the difference in its purity) at the English Mint value of gold bullion, viz., 31.17s. 10 one-half d. per ounce, such payments to commence at the period recommended by the committee.

The privilege of paying their notes as above described might be extended to the Bank for three or four years after such payments commenced, and if found advantageous, might be continued as a permanent measure. Under such a system the currency could never be depreciated below its standard price, as an ounce of gold and 31.17s. 10½d. would be uniformly of the same value. By such regulations we should effectually prevent the amount of small notes from being withdrawn from circulation, as no one who did not possess to the amount of £20 at least of such small notes could exchange them at the Bank, and even then bullion, and not specie, could be obtained for them. Guineas might, indeed, be procured at the mint for such bullion, but not till after the delay of some weeks or months, the loss of interest for which time would be considered as an actual expense, an expense which no one would incur whilst the small notes could purchase as much of every commodity as the guineas which they represent. Another advantage attending the establishment of this plan, would be to prevent the useless labor which, under our system previously to 1797, was so unprofitably expended on the coinage of guineas, which, on every occasion of an unfavorable exchange (we will not inquire by what caused), were consigned to the melting-pot, and, in spite of all prohibitions, exported as bullion. It is agreed by all parties that such prohibitions were ineffectual, and that whatever obstacles were opposed to the exportation of the coin, they were with facility evaded.

An unfavorable exchange can ultimately be corrected only by an exportation of goods, by the transmission of bullion, or by a reduction in the amount of the paper circulation. The facility, therefore, with which bullion would be obtained at the Bank cannot be urged as an objection to this plan, because an equal degree of facility actually existed before 1797, and must exist under any system of bank payments. Neither ought it to be urged, because it is now no longer questioned by all those who have given the subject of currency much of their consideration, that not only is the law against the exportation of bullion, whether in coin or in any other form, ineffectual, but that it is also impolitic and unjust; injurious to ourselves only, and advantageous to the rest of the world.

The plan here proposed appears to me to unite all the advantages of every system of banking which has been hitherto adopted in Europe. It is in some of its features similar to the banks of deposit of Amsterdam and Hamburg. In these establishments bullion is always to be purchased from the Banks at a fixed invariable price. The same thing is proposed for the Bank of England; but in the foreign banks of deposit they have actually in their coffers as much bullion as there are credits for bank money in their books. Accordingly there is an inactive capital as great as the whole amount of the commercial circulation. In our Banks, however, there would be an amount of bank money under the name of bank notes as great as the demand of commerce could require. At the same time there would be more inactive capital in the bank coffers than that fund which the Bank should think it necessary to keep in bullion to answer those demands which might occasionally be made on them. It should always be remembered, too, that the Bank would be enabled, by contracting their issues of paper, to diminish such demands at pleasure. In imitation of the Bank of Hamburg, who purchase silver at a fixed price, it would be necessary for the bank to fix a price below the Mint price, at which they would at all times purchase, with their notes, such gold bullion as might be offered to them.

The perfection of banking is to enable a country, by means of a paper currency (always retaining its standard value), to carry on its circulation with the least possible quantity of coin or bullion. This is what this plan would effect. *And with a silver coinage on just such principles, we should possess the most economical and the most invariable currency in the world.* The variations in the price of bullion, whatever demand there might be for it on the Continent, or whatever supply there might be poured in from the mines in America, would be confined within the prices at which the Bank bought bullion and the Mint price at which they sold it. The amount of the circulation would be adjusted to the wants of commerce with the greatest precision; and if the Bank were for a moment so indiscreet as to overcharge the circulation the check which the public would possess would speedily admonish them of their error. As for the country Banks, they must, as now, pay their notes, when demanded, in Bank of England notes. This would be a sufficient security against the possibility of their being able too much to augment the paper circulation. There would be no temptation to melt the coin, and consequently the labor which has been so uselessly bestowed by one party in recoining what another party found it their interest to melt into bullion would be effectually saved. The currency could neither be clipped nor deteriorated, and would possess a value as invariable as gold itself, the great object which the Dutch had in view, and which they most successfully accomplished by a system very like that which is here recommended.

From "*Proposals for an Economical and Secure Currency;* with Observations on the Profits of the Bank of England as they regard the public and the proprietors of bank stock." Second edition. London, 1816.

SECTION III.

While a standard is used, we are subject to only such a variation in the value of money as the standard itself is subject to; but against such variation there is no possible remedy, and late events have proved that, during periods of war, when gold and silver are used for the payment of large armies distant from home, those variations are much more considerable than has been generally allowed. This admission only proves that gold and silver are not so good a standard as they have been hitherto supposed—that they are themselves subject to greater variations than it is desirable a standard should be subject to. They are, however, the best with which we are acquainted. If any other commodity less variable could be found, it might very properly be adopted as the future standard of our money, provided it had all the other qualities which fitted it for that purpose; but while these metals are the standard, the currency should conform in value to them, and whenever it does not, and the market price of bullion is above the mint price, the currency is depreciated. This proposition is unanswered, and is unanswerable.

Much inconvenience arises from using two metals as a standard of our money; and it has long been a disputed point whether gold or silver should by law be made the principal or sole standard of money. In favor of gold it may be said, that its greater value under a small bulk eminently qualifies for a standard in an opulent country; but this very quality subjects to greater variations of value during periods of war or extensive commercial discredit, when it is often collected and hoarded, and may be urged as an argument against its use. *The only objection to the use of silver as the standard is its bulk, which renders it unfit for the large payments required in a wealthy country; but this objection is entirely removed by the substituting of paper money as the general circulation medium of the country. Silver, too, is much more steady in its value, in consequence of its demand and supply being more regular; and as all foreign countries regulate the value of their money by the value of silver, there can be no doubt that, on the whole, silver is preferable to gold as a standard, and should be permanently adopted for that purpose.*

SECTION IV.

In the next session of Parliament, the subject of currency is again to be discussed; and, probably, a time will then be fixed for the resumption of cash payments, which will oblige the Bank to limit the quantity of their paper till it conforms to the value of bullion. * * *

If the Bank should be again called upon to pay their notes in specie, the effect would be to lessen greatly the profits of the Bank without a correspondent gain to any other part of the community. If those who use one and two, and even five-pound notes, should have their option of using guineas, there can be little doubt which they would prefer; and thus, to indulge a mere caprice, a most expensive medium would be substituted for one of little value.

Besides the loss to the Bank, which must be considered as a loss to the community, general wealth being made up of individual riches, the State would be subjected to the useless expense of coinage, and on every fall of the exchange, guineas would be melted and exported.

To secure the public against any other variations in the value of the currency than those to which the standard itself is subject, and, at the same time, to carry on the circulation with a medium the least expensive, is to attain the most perfect state to which a currency can be brought, and we should possess all these advantages by subjecting the Bank to the delivery of uncoined gold or silver at the mint standard and price, in exchange for their notes, instead of the delivery of guineas; by which means paper would never fall below the value of bullion without being followed by a reduction of its quantity. To prevent the rise of paper above the value of bullion, the Bank should be also obliged to give their paper in exchange for standard gold at the price of £3 17s. per ounce. Not to give too much trouble to the Bank, the quantity of gold to be demanded in exchange for paper at the mint price of £3 17s. 10½d., or the quantity to be sold to the Bank at £3 17s. should never be less than twenty ounces. In other words, the Bank should be obliged to purchase any quantity of gold that was offered them, not less than twenty ounces at £3 17s. per ounce,* and to sell any quantity that might be demanded at £3 17s. 10½d. While they have the power of regulating the quantity of their paper, there is no possible inconvenience that could result to them from such a regulation.

The most perfect liberty should be given, at the same time, to export or import every description of bullion. These transactions in bullion would be very few in number, if the Bank regulated their loans and issues of paper by the criterion which I have so often mentioned—namely, the price of standard bullion, without attending to the absolute quantity of paper in circulation.†

---

* The price of £3 17s. here mentioned, is, of course, an arbitrary price. There might be good reasons, perhaps, for fixing it either a little above or a little below. In naming £3 27s. I wish only to elucidate the principle. The price ought to be so fixed as to make it the interest of the seller of gold rather to sell it to the bank than to carry it to the mint to be coined. The same remark applies to the specified quantity of twenty ounces. There might be good reason for making it ten or thirty.

† *I have already observed that silver appears to me to be the best adapted for the standard of our money. If it were made so by law, the Bank should be obliged to buy or sell silver bullion only.* If gold be exclusively the standard, the Bank should be required to buy or sell gold only; but if both metals be retained as the standard, as they now by law are, the Bank should have the option which of the two metals they would give in exchange for their notes, and a price should be fixed for silver rather under the standard, at which they should not be at liberty to refuse to purchase.

THE END.

XI.

MR. GOSCHEN'S PROPOSALS, WITH AN INTRODUCTORY STATEMENT CONCERNING THE PROGRESS MADE IN ENGLAND.

Mr. Goschen's Proposals, as set forth in his address before the London Chamber of Commerce, December 2, 1891, embody the first actual Governmental step forward made since the last International Conference (1881-2). They are, however, only a renewal of the conditional offer communicated on the part of the Gladstone Government to the Conference in Paris in 1881 (see pp. 21, 71-2, 297), and it may therefore seem that after all no progress has been made in these ten eventful years. But this inference, however plausible, would be a mistake.

A brief analysis will outline the decade's progress in the practical politics of silver, and show that in spite of appearances "the world does move" in this respect.

First we must take account of a retarding influence, which in detail comes home to every one's personal experience, but which few take the trouble to appreciate as applied on a grand scale, to the conduct of nations. Our great project of getting silver remonetized in Europe has its theoretical side ; opening a vista for argument of almost limitless extent. The subject is in fact so extensive that, if dealt with excursively in a pedantic spirit, it may be made to resemble a morass of problems with lakes here and there that have no bottom. What the outcome may be for those who would sound all depths is suggested by the well-known saying that couples the currency with love and religion as the favorite path by which feeble or overwrought minds fall into lunacy.

On the other hand, our project of joint action of nations is practical, a project of action. It is action on a large scale, it is true, a union not of individuals, nor of corporations, but of nations. Still it is only joint action to obtain a common benefit. To bring it about, requires of course a certain effort. Brains and will must be bent to the work, trouble must be taken, travelling be done, the peculiar interests of various countries studied, the "personal equation" of their controlling forces learned, and conversations must go on in the several languages required, etc., etc. All this is within the means at hand. The agents can be put in the field, provided existing powers and resources are employed to that end.

But initiative is necessary; if a thing is to be done, it will not do itself; some one must do it. This "some one" ought to be a government—for who else will take the trouble? If the governments do not all rush forward to transact the necessary business of establishing their silver syndicate, then one or more of them must begin the work, and maintain it consistently, and upon that the history of the decade will depend.

Now there has been no such persevering initiative!

In 1878 the United States did indeed take the lead by Act of Congress, and its proposals were made to delegates of the nations and recommended by arguments which, I may be allowed to say, were not unequal to the occasion. Important events occurred in sequence. In 1879 Germany stopped her sales of silver, and in 1881 France joined us in calling another Conference in Paris to promote joint action for free coinage of silver. England and Germany having offered substantial aid on condition that the others should open their mints, the Conference was postponed, looking to the prosecution of the project through personal negotiation, which should prepare a practical scheme and get it agreed to at least provisionally or partially, in which case the Conference might be reconvoked, for such further discussion as might be needed, or for purposes of ratification.

That scheme has never been devised! Why not? The obvious reason is *that at this point, in 1882, the United States Government suddenly dropped the subject!*

As the Resolutions of the Conference will indicate (they are reprinted on pp. 260-1-2), it was expected that informal conferences of proficient representatives, meeting in the different capitals where they could talk directly with men in power, and with the frankness of privacy discuss new points as they arose, would be productive of results which were in fact lacking to a formal Conference of Delegates in which speeches were in order, and which, as it met only in one place, could be convenient only to a few persons, and could not remain long in session awaiting discussions by letter between nonproficient officials remote each from the other.

But the expectation was never brought to the test of reality, for the United States suddenly abandoned the project altogether.

The result may be easily imagined. France lapsed into her former indifference. After this ground had been taken by the Great Powers who had invited the others to join, no lesser Power could move, for to do that was to invite a rebuff, and no Power can afford to be careless in matters relating to its financial standing.

What were the individuals in Europe who took an interest in silver, to do? As the only champions left in Europe of the project thus indefinitely postponed by the nation which had proposed it, they were, so to speak, turned out into the swamp to debate the Silver Question on general principles. It was under these circumstances that it came to pass that in England the Silver Movement remained so long in the academic stage. Some incidents of this situation I have satirized under the name of "Bemuddleism," as will appear on page 160.

In time, however, the unsteadiness of the money metals brought its revenges. The Government was finally moved to call a Royal Commission to investigate a Depression of Trade and Industry (1884-6), which had been aggravated, admittedly I might say, by the non-adoption of the project to restore Silver as Money. Later, the subject grew rapidly into notice with the

Commission on Gold and Silver appointed in 1886. The outcome of the latter (Nov., 1888), being in substance favorable to silver, the time drew near when the Silver Party in England were at length enabled to exercise themselves in the evolutions of practical politics.

Of their efforts, Mr. Goschen's attitude, assumed December 2d, 1891, is one result, the first overt result, so to speak. It was evidently a preordained move in their campaign that the Tory Government should (upon warrant of public opinion) be induced to march forward to the position assumed by the Liberal Government in 1881. To be sure, neither Mr. Gladstone nor his lieutenants had made sign that they felt committed by what happened in 1881. Indeed, the incident of 1881 had quite passed from memory, and its significance was ignored by those who remembered the bare fact. So far as the Liberal party chiefs were concerned, the efforts made by the Liberal silver men to interest them in the Movement had all along failed. But education was going on, and the "record" promised the Liberal an advantage in any constituency interested in silver (see page 317)—an advantage which the Conservative could not allow them to retain.

The result, then, was an achievement of the Silver Party, a matter of management.

The future, likewise, is a matter of management. The advantageous position gained is a fulcrum for leverage, to push farther. Here, then, is progress, and in this direction for the future lies the "way out"!

MR. GOSCHEN'S PROPOSALS.

EXTRACTS FROM THE SPEECH OF THE CHANCELLOR OF THE EXCHEQUER ON THE METALLIC RESERVE OF THE BANK OF ENGLAND AND A METHOD OF INCREASING IT BY THE ISSUE OF ONE-POUND NOTES, BEFORE THE LONDON CHAMBER OF COMMERCE AT A SPECIAL GENERAL MEETING DECEMBER 2, 1891. SIR JOHN LUBBOCK, M.P., IN THE CHAIR, AND ABOUT 750 PERSONS PRESENT.—FROM THE LONDON "TIMES," DEC. 31, 1890.

You will observe I have made no allusion to the 10s notes. I took such pains as I could to ascertain whether the 10s notes would or would not be acceptable to the community at large, and the result I arrived at was this—that they would be extremely unpopular in most parts of the country, but that there was one part of the country—Lancashire—where they would value the 10s notes, not entirely on account of the note itself, but because of its being, at all events, some recognition of silver performing a part in the currency. It is from that point of view that they value the 10s note. It would not have increased the use of silver much, for it would have been necessary to hold only a very small portion of silver against these notes if they were issued. It was however considered a valuable recognition, and in telling you that I feel that I could not recommend, after the evidence I have had, the adoption of 10s notes, at all events until we have had very considerable experience of the 1£ notes: at the same time my dropping that part of my plan must not lead any one to suppose that I recede in any way from the position which I have always maintained of being anxious to see the use of silver extended as far as it was possible to be done under our existing system. I have done what I could to increase the use of silver. There is a section in the country who are showing a growing interest in the silver question that cannot be ignored.

They may ask this: If you will not do what we want—namely, make any real forward movement in establishing a parity between gold and silver—if you will not do that yourselves as a Government, would you do what you could in conference with other Governments to promote the use of silver in those other countries by offering as much as you can do without an abandonment of your own principles? Well, I think that that is a demand that may be made now, but which has not been made for the first time. It was made in 1881, and at that time a Monetary Conference was held, at which Sir Charles Fremantle and another gentleman represented this Government, and they were authorized to make this declaration to the Conference: That if the Mints of France, the United States, and other countries were open to the free coinage of silver, the Bank of England should be asked to act upon that portion of the Bank Charter Act which enables it to hold a portion of its bullion in silver. The Bank acceded at that time to that request, and the result was a letter, which I will read, from the Secretary to the Treasury to the Bank of England. It was as follows:

TREASURY CHAMBERS, *July* 1, 1881.

GENTLEMEN:

I am directed by the Lords Commissioners of Her Majesty's Treasury to acknowledge the receipt of your letter of the 30th ultimo, in which you state that the Bank Court see no reason why an assurance should not be conveyed to the Monetary Conference at Paris, if the Treasury think it desirable, that the Bank of England, agreeably with the Act of 1844, will be always open to the purchase of silver, provided that the Mints of other countries return to such rules as would ensure the conversion of gold into silver and silver into gold.

My Lords are of opinion that such an assurance is desirable, provided always that it be understood that the silver-using countries are to permit a free coinage of silver; and, as they note the opinion of the Bank Court that the exercise of that power by the Bank would not involve a risk of infringing the principle of the Act of 1844, they have communicated a copy of your letter to the Secretary of State for Foreign Affairs, and have requested him to convey to the Monetary Conference the intimation that the Bank of England, agreeably with the Act of 1844, but under the condition which you describe, will be open to the purchase of silver.

I have, &c.,
  (Signed)   F. CAVENDISH.
The Governor and Deputy Governor
 of the Bank of England.

This was the letter which was sent in 1881 from the Treasury to the Bank of England, and at that time the Government of India further suggested that if these countries would agree to open their Mints to silver, India would agree that so long as that system was maintained, she, too, would keep her Mint open to silver. Those were practically the only two things which this country could offer. I believe another point was mooted, namely, whether the legal-tender limit could be raised from 2£ to 5£, but I have no accurate information on that point. What I have got to say is this, that so far as the Government of 1881 went, we might safely go again if the necessity arose. I know there is considerable stir and anxiety upon the part of other countries. I know there is considerable desire for a conference. I am anxious for the increased use of silver, and personally—I am speaking without communication with my colleagues or the Bank of England on the subject—I have been always anxious to see the use of silver extended as far as it could be done compatibly with our general arrangements. I have stated this, and have stated it without knowing whether the Bank of England hold at present the same opinion that they held then; but I was anxious, as great interest has been expressed on this matter, to show how far I consider personally the Government might be able to go. And do not let it be thought that if such an arrangement were carried out, and the Bank of England were to hold a portion of their reserve in silver, on the express condition that other countries would keep their Mints open for silver as well as gold, it would be in any way in contradiction to the policy we all desire to see followed, that the stock of bullion in the Bank of England should be largely increased, because, by the adoption of free mintage in other countries, the pressure upon our stock of gold would be considerably avoided. The pressure upon our stock of gold naturally has been increased and intensified when other countries passed to a monometallic system instead of a bimetallic system. Therefore, there is no contradiction whatever in saying that on that condition, but, let it be fairly understood on that condition only, I do not see why the Bank of England might not be invited to repeat such a declaration as that of 1881.

* * * * * * *

Now I want you to understand this—probably you understand it, but I want the public to do so—that the Government as a government have no power to force any particular kind of circulation on the country. The letters I have received about the supply of silver, for example, have been innumerable. 'Why don't you let us have more silver?' Good heavens, I wish every one would take as much silver as possible, considering the enormous profit the Exchequer makes by it. We have untold sums at the Bank of England and at the Mint waiting to be circulated, anxious to travel [laughter], but they are not invited. I do not know who the persons are who do not extend the invitation to these silver coins to pay a visit to the country; but at all events some of those who spread the circulation of the country —all of them—have got far more power to determine what circulation there shall be in the country than the Government.

XII.

A TRACT ON SILVER POLICY.

DISTRIBUTED BY THE PARLIAMENTARY SILVER COMMITTEE TO MEMBERS OF PARLIAMENT (APRIL, 1891).

The paramount issue is whether stable parity of silver and gold is or is not a great interest of the British Empire.

Of course we think the affirmative is true, and indeed obviously true. We think that the importance of that interest is above and beyond all local preference or petty convenience as to yellow metal or white, or light or heavy, and as England is the leading centre of international trade and international investment, we believe that here is the spot where that truth ought to be recognized. How, then, does the case stand? How far is our affirmative recognized?

I find the difference of opinion a difference mainly of degree, not of kind. The chief point unsettled is *how much it is worth while for England* to do in order to obtain the benefits of stable parity.

Between the anti-silver policy looking to demonetization and the pro-silver policy looking to remonetization, the choice is made. England is in favor of the Restoration of Silver. Only as to the quota of action to be furnished in England—the United Kingdom's share in the sum of co-operation required—there are differences of opinion.

So far as the point of *principle* is concerned, that has been admitted by the Government of the United Kingdom. Its representation at the International Monetary

Conference of 1881 had that effect. England was in favor of the Restoration of Silver. I refer not merely to the attitude of India as presented by Sir Louis Mallet and Lord Reay. The communication by Sir Charles Fremantle to the effect that the Bank of England would hold silver bullion against its notes up to the legal limit (one part of silver to four of gold), in case free coinage of silver should be resumed by other countries, was a recognition on the part of the Government of its interest, and of its faith in the practicability of the measures proposed for the maintenance of parity, and that its interest was an important interest. I have further been informed that it was understood at the time, though not formally offered, that parliamentary authority would be asked and obtained, in case of need, to raise the legal-tender limit of English silver coin. The object of the offer made was to induce France and the United States to establish free coinage.

Are our friends fully aware of this? I fear they are not. To ensure attention I bring to your notice the accompanying letter (page 317), in which no less an authority in the Government of the United Kingdom than the Lords Commissioners of Her Majesty's Treasury will be found to have stated the point very clearly.

Unfortunately the quota of co-operation thus offered on the part of the United Kingdom was not regarded as sufficient to warrant the other Powers in undertaking the measures needed to establish the desired parity.

Then came the establishment of your League. What was its object? It was established with a practical end, namely, to bring about such co-operation of the United Kingdom as should be needed, an end to be attained by the obvious means of enlightening public opinion as to the degree of its importance. These offers already made were of course to be kept in validity. In marking out in its platform what was believed to be the proper quota for the United Kingdom, the League assigned no limit. They were for free coinage of silver, asking no less from England than from the United States and France. Such then was the task assumed by the League.

But little time elapsed after its foundation before events began to force themselves upon public attention which justified its views in a very practical way. The depression of trade and industry in Great Britain attained such depth as to necessitate a Royal Commission of inquiry, which in time gave way to a Royal Commission on Gold and Silver.

What was the result of all these years of discussion in which the League bore its share? The minimum result is to be found in the admission on the "gold side" (so called) of the Royal Commission; the maximum is to be found on the "silver side." Of the latter I need only say their ground was the ground of the League; that the degree of importance they assigned to this interest of the Empire was a very high one, and it was urged that diplomatic initiative of Her Majesty's Government be brought to bear to push joint action of nations to restore silver to general free coinage (Part III., section 36).

In estimating the attitude of the "gold side" of the Royal Commission account must naturally be taken of the strategic bearings of their position. Predispositions and presumptions, as well as prejudices, were in favor of inaction. Nothing was easier than to shrink from "a leap in the dark" without realizing that this leap was after all but a step from a bed to a carpeted floor. It was thus in spite of all temptations that they were willing to do what they did, and that was nothing less than to undertake a certain initiative in favor of silver.

What were the avowed objects in view? I find the purpose avowed to "relieve tension of the present situation." I also find the purpose avowed to prevent "an apprehended further fall in silver," and to keep its "value, relatively to gold, more stable." Here are purposes in sympathy with our own. But is there not, beyond and behind all this, implicitly present, though not avowed in plain terms, the very practical and diplomatic idea that if the joint action so recommended be set on foot, free coinage of both metals in other nations, and hence parity of the money metals, will be the result? I find that very practical and diplomatic idea to have been entertained in manner and form as set forth in the sequel to this paper.

I speak here seriously of what is suggested as well as of what is incisively avowed. I see in these suggestions the shadows of coming events, the arrival of which it is the business of reformers to hasten. The "London Times" states editorially to-day that "free coinage in the United States would fix the ratio all over the world," and yet you can remember the day when men were called "lunatics" in London for saying that Great Britain, France, and the United States together could accomplish that same result. But I have seen all along, from the very inception of the struggle against and for silver, the desire that some other nation should establish parity between the money of England and the money of India has been a potent factor in the *expression* of opinions as well as in their *formation*.

What then were the actual proposals made on the "gold side" of the Royal Commission? They lie in part within and in part outside of the range of the proposals made in 1881 to the representatives of the nations in Paris.

First, I mention their recommending *English initiative to bring about concerted action of nations.* This is beyond the position taken in 1881, for that position was taken not on the initiative of England, but upon the invitation of two other Powers. Thus we see the Royal Commission *in effect unanimously* recommended that *the Government should initiate a movement* (of one or the other kind) and actively promote joint action of nations. But while in respect to initiative this goes beyond the attitude of 1881, still, at the same time, the "gold side" of the Royal Commission by their statement of detail held themselves, in a sense, within the limit of 1881, because they seriously speak of using, I will not say a threat, but a recognized possibility, of stopping the coinage of silver in India, as an inducement to other Powers to act.

Their proposition "for relief of the tension of the existing situation" goes quite beyond the propositions of 1881. They propose small notes based on silver, issued either by the Treasury or the Bank, as a measure to be taken independently, a quota to be offered voluntarily, without demanding from other nations a *quid pro quo.*

In fine I ascertain that Lord Herschell and his colleagues stood in this position.

They repudiate the demonetization policy. On the contrary, they desire the Restoration of Silver to its former general legal equality with gold—provided it is accomplished by other nations, with only limited co-operation from England herself.

What is their upper limit of co-operation?

I fix it as follows:—

They were willing (*see* page 28, C)* that full legal-tender bank notes should be based on silver, in replacement of gold, to a limited amount (one part of silver to four of gold). (This means that, let us say, four million sovereigns are exported and so-and-so many million ounces of silver are imported.)

2. They indicate a willingness (*see* page 27, A) that the silver coinage should be increased. (Something has been done in this line, and thereby a profit of nearly a million sterling registered by the Treasury.)

3. They also indicate a willingness (*see* page 27, B) that the legal-tender limit of the silver coin be raised.

4. They recommend an issue of small notes based on silver bullion. (*See* page 29, D.) (That might be intended in part to take the place of the proposition as to the Issue Department bullion.)

5. *The proposed attitude of the Ministry referred to, their favorable disposition and initiative in promoting joint action with other nations,* may be held to have *all* these views as its background. (*See* passages italicized on pages 26–32.)

The next well-marked stage of *possible active co-operation above these* is the acceptance of a limited amount of silver coin as full legal tender in England. This, I assume, they reject, and of course *a fortiori* they reject free coinage of silver in England. (*See* page 30 and author's note.)

It is important to note, however, that there is a wide range for give and take between the last-mentioned stage of co-operation and the former. In each there is a question of *amount*.

I find nothing in the *principles of public policy* laid

* These page references are to the Appendix of the Tract, which is not reprinted.

down by Lord Herschell and his colleagues on the gold side which should prevent their consenting that the figures be raised to some extent.

For example, a relaxation of the present statutory bar to the proportion of silver bullion to be held in the Issue Department would be regarded in other countries as of first [importance. Suppose the law were relaxed, and silver in the Issue Department should be allowed not in the proportion of one to four, as at present, but as one to three or one to two. What harm would that do (from the point of view of the Commissioners) either to the Bank or the public? None at all! With silver "as good as gold" in Paris and in New York such a holding could bring no risk of suspending gold payments, and the maintenance of gold payments is the main point in view. If a silver fifth was safe in 1844 when there was no treaty and no identity of ratio between Paris and New York, why should not a silver third be safe with New York and Paris bound in alliance and uniformity?

I may also repeat here my statement that if the power of the Crown should be fully used by the Treasury to further that Restoration of Silver which Lord Herschell and his colleagues recognize as "the right direction," the holding of silver coin in England could be enormously increased without parliamentary action.

The questions you addressed me, then, as I define them, refer to the pro-silver movements recommended by Lord Herschell and his colleagues, going beyond, as well as including, the propositions of 1881.

I frankly say I am unable to see why the League should not, upon proper occasion, impress upon the Ministry and Parliament that the action thus recommended is but the minimum imposed by its duty upon the Government. I recall also that this position is naturally strengthened at the present time by the fact that the "tension" referred to has again asserted itself in unequivocal form.

In reference to the Royal Commission's view concerning the "tension of the present situation," in 1888, it is important to realize that the Baring crisis, though it came two years later, is corroboration absolute.

Of course this means no palliation of the business mistakes that led to the crisis, whether made in Argentina or in London. *Bad driving is bad driving, whatever the color of the horse.* Financiering can be reckless, whether its monetary instrument be gold, or silver, or paper, or the several kinds of money together, under divers conditions.

But in last November Buenos Ayres and London, and then in sympathy with London, all financial nerve-centres of the world, felt a "tension" of a particular kind. There was a tension which full compliance with the recommendations of the Commission would have allayed, an intense desire and need of laying hold, not merely of capital, but of cash, and not merely of cash, but of a particular kind of cash—the yellow kind. If the world's entire stock of money had been available where the pressure was hottest, there would have been elasticity instead of rigidity. It was this rigidity which sharpened the crisis, a crisis "whose gravity no fertile imagination could exaggerate," as Mr. Goschen has authoritatively observed, "a crisis which risked the supremacy of English credit, risked the transfer of business to other centres."

From this point of view it is plain that it would have been well for the City of London if the advice of the Royal Commission had been adopted by the Government at once in 1888 and after.

As for the future, the abnormal monetary conditions maintained by the doctrinaire anti-parity laws now in force are a standing danger. Of this the City is notified every time a little gold leaves the Bank. The notification may not be fully understood, but it is there.

While, then, the crisis owed its *existence* to bad business, its *gravity* in London was due, in important measure, to bad laws, to laws which had created an artificial rigidity, a sort of lop-sided and top-heavy system, whose purely gratuitous excrescences of the doctrinaire order enhance the normal risks of business. So this pet of the doctrinaires, the policy of preventing parity of moneys, has its revenges. When will the lesson be learned—the lesson presented by the spectacle of last November, "money" at 7 per cent in London, with a prospect of widespread ruin that would have devastated the land but for that rare phenomenon, a loan *in specie* from the Bank of France, *and yet at the same time millions sterling worth of specie were lying idle in Bombay and Calcutta, "money" being a drug there at less than 2 per cent!*

Further light may be thrown on the situation if we inquire what would be the effect to-day if the gold in Argentina could be brought to Europe, its place being taken by new silver coin of equal value. There are 11,000,000 (gold) dollars' worth of gold there—at least, so I am informed by a member of the Argentine Committee—mostly in the form of foreign coin.

What would be the effect of the transfer? It would take a load off the silver market, and a load off the gold market, and the banks would feel as if rain were descending after drought.

And yet there are naïve casuists who maintain the Argentine crisis has nothing to do with the silver and gold question!

Postscript.

Sir David Barbour's review of the Indian silver trouble (in his financial statement) is a renewal of testimony, from a former member of the Royal Commission, of most grave effect. It raises the question of the further demonetization of silver; it marks the present as a turning point in history. No co-operation being given as yet in Europe to second the late Act in relief of silver passed in Washington, it is not strange that the future should look dark in Calcutta. The silver that Roumania sold last summer is represented by a surplus in New York, still operative in cutting down the proceeds of Indian taxation! And how is it with the increasing gold accumulations in Russia? What of the promise of gold payments in Austria-Hungary, and gold payments in Persia? If such things are done or promised, why not then in India, seeing that America refuses free coinage for silver?

Sir David Barbour sees that the United States definitely refuse to make changes in their monetary system which would bring about an agio on gold or an undue efflux of it from the country. Having refused this from the start, and maintaining that refusal under conditions which now cut off all chance of yielding—the refusal has already gone so far that candidates marked out for the coming Presidential contest are regarded as pledged against the free coinage of silver (unless, of course, in union with Europe)—the alternatives left for the Indian Finance Minister's consideration seem to be only the following:

Either the pro-silver recommendations of the Royal Commission shall be adopted by the English Government (and by Parliament where necessary), and a co-operative movement of nations to restore silver set on foot—

Or events will take their onward course toward the rejection of silver and adoption of gold in India.

And then perhaps in China?

The consequences would be very serious, as Sir David Barbour recognizes. Most serious! Still, the situation is created not by India, but by the refusal of those in Westminster upon whom action is incumbent, to give sequence to the recommendations of a Royal Commission which made its Report more than two years ago, after more than two years' study.

But who is to suffer the terrible consequences that would follow a new series of fluctuations in the exchanges, and a new series of imperious drafts upon that stock of gold which the city of London now watches with such anxious eyes? *Who can suffer more than England?*

In 1878, when, during the Premiership of Lord Beaconsfield, Mr. Goschen attended the Conference on Silver and Gold convoked by the United States Government at Paris, his testimony was given to the importance of stopping the demonetization movement. It was then a publicly recognized interest of England to do this. Germany was then selling silver, and in other nations efforts were making to set new sales on foot. Germany stopped her sales not long after, and no sales were undertaken elsewhere. If Mr. Goschen's monitions in 1878 had this effect, is not the same tendency to be followed now? It would seem to be all the more justified "by the tension of the present situation."

I am in position to recall certain facts which bear rather closely upon that point. I refer to bright hopes that flourished, I had reason to think, in the hearts of leading men in those days, hopes which since have shown themselves *nil*. One hope was, that "poor nations" would take more silver, so that "rich nations" might use gold without suffering any disadvantage! Another hope was, that "other countries" would establish free coinage of silver, that they would establish Parity by a new Monetary Union, without England's doing anything more than to maintain silver in India.

These hopes to-day seem very naïve; there is simplicity about them which it is difficult to associate with grave and potent men. But they were very firmly held, and were, I believe, most effective in determining the attitude of governments in the early stages of discussion.

Now experience throws strange light upon these illusions. I observe that it is the so-called "poor" countries that get rid of silver money. The Bank of England would have been only too happy to get the gold that Russia received for silver sold in 1890. And yet Russia, whose official unit is the silver rouble, and whose paper régime indicates monetary weakness, would have been classed in 1878 among those nations predestined *not* to take gold. Instead of that her stock is becoming a large one. I have spoken of Roumania having exchanged silver for gold, and of the gold in Argentina; and as I speak of Argentina, so I might speak of Brazil, and of other countries beside.

As for other countries establishing free coinage, they have been waiting for many years for the English Government to recognize England's interest in joining them in that great work of common benefit. I should suppose late events would put a quietus upon the expectation that they will perform that task without England's co-operation. That expectation cannot reasonably survive the gold loan made in 1890 to the Bank of England by the Bank of France.

In general the mistakes that are made on these points in 1891 and after, are likely to receive attention they have hitherto missed. The pardon they could hitherto look to will hardly be accorded in the future.

APPENDIX OF THE TRACT.

THE ISSUE OF ENGLISH FULL LEGAL-TENDER NOTES ON A DEPOSIT OF SILVER BULLION, OFFERED BY MR. GLADSTONE'S GOVERNMENT TO OTHER NATIONS TO INDUCE THEM TO ESTABLISH FREE COINAGE OF SILVER.

Extract from "Return, Paris Monetary Conference, 1881," ordered to be printed by the House of Commons, August 19, 1881.

Twelfth Session. 6th July 1881.

Mr. Magnin [the Finance Minister of France] presided, and there were present the delegates of

Austria-Hungary,
Belgium,
Denmark,
Germany,
Great Britain, British India,
Greece,
Italy,
The Netherlands,
Portugal,
Russia,
Sweden,
Norway,
Switzerland,
United States of America, and
France.

* * * * * *

Mr. Fremantle read the following declaration:—

Declaration of the Delegate of Great Britain.

In pursuance of the announcement made to the Conference at last Saturday's session, I have the honor of making the following communication on behalf of my Government:—

OFFER BY MR. GLADSTONE'S GOVERNMENT. 315

The United States Minister at London, in the course of a conversation with Her Majesty's Secretary of State for Foreign Affairs, having expressed an opinion that it would be possible to arrive at an agreement between the other Powers on the monetary question if (*inter alia*) the Bank of England should agree to exercise the powers conferred on it by the Bank Charter Act of 1844 (7 & 8 Vict. c. 32, ss. 2 and 3), and if the Treasury would put a question to that effect to the bank directors, Lord Granville applied to that department, and through that channel obtained a reply from the bank directors. In this reply the bank declares its readiness to exercise the power above mentioned, *on condition that the Mints of other nations revert to the observance of rules ensuring the exchange of gold for silver, and of silver for gold, at a legal rate.**

Her Majesty's Government, having subsequently learned that Mr. Lowell's action was in no way the result of instructions from his Government, did not deem it proper to follow up the declaration of the Bank of England by communicating it to the Conference through its delegate.

A similar proposal having, however, within the last few days been submitted by the Ambassador of His Majesty the King of Italy at London, on behalf of his Government, Her Britannic Majesty's Government has promptly given it the respectful reception it will always accord to the representations of one of the great Powers of Europe.

I have, therefore, the honor of laying on the table of the Conference the exact words used by the Bank of England in the above-mentioned communication :—

---

* Not italicized in the original.

"The Bank Charter Act permits the issue of notes upon silver, but limits that issue to one-fourth of the gold held by the bank in the issue department.

"The purchase of gold bullion is obligatory and unlimited, the purchase of silver bullion is discretional and limited, the distinction being enforced by the necessity of paying all notes in gold on demand.

"The reappearance of silver bullion as an asset in the issue department of the Bank of England would, as is understood by the Foreign Office letter, depend entirely on the return of the Mints of other countries to such rules as would ensure the certainty of conversion of gold into silver and silver into gold. The rules need not be identical with those formerly in force; the ratio between silver and gold, and the charge for mintage, may both or either of them be varied, and yet leave unimpaired the facility of exchange, which would be indispensable to the resumption of silver purchases by a bank of issue whose responsibilities are contracted in gold.

"Subject to these considerations, the Bank Court are satisfied that the issue of their notes against silver, within the letter of the Act, would not involve the risk of infringing that principle of it which imposes a positive obligation on the bank to receive gold in exchange for notes, and to pay notes in gold on demand.

"The Bank Court see no reason why an assurance should not be conveyed to the Monetary Conference at Paris, if their Lordships think it desirable, that the Bank of England, agreeably with the Act of 1844, would be always open to the purchase of silver under the conditions above described."

EXTRACT FROM EXPLANATORY CORRESPONDENCE.*

ORDERED PRINTED AUG. 27, 1881.

TREASURY to BANK OF ENGLAND.

(11,504/81.)

Treasury Chambers, *July* 1, 1881.

GENTLEMEN,

I am directed by the Lords Commissioners of Her Majesty's Treasury to acknowledge the receipt of your letter of the 30th ultimo, in which you state that the Bank Court see no reason why an assurance should not be conveyed to the Monetary Conference at Paris, if the Treasury think it desirable, that the Bank of England, agreeably with the Act of 1844, will be always open to the purchase of silver, provided that the Mints of other countries return to such rules as would ensure the conversion of gold into silver and silver into gold.

My Lords are of opinion that such an assurance is desirable, provided always that it be understood that the silver-using countries are to permit a free coinage of silver;† and, as they note the opinion of the Bank Court that the exercise of that power by the Bank would not involve a risk of infringing the principle of the Act of 1844, they have communicated a copy of your letter to the Secretary of State for Foreign Affairs, and have requested him to convey to the Monetary Conference the intimation that the Bank of England, agreeably with the Act of 1844,

---

* Five pages are omitted here.
† Not italicized in original.

but under the condition which you describe, will be open to the purchase of silver.

I have, &c.,

(Signed)   F. CAVENDISH.

The Governor and Deputy Governor
of the Bank of England.

The further pages of the Appendix of the Tract are here omitted. Their titles are as follows:

THE PRO-SILVER RECOMMENDATIONS OF LORD HERSCHELL AND HIS COLLEAGUES ON THE "GOLD SIDE" OF THE ROYAL COMMISSION, BOTH INCLUDING AND ADDITIONAL TO THE QUOTA OF CO-OPERATION OFFERED TO OTHER NATIONS BY MR. GLADSTONE'S GOVERNMENT IN 1881.

EXTRACTS FROM THE FINAL REPORT OF THE ROYAL COMMISSION ON GOLD AND SILVER

The citations are from the Report of the "gold side" of the Royal Commission, sections 134, 135, 136, 137, 138, and are accompanied with a comment which seeks to bring out a veiled intent ascribed to the "Gold" members to promote the Restoration of Silver to general legal equality with gold by means of furthering the action of other nations, with only a limited quota of co-operation from England itself.

EXTRACT FROM AN EDITORIAL ARTICLE IN THE "LONDON TIMES," JANUARY 20, 1891.

EXTRACTS FROM SIR DAVID BARBOUR'S FINANCIAL STATEMENT FOR 1891-92.

XIII.

SILVER AND THE ENGLISH ELECTIONS.

I. Memorial of the Leaders of the Northern Operatives.

The Legislative Council of the United Textile Factory Workers Association on Silver issued the following declaration at the close of November, 1891 :—

The Council of this Association have for a considerable period given much attention to the effect upon the permanent interests of the textile industry of this country of the demonetization of silver, and consequent absence of a par of exchange between gold and silver moneys. The conclusion they have come to, which has been much strengthened by the events of the last twelve months, is that the prosperity of the trade —in some branches probably its very existence—is involved in the question. In the interest, therefore, of the operatives and others employed in the textile industry whom they represent, and whose well-being the Association has specially to safeguard, a clear duty is imposed upon them which they cannot and must not evade. That duty is to press by every legitimate means in their power upon those who have or seek any parliamentary influence the imperative necessity of insisting that Government and Parliament should at once seriously grapple with the evils of our present monetary system, and take such immediate steps as shall ensure the recognition of silver as standard money throughout the British Empire and between this and other nations. Whatever other question of importance may be before the country, the urgent need of this reform demands that it shall be promptly dealt with, and it is pressed upon this Council that they should, without loss of time, inform you that the circumstances connected with the trade and with the well-being of those employed in it render it imperative that the whole force—political and moral—of the industrial classes of this country shall be exercised to promote it to successful conclusion.

II. CORRESPONDENCE WITH CANDIDATES AT THE ROSSENDALE ELECTION.

The following is an extract from the *Manchester Courier* of January 21, 1892:

THE CURRENCY QUESTION.

The following correspondence has been passed between Mr. F. Birtwistle, Secretary of the United Textile Factory Workers, and the two candidates:

UNITED TEXTILE FACTORY WORKERS, EWBANK CHAMBERS,
17, ST. JAMES' STREET, ACCRINGTON, January 6, 1892.

DEAR SIR,—I beg to enclose a circular which, by instruction of our Legislative Council, has been sent to members of Parliament and candidates in the textile districts of the North of England.

The currency question is of vital importance to this district, and it will give great satisfaction to a large number of our members in the Rossendale division if we can advise them that, if returned to Parliament, you will give your support to the movement for the recognition of silver as standard money throughout the British Empire and between this and other nations.—Yours faithfully, T. BIRTWISTLE.

Sir Thomas Brooks.

CRAWSHAW HALL, RAWTENSTALL, January 13, 1892.

DEAR SIR,—Owing to so many engagements I regret I have been unable to reply to your letter earlier. Any movement which would be a real benefit to the commercial and industrial interests of the United Kingdom I would do anything in my power to aid, but the question to which your letter refers is such an abtruse question, and so involved in technical difficulties, that I have not yet had an opportunity of studying it so much as I should wish. I have observed, however, that this is a question to which Mr. Chaplin, Minister of Agriculture, has devoted and is devoting considerable attention, and also that Mr. Goschen himself regards it in a favorable light, and I feel sure that the result of their considerations will be to produce a plan which will mitigate, if not obviate, the present difficulties surrounding the matter, and to this end I shall be very glad to give my support.—Yours truly,

THOMAS BROOKS.

T. Birtwistle, Esq.

UNITED TEXTILE FACTORY WORKERS, EWBANK CHAMBERS,
17, ST. JAMES' STREET, ACCRINGTON, 15th January, 1892.

DEAR SIR,—I am much obliged for your favor of the 13th instant, from which I am glad to note that you appreciate the difficulties attendant on our present system of monetary laws, and that you will support the application to them of an effective remedy.

There is every reason to believe, from their public observations, that several members of the present Government regard favorably the remedy advocated by our United Textile Factory Workers Association and many other organizations, but we have found, from long experience that, however evidently desirable a reform may be, it is frequently necessary to bring some moral pressure upon whatever Government may be in power, and also on Parliament, in order to make sure that they will take prompt action.

We should therefore like to be able to assure our members in the Rossendale division that, if returned, you will press on Government and Parliament the views we support as necessary to our welfare, viz., the necessity of arranging for the opening of the leading Mints of the world for the free coinage of silver as well as gold at a fixed ratio. Our members will expect some information from us on this point, and I hope you will put us in a position to inform them that you are prepared to do so.—Yours faithfully, T. BIRTWISTLE.

Sir Thomas Brooks.

CRAWSHALL HALL, RAWTENSTALL, January 19, 1892.

DEAR SIR,—In further reply to your letter, although I am wishful to support your views, and think, if I am returned to Parliament, that I can be of some service in promoting them, you must kindly excuse my pledging myself further until I have had an opportunity of learning more on such an important subject.—Believe me, yours sincerely,

THOMAS BROOKS.

T. Birtwistle, Esq.

UNITED TEXTILE FACTORY WORKERS, EWBANK CHAMBERS,
17, St. James' Street, Accrington, January 20, 1892.

DEAR SIR,—I am in receipt of your favor of yesterday, and note you wish for further time for studying the currency question, but that in the meantime we are to take it that you are desirous of supporting the views advocated by our association on the subject, and that if returned to Parliament you would devote some service to promote them. Yours faithfully, T. BIRTWISTLE.

Sir Thos. Brooks.

XIV.

DEMONETIZATION IN GERMANY AND IN AUSTRIA-HUNGARY.

An Act of the German Reichstag introduced by Count Caprivi November 7, 1891, and passed in February, 1892, authorizes the Government to retire the "Dollars of the Union," one-thaler and two-thaler pieces coined in Austrian Mints under the Coinage Treaty of Vienna of 1857. The total amount so coined was 31,115,849 thalers. Of these about 25,000,000 are estimated to be in circulation in Germany, equivalent in face value to 17,500,000 of our dollars. There are various plans in view for the operation so contemplated, one of them being the acceptance, under arrangement supplementary to the new Commercial Treaty, of a part of the sum by Austria-Hungary, where the thalers are legal tender for $1\frac{1}{2}$ gulden.

The long-debated plans in Austria-Hungary for resumption of specie payment—or establishing parity between the paper money, silver coin, and gold coin of the dual empire—have lately assumed more definite form through the appointment and deliberations of Austrian and Hungarian Imperial Commissions, which have not yet closed their labors. The eventual adoption of a Gold Unit of Coinage is regarded as nearly certain, and it is generally understood that this measure will necessitate a considerable acquisition of gold from other countries, and also a considerable demonetization and sale of silver now in use as coin.

BY THE SAME AUTHOR.

SILVER AND GOLD, and their Relation to the Problem of Resumption. (Cincinnati: Robert Clarke & Co., 1876.) [Presented as a printed deposition to the Congressional Monetary Commission of 1876.] New edition, January, 1877, 200 pp.; with Appendix containing papers on—
The Laissez-faire theory and Iwan Possoschkow, &c., and reprint of An ADDRESS TO CONGRESS against the Bland Bill, Dec., 1876.
Monetary Malaria, or the Health of Nations, 1877.
The MONETARY SITUATION. (Cincinnati: Robert Clarke & Co., May, 1878.) Being an Address before the American Social Science Association, and containing also as Appendix papers on—The Prussian Anti-Silver Theory, and its origin in an historical error.—General Restoration of Silver, a condition precedent to successful cancellation of paper money (1877). A Vindication of the practicability of Bimetallic Union (1877).
SPEECHES IN THE INTERNATIONAL MONETARY CONFERENCE OF 1878, and DOCUMENTS presented.—In " Procès-Verbaux," or Report [original in French] of the Proceedings of the Conference, etc. (Paris: Imprimerie Nationale, Nov. 1878, folio.) Ditto in English Translation in THE DOCUMENT OF THE CONFERENCE OF 1878. (Washington: Government Printing Office, July, 1879. 918 pp., 8vo. & 4to.) This volume comprises also the two following Titles.
HISTORICAL MATERIAL FOR THE STUDY OF MONETARY POLICY (518 pp.) Consisting chiefly of documents illustrating the monetary history of France, England, and the United States (of which many are printed for the first time from MSS., and others for the first time translated), compiled and edited as a partial DOCUMENTARY HISTORY OF MONETARY POLICY; and—
CONTRIBUTIONS TO THE STUDY OF MONETARY POLICY (125 pp.). Consisting of Historical and Doctrinal Essays and a Bibliography of Money, and including the Essay next hereinafter named.
THE POSITION OF LAW IN THE DOCTRINE OF MONEY, and other papers. (London: 1882.) La Monnaie et la Loi. Traduction par Emile de Laveleye. (Paris: Guillaumin et Cie., May, 1881.) Das Geld und das Gesetz nebst Rede über das Interesse der Vereinigten Staaten an der Silberfrage. Uebersetzung von E. Koch. Köln: Heimann, August, 1881.)
Sir Isaac Newton and England's Prohibitive Tariff upon Silver Money; an open letter to Prof. W. S. Jevons. (Cincinnati: March, 1881.)
DISCOURS PRONONCÉS ET DOCUMENTS PRÉSENTÉS DANS LA CONFÉRENCE MONÉTAIRE INTERNATIONALE DE 1881.—In Procès-Verbaux. (Paris: Imprimerie Nationale, August, 1881, (folio.) [Also separate edition, 77 pp. folio.] Ditto in English Translation: Report of Proceedings of Conference of 1881. Blue-Book. (London: Spottiswoode, September, 1881, folio), and published by Department of State (Washington: November, 1881); also in German Translation. Published by the German Government. (Berlin: 1882.)
SILVER AS AN INTERNATIONAL QUESTION. An Address to Congress; being a letter written in response to a request of Hon. A. H. Buckner, of Missouri, Chairman of the Committee of the House of Rep's. on Currency and Banking. (Washington, Feb., 1885.)

, REASONS FOR SUSPENDING SILVER COINAGE. An Address delivered in response to the invitation of the Executive Committee of the NATIONAL COMMERCIAL CONVENTION, at its meeting in Atlanta, Georgia, May 21, 1885. Also Extracts printed by the New York Board of Trade and Transportation, July, 1885.

The British Standard of Value: an Address before Section F. (Economic Science and Statistics) of the British Association for the Advancement of Science, Sept., 1885, with Appendix, of documents now first brought to notice, including Monetary Reports of JOHN LOCKE, and of SIR ISAAC NEWTON, (1701-2, *Editio Princeps*, privately printed, from MSS. found by the author of the address). Extracts read by a member of the Committee, and Abstracts printed for distribution.

Ought the National Banking System to be abolished? (*North Am. Rev.*, Sept., 1885.)

THE INTERNATIONALITY OF THE SILVER QUESTION." An Address prepared at the invitation of the Executive Committee of the American Bankers' Association, for its meeting at Chicago, September 24, 1885. (Bankers' Pub. Assoc., New York, 1885.)

A Chapter on Monetary Policy. (*North American Review*, December, 1885.)

SILVER: AN ISSUE OF INTERNATIONAL POLITICS. An Address to Congress, March, 1886. (Cincinnati: R. Clarke & Co., 1886.)

THE BANKING COMMUNITY AND THE SILVER QUESTION. An Address delivered at the Annual Convention of the American Bankers' Association, Aug. 21, 1886, at Boston. (In Report of Convention, American Bankers' Pub. Assoc.)

Silver before Congress in 1886. (*Quart. Journal of Economics*. Boston: Ellis, Oct., 1886.)

THE SILVER POUND and ENGLAND'S MONETARY POLICY since the RESTORATION; together with the HISTORY OF THE GUINEA, illustrated by Contemporary Documents. 300 pp. (London: Macmillan & Co., 1887.)

MONETARY HISTORY AND MONETARY JURISPRUDENCE: an Address before Section F. (Economic Science and Statistics) of the British Association for the Advancement of Science, Sept., 1887. Printed in "the Currency Question before the British Association," published by the Bimetallic League. (Manchester, 1887.)

Remarks upon Silver as Standard Money in England, at an interview with the members of the Board of Directors of the Manchester Chamber of Commerce, at a called meeting, Nov. 2, 1887. (Stenographic report printed for the use of the Directors.)

THE UNITED STANDARD: Answers to the Questions of the ROYAL COMMISSION ON GOLD AND SILVER, Feb., 1888. (Appendix to Final Report, Oct. 1888. Blue-Book.)

THE PARITY OF MONEYS as regarded by Adam Smith, Ricardo, and Mill. An open Letter answering a question of a Member of the ROYAL COMMISSION on Gold and Silver. By Amicus Curiae. London, June, 1888. Also read before Section I. (Economic Science and Statistics) of the American Association for the Advancement of Science, Aug. 20, 1888. (London: Macmillan & Co., 1888.)

OBSERVATIONS au Congrès Monétaire de l'Exposition en réponse à MM. Levasseur et Du Puynode. Sept. 13, 1889. (Paris: Guillaumin & Cie.)

INSTRUMENTS OF VALUATION. An Address before the American Metrological Association. Washington, April 22, 1890. (Report of Proceedings.)

RECENTLY ISSUED,

Large 8vo, 314 pp., cloth, $4.00.

THE SILVER POUND
AND
ENGLAND'S MONETARY POLICY SINCE THE RESTORATION,
TOGETHER WITH THE
HISTORY OF THE GUINEA,
ILLUSTRATED BY
CONTEMPORARY DOCUMENTS.

LONDON:
MACMILLAN AND CO.
1887.

Opinions of the Press.

THE ACADEMY [*London Weekly*], *July* 30, 1887.

Mr. Dana Horton commands a peculiarly respectful attention as the most learned and one of the ablest champions of a cause in favour of which so much ability and learning are now enlisted. The historical research and the dialectical acumen by which he is distinguished are conspicuously manifested in the work before us. Monetary history—a field neglected by most economists—has been cultivated by Mr. Horton with a rare diligence. His labours have been rewarded by the discovery of hidden treasures.

* * * * * *

Misinterpreted history is not the only idol of the market-place which Mr. Horton undertakes to clear away. The prepossession against a fixed par between silver and gold is largely due to an erroneous theory concerning the relation of law to the value of money.

* * * * * *

At many other points the bimetallist leader attacks successfully the mono-metallist intrenchments. Nor can it reasonably be denied that he has carried at least the outworks of those defences—all the loose mass of unfounded prejudices by which it has been sought to bar even the approach to a consideration of the subject. It is another question whether he makes much impression on the interior lines of defence occupied by picked champions.

From the WESTMINSTER REVIEW, *September*, 1887.

A work of original historical investigation. Considering the dryness of the subject to all but experts, it is written in a style remarkably interesting, and even picturesque, as well as vigorous. Much historical information, which we believe to be practically new, is brought to light. We decline to express any opinion as to the bearing of this new information on the main question; but undoubtedly it is important, and must be taken into account by experts. * * * As we said, the work is chiefly historical: but a valuable feature is the author's examination of the theories which he detects underlying and controlling monetary legislation. The lessons of history, as the author reads them, are clearly brought out and vigorously insisted on.

From THE WORLD [*London Weekly*], *July* 13, 1887.

A BOOK WORTH READING.—* * * The position is so critical that we have invariably made a point of calling the attention of our readers to all publications bearing on the question of currency, which seemed deserving of special notice. We deem it, therefore, to be simply our duty to briefly notice Mr. Dana Horton's latest work. After all that has been said and written on the silver question, it might seem almost impossible to produce a work which takes fresh and novel departures, and approaches and treats the subject in an original and striking manner; but in this respect Mr. Dana Horton has undoubtedly and admirably succeeded.

* * * * *

It is positively refreshing to read this last treatise of Mr. Horton, and we feel certain that no thoughtful and reflecting mind can study "The Silver Pound" without becoming not only himself convinced of the absolute correctness of the principles advocated, but without feeling himself, as an honest and useful man, called upon to sow these principles broadcast.

From THE ATHENÆUM [*London Weekly*], *August* 20, 1887.

While, therefore, we share Prof. Jevons's high opinion of Mr. Horton's ability, and rank him "quite apart from the ordinary bi-metallists," we do not think that Mr. Horton has shown that Locke's judgment on the question before us differs from what we previously believed it to be; but his readers may heartily thank Mr. Horton for the interesting and valuable historical investigation of which he has given them the benefit.

From THE STATIST [*London Weekly*], *July* 30, 1887.

It would be a mistake not to recognize that the writer is a student and scholar of rare worth. He is simply a *gold* mine of information regarding monetary history. No matter what the country is which has had such a history, Mr. Horton is at home in that history, has studied every material fact that can be ascertained, has dug up long-forgotten documents, and has, in fact, made it possible for the present generation, to comprehend past monetary arrangements, and the circumstances in which they arose, unlike as these circumstances may have been to those of the present time.

The present book constitutes a chapter of the history which much requires to be written.

* * * * * * *

For students, also, Mr. Horton's nice distinctions of the different meanings of the word Standard itself, and of other terms in monetary discussions, will be most useful. We should have liked the book better, of course, if it had not been written from a bi-metallist point of view (though Mr. Horton's bi-metallism, be it observed, is by no means of the Cernuschi type); but this difference of opinion ought not to prevent us from acknowledging the really great value of the work to the student and the scholar.

From the DUBLIN EVENING MAIL, *August* 3, 1887.

Taken as a good historic statement of an intricate subject, the history of our British monetary system and its modifications up to the present time, we can cordially recommend this work.

MONEY: A JOURNAL FOR INVESTORS AND SPECULATORS, AND REVIEW OF THE MONEY MARKET [*London Weekly*], *August* 17, 1887.

It would be difficult to conceive a more exhaustive contribution to the great monetary question of the age than this historical inquiry—the outcome of painstaking researches by the greatest living authority on the subject. * * * Such a work as this is an invaluable aid to the attainment of a right conception of the *pros* and *cons* of the question at issue. It is a masterpiece, and will be regarded, not only at the present juncture, but for all time to come, as a standard work on our monetary policy.

From THE LONDON MORNING POST, *August* 1, 1887.

Ample justification for the prevailing ignorance as to the point of the dispute that is now raging in financial circles is contained in the first words of Mr. Horton's book, in which he gives nine definitions of "Standard" (in the monetary sense of the term)—these being only "some of the various meanings attached to the word."

From the MANCHESTER COURIER, *July* 29, 1887.

There is probably no one on either Continent who can speak with greater authority on the currency question than Mr. S. Dana Horton. * * * This history of English money is of a more exhaustive and complete character than any hitherto published. * * * Its publication comes at a most opportune moment, when the Royal Commission on Gold and Silver is sitting, and when the thinking minds of the country are exercised to get a solution of the national monetary and commercial difficulties we are suffering from; and Mr. Horton's book clears away much of the obscurity which has hampered a clear understanding of many important points, and furnishes a mass of information which demands the careful study of all who desire to be well informed on the subject. Indeed, the appearance of this book marks a new stage in the currency controversy. Hitherto the literature on the subject has been fragmentary.

This book, for the first time, places the whole controversy before the public in a complete form, giving theory as well as practice its proper place.

From the London DAILY TELEGRAPH, *July* 13, 1887.

There is matter for some painful reflection just at present in "The Silver Pound," a sketch of England's monetary policy since the Restoration. It deals with the traditions and virtues of good money at a moment when our Mint has put forth a coinage which, so far as image and superscription go, is a disgrace to an artistic age, and a sorrow to numismatists.

* * * * * * *

As such the volume cannot hope to interest everyone; but to the initiated, who appreciate the rivalry of precious metals, and comprehend the fine perplexities of single and double standards, dual money and elder systems, the author's researches must prove attractive. A History of the Guinea follows, and concludes what bears all the appearance of being a careful and erudite treatise on these difficult and complex subjects.

From THE MANCHESTER GUARDIAN, *September* 3, 1887.

Mr. Horton has brought to light some most important facts which will undoubtedly expand our views as to the importance and the true objects of monetary legislation.

In no other direction, probably, are the teachings of history so fatally neglected as in that of monetary legislation. The Act of 1816, by which for the first time in this country or anywhere else gold alone was made the sole standard of value, seems to be accepted by many as the final expression of the wisdom taught by all previous experience. It was, in truth, a great experiment, the lessons of which we are just beginning to understand.

From THE MANCHESTER GUARDIAN, *October* 8, 1887.

That the best book which has appeared in our times on English monetary history should have been written by an American is, at first sight, not creditable to English economists. But there is a justifying explanation. In the United States currency questions have for many years been "living issues" in consequence of the existence of inconvertible war paper money from 1862 to 1878, and the importance of arranging for the return to a specie basis after the war was ended. The situation was, in fact, not unlike that in which our forefathers stood during and after the Napoleonic wars. It is natural, therefore, that the more studious of American writers upon the problems immediately before them should have turned their attention to English experience for teaching and guidance.

* * * * * * *

To readers on this side the Atlantic this work is doubly valuable. It appears at a time when circumstances are rapidly forcing into prominence a currency problem in this country, and it sets forth precisely the kind of information which is absolutely indispensable to a clear understanding of it, at least on its historical side.

From THE MANCHESTER GUARDIAN, *October* 11, 1887.

The whole book will be read by all who occupy their minds with one of the most important, perhaps the most important, of the economic questions of our day.

From THE BEACON, *Boston, Mass., Sept.* 10, 1887.

Mr. Horton's "Silver and Gold" was published in 1876 by Robert Clarke & Co. at Cincinnati; he made weighty contributions to the International Monetary Conferences of 1878 and 1881, where he represented the American Government with consummate ability, to the confusion of the European mono-metallists; and now he publishes "The Silver Pound, and England's Monetary Policy since the Restoration," together with the History of the Guinea. * * *

It is extremely desirable that Congress, the members of the administration, bankers, politicians, and students should read and master this noble monograph. * * *

And even a mono-metallist will not wish to take leave of it without paying a tribute of hearty admiration to the distinguished author, now unquestionably the greatest of all American publicists.

From THE FINANCIAL AND COMMERCIAL CHRONICLE [*New York Weekly*], *October* 1, 1887.

A very interesting volume. * * * It may turn out that Mr. Horton's book is timely in a wider sense than at first appeared. In any view, the sitting of the Royal Commission made the moment of its issue very opportune.

From the SPECTATOR, *September* 1*st*, 1887.

Mr. Dana Horton, in a very elaborate style, and with a still more elaborate array of historical research, delivers an attack on the gold standard.

From THE GLASGOW HERALD, *November* 3, 1887.

A very important addition to the literature of currency, and it should be carefully studied by all who desire to understand that complicated question.

From the SATURDAY REVIEW [*London Weekly*], *Nov.* 19, 1887.

The case is now being argued as it ought to be, and thoroughly reasoned out, and we may hope, though scarcely expect, that the Commission will come, in their Report, to a definite conclusion. * * * Mr. Horton insists * * * inasmuch as gold was legally rated to silver under the monetary administration of Locke and Newton, both metals were equally money of the country. Mr. Horton says:—

Not only in England, but generally, silver was the standard. Both metals were money, but the fixed money, the rating money, so to speak, was silver: the rated money was gold.

Sir Robert Peel was, no doubt, misinformed. * * * Mr. Horton enumerates nine different senses of the word standard. * * * Applying these definitions to Holland [it appears that] Holland has, at one and the same time, (5) a silver standard, (6) a silver and gold standard, (7) a silver standard, (8) a gold standard, (9) a limping standard, according to the sense in which we use the word. No wonder that the arguments *pro* and *con* in the monetary controversy fall often *à tort et à travers*, and that the arguers are mostly at cross-purposes with each other. The knights of the fable persist in looking some at the gold, some at the silver, side of the shield. * * * Mr. Horton concludes that there is a monetary *solidarité* between the nations, and a necessity pressing upon each of them to establish an accord on the principles and practice to be followed; and he has much to say on the responsibility of England for the present dislocation, and her paramount interest in leading the way to a reasonable adjustment. * * * The whole book is well worth study, both by those who agree with Mr. Horton's conclusions and by those who dissent from them. Both classes of readers will find much that is new to them, and much matter for reflection, and the quotation from Nicholas Oresme's tractate *De mutationibus monetarum* (1382) with which he concludes may well conclude our article:—

Se aucum doncques pour amour de verité enquerre, vouldroit contredire à icelles ou escripre contre, bien sera, mais se j'ai mal parlé porteige tesmognage du mal avec raison, affin qu'il ne soit veu pour néant et de sa singulière voulenté temerairement condemner ce que bonnement ne se peult impugner ne contredire.

[If any one for the love of truth to be sought out shall desire to contradict these pages or to write against them, it is well. But if I have spoken ill let him bring evidence of the wrong, giving his reason, so that it be not seen that for naught and out of mere wilfulness one rashly condemns that which cannot rightfully be impugned or contradicted.]

From the London GRAPHIC, *April* 28, 1888.

The "Silver Pound" is regarded as the most authoritative book on this subject ever written.

www.ingramcontent.com/pod-product-compliance
Lightning Source LLC
Chambersburg PA
CBHW030316240426
43673CB00040B/1180